Soundings on
SOUTH ASIA

Soundings on
SOUTH
ASIA

Syed Ali Mujtaba

NEW DAWN PRESS, INC.
UK • USA • INDIA

NEW DAWN PRESS GROUP

Published by New Dawn Press Group
New Dawn Press, 2 Tintern Close, Slough, Berkshire, SL1-2TB, UK
e-mail: ndpuk@newdawnpress.com

New Dawn Press, Inc., 244 South Randall Rd # 90, Elgin, IL 60123, USA
e-mail: sales@newdawnpress.com

New Dawn Press (An Imprint of Sterling Publishers (P) Ltd.)
A-59, Okhla Industrial Area, Phase-II, New Delhi-110020, India
e-mail: info@sterlingpublishers.com
www.sterlingpublishers.com

Soundings on South Asia
© 2005, Syed Ali Mujtaba
ISBN 1 932705 40 6

All rights are reserved. No part of this publication may be reproduced, stored in a retrieval system or transmitted, in any form or by any means, mechanical, photocopying, recording or otherwise, without prior written permission of the original publisher.

PRINTED IN INDIA

Preface

South Asia is a huge landmass home to about one quarter of the world's population. It comprises seven nations in a geographical continuum with only Sri Lanka and Maldives separated by a narrow strip of sea. The region is marked by an asymmetry of power structure, differential system of governance and interstate conflict. At the same time, the region also exhibits a great deal of harmony in ethnic composition, food habits, language, values, mores and norms.

It is generally being felt that while rest of the world has removed regional impediments and are moving ahead through regional cooperation, South Asia remains a disjointed and disorganised region. The countries in the region remain mostly in conflict since independence, and suffer from high degree of insecurity and underdevelopment.

There are many reasons why South Asia has not been able to hem a regional identity. My interaction with Samuel Paul Huntington, the celebrated author of the book *Clash of Civilisations* in Chennai, in 1998 provided some insights to this problem. Huntington says, since South Asia comprises of two principle religions, Hinduism and Islam representing two civilisations which are basically antithesis of each other, there cannot be a regional grouping based on them.

He gave me the hackneyed two nation theory, of Islam and Hinduism representing mutually antagonistic forces—one a monotheist, the other a polytheist; one worships idols, to the other physical manifestation of God is a sin; one religious group is untouchable to the other; the two never share meal and matrimonial ties among them are considered sacrilegious. Huntington says the two civilisations that have remained in conflict since antiquity, would continue to be so, no matter how much progress these countries make. He said, the main reason that obstructs regional cooperation in South Asia is the clash of civilisations.

I tried to convince the celebrated author that his arguments were detached from the objective realities and suggested that Islam in many ways is unique in South Asia. I asked him to visit the Vaishno Devi shrine in Kashmir and see for himself how Muslim Gujjars since time immemorial had been taking Hindu pilgrims on their ponies to the holy caves of Vaishno Devi, the divine consort of Lord Shiva. I also requested him to visit any Muslim shrine in this country and see for himself how many Hindu devotees throng such places round the year. Huntington was not convinced.

To my mind, the root cause that blocks formation of a regional identity is the rigidity of the nation states to guard the hard won national identity. These countries feel that dilution of the national identity would give rise to fissiparous tendencies leading to disintegration of the national unity. The general apprehension remains that regionalism would prove counter productive to the idea of nation state.

Historically South Asia had never been one unit in the sense of a nation state. The central authority of the Mughals and the British empires bonded the region together through administrative paraphernalia whose underlying principle was 'larger the sword the longer the claim.' Nationalism in South Asia surfaced as a reaction to colonialism and formation of national identity was its logical corollary.

During the time of the formation of national identity, the sub-nationalistic forces merged their differences under the canopy of larger nationalism assuming fair play and justice after freedom from the colonial bondage. This however did not happen and in the process of nation building, the new nation states became over-centralised and subsequently gagged the aspirations of their specificities. This led to a cacophony of separatist demands. Though they were brushed under the carpet of national identity, these issues became the source of all troubles. As such, it remains debatable,

Preface

whether the enormous amount of regional diversity could continue to be lumped together into the restricted format of a nation state and be peddled along like a moving anarchy, or some serious efforts should be made to harmonise the subcontinental differences, without diluting the national identity. The choices have to be made.

Soundings on South Asia is an attempt to provide a compendium of the region's development through short essays and help in understanding the regional dynamics which blocks regional integration. This book is an outcome of over seventy articles, written over the period of last one decade, that provides a panoramic view of the developing themes in the region. Since most of the issues remain still relevant, the book delves into its background and circumstances to put them in proper perspective.

The book contains fifteen chapters including "Soundings on South Asia" and "Resounding on South Asia" as the first and the last chapters respectively. It begins with the hypothesis: can South Asia ever become United States of South Asia (USSA) and answers that the job is difficult but not impossible. The core argument of the book is that salvation of South Asia lies alone in mitigating the subcontinental differences.

Chapter two which sets the tone of the book is called "Partition of India and Its Aftermath". It comprises six articles that delves into partition process and its nuances, changing profile of Muslims in independent India and about those who migrated to Pakistan. There is an interesting interview of two Pakistanis taken in London who, as children had first migrated to Pakistan, then went to UK as students, where they settled down with jobs.

Chapter three dwells upon the India-Pakistan relations. An article in this chapter calls upon India and Pakistan to break the shackles of history. Another article highlights the growing international focus on India-Pakistan relations. The predicament of the US in South Asia is yet another theme of discussion in this chapter. What compelled India and Pakistan to resume talk is reasoned here. Indo-Pak dialogue caught in optimism-pessimism syndrome highlights the mood in which Indo-Pak bilateral relations is moving forward.

The focus is on Kashmir in the fourth chapter and opens with the discussion on the genesis of this dispute. It then goes to chronicle India-Pakistan bilateral talks over resolving the Kashmir issue. That Kashmir needs to look beyond the healing touch policy is another theme of discussion. India's road-map to Kashmir talks about the flawed assumptions by India and lays emphasis on the primacy of people's aspirations to the territorial sovereignty. The last article in this chapter is an exclusive interview with the slain Hurriyat leader Abdul Ghani Lone, which reflects Kashmiri's viewpoint on this issue.

The fifth chapter is on Sri Lanka, which begins with the nuances of the Tamil ethnic problem. It goes on to discuss, why peace as an option is preferred to war and also makes assessment of President Chandrika Kumaratunga's two terms in office. The central focus of this chapter is the LTTE's counter proposal or the demand of one state and two nations in Sri Lanka. A special interview with Sri Lanka Muslim Congress leader Rauff Hakim discusses the current peace initiatives and Muslim's position in the ethnic rigmarole of the island. India-Sri Lanka relationship, Tamil Nadu fisherman's problem and the Sri Lankan refugees in Tamil Nadu wraps up this chapter.

Keeping the contours of South Asian geography, the Maldives occupies the sixth slot in this book. The first article discusses the pace of development in the Maldives. The nascent economy of Maldives needs diversification is an argument put up for consideration. An article assesses the Maldives' foreign policy to be based on pragmatism. The most controversial write-up is about the political situation in the Maldives, which highlights that the nation of islands is yearning for political reforms. It is being stressed in the last article how other countries of the subcontinent can take a cue from India-Maldives relations.

Bangladesh features in the seventh chapter and chronologically accounts from the nuances of its emergence, quoting declassified papers from the British archives. Internal political dynamics of the country, parties and politics in Bangladesh are discussed in the article. The need for adopting a positive approach in India-Bangladesh relations is stressed even as the chapter discusses the border tension between the two countries over the illegal immigrant issue. An offbeat write-up on Bangladesh's achievements in health care concludes this chapter.

The developments in Nepal are looked at in the eighth chapter, which begins with the description of political situation in the Himalayan Kingdom now at a crossroad. It discusses the wrangling among the political parties as reasons for monarchy to gain strength in Nepal. The Maoist insurgency that is now plaguing Nepal is discussed separately in this chapter. Two articles are devoted to India-Nepal relations. One talks about allaying India's security concerns and the other stresses on India-Nepal relationship to be built on pragmatism.

Followed by an insight, the ninth chapter begins with some thoughts on why Bhutan's ruling elite is facing an identity crisis. The steps towards democratisation by drafting new constitution and the winds of democracy blowing over Bhutan are subjects of discussion in this chapter. The uncertain future of Bhutan's refugees and 'foreigner's issue' are also separate themes of comment here. The chapter closes with the 'India-Bhutan relationship' and 'Operation All Clear' by Royal Bhutan Army to flush out anti-Indian insurgents hiding in Bhutan.

In Chapter ten, Myanmar is deliberately dealt with, as historically this country has remained an integral part of South Asian identity. The chapter opens with Myanmar having no respite from military rule and the struggle for democracy continues under Aung San Suu Kyi. This chapter also salutes those students who laid down their lives in the youth protest of 1988. The development of a new diplomatic track in India-Myanmar relationship concludes the segment.

Chapter eleven is on Afghanistan, which is again included due to its historical antecedents with South Asia. It begins with the current plight of Afghanistan and links it to the invasion and withdrawal of Soviet Union that has left the country fragmented. New parameters in India-Afghan policy and Hamid Karzai government's reconstruction of a new Afghanistan are discussed here. The US war against global terrorism remains foggy, even after change of regimes in Afghanistan and Iraq, is another contention in this chapter. There is an interesting discussion on the Islamic resurgence in the twenty-first century in the end.

The twelfth chapter talks about collective regional issues. It begins with reasons of insecurity plaguing the region and India's role in South Asia. There is discussion on insecurity and nuclearisation of South Asia. India and nuclear proliferation debate raises the question whether South Asia could ever be made a nuclear free zone. The security discussion is stretched to nuclear safety in India and questions how unsafe are India's nuclear power plants. The combined problem of South Asia is also discussed in the thirteenth chapter. There are some interesting themes lined up like the problem of ethnicity, rising tide of religiosity, issues of refugees, and human rights abuse. The plight of women in the region and their under representation in politics is also discussed. The chapter has a discussion on impact of information technology on the region and emphasises that the salvation of the region could only be possible through its economic integration.

The last but one, chapter is on SAARC (South Asian Association for Regional Cooperation). There are articles, which traces how regionalism is being promoted through SAARC and argues for more vigorous economic cooperation to give the concept a boost. This chapter highlights that bilateralism remains the Achilles heel of SAARC. The retrospect and prospects of SAARC is looked at in another write-up. The discussion in this chapter leaves a food for the thought on shades of subregional grouping emerging in South Asia.

Soundings on South Asia has some highlights. The book argues for the inclusion of Myanmar and Afghanistan in some capacity in the regional grouping. The argument is based on the assumption that the subcontinent, since its transition from civilisations to empires, to nation states, has seen these two countries as its geographical frontiers. To detach them at a time when the nation states are striving for regional grouping would be improper reading of history.

In the initial stages of the formation of SAARC, the idea of inclusion of Myanmar and Afghanistan was considered. However, Myanmar opted out of SAARC fearing democratic tremors from it in its country. Afghanistan was deliberately kept out of SAARC for having a reactionary regime there. With the subregional grouping now east of South Asia attracting attention, inclusion of Myanmar, in some capacity, may add dynamism to SAARC; even as it may continue to be member of ASEAN. Similarly, with a stable government now in Kabul, the region would greatly benefit with the inclusion of Afghanistan into SAARC.

The other highlights of the book are the chapters on the Maldives and Bhutan. The general perception that Bhutan and the Maldives are insignificant countries is dispelled in this book by providing a bit of information about these two countries. The write-ups talk about the development taking place in both countries and the nature and direction of changes taking place there. The chapter on Bhutan highlights the code of edict being promulgated by the ruling elite to maintain its distinct identity and a constitution being drafted to stem the tide of democratic upsurge in the Kingdom. Similarly, the political discontentment brewing in the Maldives is highlighted, which is necessitating political reforms in the nation of islands. The information on the Maldives, which readers may find interesting in many ways, has come after a great deal of difficulty.

Soundings on South Asia tries to critically understand the regional dynamics and the subcontinental differences. The sole purpose of this book is to build a case for regionalism in the subcontinent where I have tried to shore up the idea that if European Union or ASEAN could become a success story then what holds South Asia from becoming United Sates of South Asia (USSA). The day, Indian, Pakistani, Sri Lankan, Bangladeshi, Nepali, Bhutani and Maldivian would start feeling that their national identity would not be an impediment in sewing a common South Asian identity, the purpose of writing this book would be served.

Last, but not the least, the opinion expressed in this book is a reflection of my multilayered identity and for which I am solely responsible.

Syed Ali Mujtaba
syedalimujtaba@yahoo.com

Chennai, 2005

Acknowledgements

I begin my acknowledgements by thanking Mr S K Ghai, CMD, Sterling Publishers for publishing this volume. The moment I sounded him on the idea, he agreed to it enthusiastically and asked me to proceed with the drafting of the manuscript. My special acknowledgement goes to him for showing confidence in my abilities and giving me complete liberty regarding the contents of this book.

Since this book contains more than seventy articles written over a period of decade it is difficult to mention the names of all the publications in which they first appeared. My acknowledgement goes to all of them for providing space to my writings in their publications. Here I may add that the articles in the book have been revised, updated, rewritten to keep pace with the times. More than half of the contents are new additions to suit the requirement of the book.

The foundation of this book was laid when I was a student in the early nineties at the South Asia Division, School of International Studies, Jawaharlal Nehru University, New Delhi. I thank the Division's teachers and students with whom I interacted and who helped me in formulating the ideas of this book. My acknowledgement in a very profound sense goes to all those Pakistani, Bangladeshi, Sri Lankan, Nepali, Maldivian and Bhutaneses citizens with whom I interacted in pursuit of my academic interests.

My personal acknowledgement goes to Mrs Dhanalakshmi Ayyer, a freelance writer who had taken pains to go through the manuscript at its initial stage. I may also thank the editor of Sterling Publishers for carrying out a massive revision in the final proof copy of the manuscript. I would fail in my duties if I do not thank Biju K F who had helped me in dusting my old files and coaxing me to embark on this project. Lastly, my special thanks go to my wife Rubina for her silent and stoic support in helping me complete this project.

Chennai 2005

Contents

	Preface	v
	Acknowledgements	xii
1.	**Soundings on South Asia**	1
2.	**Partition of India and Its Aftermath**	8

• Did Jinnah Want Pakistan? • Pakistan – The Unfulfilled Dream • Changing Profile of the Indian Muslims • Mohajir Imbroglio in Pakistan • Peace Battles in Karachi • Mohajirs Remote Controlled from London

3.	**India-Pakistan**	26

• Breaking the Shackles of History • Growing International Focus • US Predicament in South Asia • Compulsions for Composite Dialogue to Begin • Caught in Optimism-Pessimism Syndrome

4.	**Kashmir**	40

• The Genesis of Kashmir Issue • India-Pakistan Bilateral Talks • Beyond the Healing Touch • India's Road-map to Kashmir • Remembering Abdul Ghani Lone

5.	**Sri Lanka**	55

• Nuances of Sri Lanka's Ethnic Problem • Peace Gets Past War in Sri Lanka • Assessment of Chandrika's Rule • Bargaining for Two Nations • The Muslim Factor in Sri Lanka • India-Sri Lanka Relations • Tamil Fishermen's Problem • Sri Lankan Refugees in Tamil Nadu

6.	**The Maldives**	80

• The Maldives on Developmental Path • The Maldives' Economy Needs Diversification • Pragmatism Marks the Maldives' Foreign Policy • The Maldives Yearns for Political Reforms • India-Maldives Relationship

7. **Bangladesh** — 95
   - Bangladesh: Emergence and Lessons • Parties and Politics in Bangladesh • India-Bangladesh Relations • Bangladeshi Immigrants Issue • Bangladesh Health Care Scene
8. **Nepal** — 110
   - Nepal at Crossroads • Nepal: Monarchy Gains Strength • Maoist Insurgency in Nepal • India-Nepal Relations • India-Nepal Allay Security Concerns
9. **Bhutan** — 124
   - Bhutan Faces Identity Crisis • Democracy Knocks Bhutan • Democratisation of Bhutan • Bhutanese Refugees Issue • India-Bhutan Relations • Bhutan's 'Operation All Clear'
10. **Myanmar** — 139
    - Military Rules Myanmar • Aung San Suu Kyi – Myanmar's Icon • Myanmar's Students Struggle • India-Myanmar Relations
11. **Afghanistan** — 150
    - Afghanistan after Soviet Withdrawal • Reconstruction of Afghanistan • India and Afghanistan Relation • Islamic Resurgence in the 21st Century • War against Global Terrorism
12. **South Asia I** — 163
    - Insecurity Plagues South Asia • India's Role in South Asia • South Asia after the Nuclear Tests • India and Nuclear Proliferation Debate • Nuclear Safety Standards in India
13. **South Asia II** — 178
    - South Asia: Problem of Ethnicity Conflagrates • South Asia: Religion versus Reason • Refugees in South Asia • Human Rights in South Asia • Women Struggle in South Asia • Information Technology in South Asia • Economic Integration of South Asia
14. **SAARC** — 198
    - Regionalism through SAARC • Economic Cooperation and SAARC • Bilateralism and SAARC • SAARC – Retrospect and Prospects • Sub-regionalism in South Asia
15. **Resounding on South Asia** — 214
    Index — 222

1
Soundings on South Asia

International relation in the new millennium is gravitating towards a more complex world order where the forces of conflict and cooperation are simultaneously at work. While on the one hand, there is consensus for peace and development, on the other, strife and conflict are disturbing the international balance. This global reality is also impinging upon the South Asian scene.

The post-colonial states in South Asia have become monolithic political entity while their societies remain multiethnic. In the absence of redress of their grievances the specificities feel gagged, and clamour for distinct political identity. They have taken the shape of sub-nationalism which is having separatist tendencies. This intra-state conflict coupled with interstate tension has vitiated the security environment of the region.

At the same time, the forces of integration are also at play in South Asia. Issues of environment, food, energy and human security, are all clamouring for regional cooperation. Economic and communication network are also catapulting the cause of regionalism. The fragmented mosaic of South Asia yearns to be cemented by the traditional bond of cultural cohesiveness of the region.

It is very difficult to predict how long these opposite forces would remain in a tug-of-war. However, the balance sheet of the forces of conflict and consensus makes an interesting case study in South Asia.

South Asia is a conglomeration of ethnic plurality. Many ethnic, linguistic, and tribal groups demand political and cultural rights from their respective countries. In case of their non fullfilment, they scale up their demand which varies from autonomy to separatism.

For instance in India, the Sikhs demand maximum cultural and political autonomy for Punjab. So do, Nepalese, living in the hill districts of West Bengal. In Pakistan, the Punjabis, Baluchis, Pushtuns, Sindhis and Mohajirs demand greater political autonomy for being a distinct nationality. Similar demand is made by those living in the hill tracks of Chittagoan district in Bangladesh.

The demand for autonomy gives way for the total separatist demands. The Jammu and Kashmir Liberation Front (JKLF) and United Liberation Front of Assam (ULFA) want complete independence from India. In Sri Lanka, the LTTE, representing the Tamils, demand a separate homeland in the northeast of the country.

In this context, the question of right to self-determination assumes greater complexity when religious, ethnic and linguistic groups are described as nationalities. As every odd group claim to be a nationality, the dilemma of what constitutes a nationality remains undefined in South Asia.

Since there are porous borders, the South Asian states, faces the problem of migration which is causing interstate conflict. The influx of Bangladeshi refugees in Assam and West Bengal is one such case. Tamil Nadu too houses a large number of Sri Lankan refugees which is worrying the Indian government. The influx of Nepalese population in Bhutan has raised the foreigners issue and is a cause of tension between the two countries.

South Asia is also witnessing the phenomena of religious bigotry. In India, the forces of Hindutva are disturbing the communal peace in the country. The issues centering on Ayodhya and 2002 Gujarat riots are testimony to this fact. The drive for Islamisation is taking Pakistan towards religious extremism. In Bangladesh too religious fundamentalism has been on the rise. In Sri Lanka, numerous sectarian riots have been taking place due to religious chauvinism.

The domestic politics in South Asia is played through the blame game on each other. This is done to safeguard the regimes, prove patriotic credentials and cover the shortcomings. India talks at length against Pakistan on cross border terrorism in Kashmir and the activities of the ISI. Against Bangladesh, India rakes up the issues of illegal infiltration and support to insurgency in the northeast of the country. India also accuses Kathmandu of giving shelter to anti-Indian forces in Nepal.

However, it is the Indo-centric nature of the region that makes the neighbours blame India for all their domestic problems. Sri Lanka holds India responsible for the Tamil militancy and takes exception to increasing Indian interference in its domestic politics. Bangladesh harps upon the overwhelming size of India and hold it responsible for its water and Chakma problems. Nepal blames that the Maoist insurgency in its country is being perpetrated by India. Islamabad accuses India's RAW to be responsible for many disruptive activities in Pakistan.

All the neighbouring countries with the exception of the Maldives blame India to be impinging on their national sovereignty. In recent years, the prevailing perception has been allayed by India during I K Gujral's regime and subsequently by the other governments as well, but a sense of insecurity persists among the neighbours in the region.

There are many irritants that reflect upon the interstate relations in South Asia. Between India and Pakistan, there are issues of terrorism, drug-trafficking, Walur barrage, Sir Creek, Siachin glacier and Kashmir. Between India and Bangladesh, Talpatty, New Moor Island, Chakma, illegal immigration, water sharing and northeast insurgency are the contentious issues. With India and Nepal, the trade and transit treaty, and the Kingdom becoming a sanctuary for forces unfriendly to India are being contended. The fishermen problem in the Palk-strait, Kachatheevu Island and Tamil refugees impinge on India- Sri Lanka relations.

Though, there is global consensus against terrorism, this phenomena fails to recede in the region. Aiding and abetting armed struggle continues to be an instrument of state policy in South Asia. It began with Indian policy of encouraging the armed struggle of the Tibetans against China in 1950s. The Indian policy manifested against Pakistan during the course of the liberation of Bangladesh in 1971. The same policy was put in operation in 1980s when India supported the cause of Tamil 'Eelam' by the LTTE in the northeast of Sri Lanka.

The echoes of terrorism had its resonance on India when Pakistan started aiding and abetting militant activities first in Punjab and then in Jammu and Kashmir. Similarly, India also felt the heat of armed struggle in its northeast region, which it alleges to be abetted from outside soil. In the same pattern Nepal places the Maoist insurgency and alleges it to be perpetrated from outside.

The resultant interstate tension has vitiated the security scenario of the region. It is conspicuously reflected in the defence spending of the seven nations of South Asia. About 40 million US dollars are spent by Nepal on its security. Bangladesh spends about 400 million US dollars, Sri Lanka about 500 million US dollars. Pakistan's defence budget is about 4.5 billion US dollars and India's defence budget is 7.5 billion.

There has been a steady increase in defence spending by both India and Pakistan for replacement of outdated weapons and procurement of new ones, which has led to further increase in their defence budget.

Senior officials of India and Pakistan have been paying regular visits to US, Russia and Israel for arms negotiations. India signed a defence protocol with Russia and procured early warning radar system, "Falcon" from Israel. Fresh negotiations with US were made during the Vajpayee government and Defence Minister George Fernandes visited America several times to strike a defence deal.

Pakistan too has been alive to the realities of its security concerns. President Musharraf has been visiting several countries for armament purchase. Pakistan has become eligible to acquire fresh weaponry from the US after the US Secretary of State Colin Powell announced granting non-NATO ally status during his Islamabad visit in 2004. However, there has been no fresh announcement of armament supply to Pakistan by the US as yet.

The growing trend of enhanced defence spending by India and Pakistan has raised the security concerns of the other countries in the region. Even Sri Lanka, Bangladesh and Nepal are looking beyond South Asia to keep themselves secure. The most conspicuous feature is that China has become the main supplier of arms to Islamabad, Dhaka and Colombo.

Added to the security dimension is the nuclear issue that has exacerbated the insecurity scenario in South Asia. The risk of inadvertent or accidental nuclear use due to unsophisticated nuclear command and control systems and poorly defined nuclear doctrines has made the region vulnerable. However, there are some who believe that the nuclear deterrence has helped in establishing long-term peace in South Asia.

Overriding the forces of divisiveness are the economic compulsions that are undermining the tensions and turbulences in the region. It is widely believed that peace and stability could be achieved only by following the path of economic cooperation. India and Bangladesh have identified some products for trade which can be conducted on free convertible currencies. India and Nepal have relaxed custom regulation to facilitate the volume of trade. There are joint ventures between India-Nepal and India- Sri Lanka. Even India and Pakistan registered an impressive growth in bilateral trade during 2000-2001, despite the border tension. However, at the moment the total export within the SAARC countries remains at a dismal figure of 3.5 per cent.

In South Asia, there is a vicious circle of poverty, hunger, malnutrition, and population explosion being witnessed. There is a need for a combined approach to tackle them. The handling of water resources remains a serious issue in the region. Bangladesh complains that India's construction of the Farraka barrage on the river Ganga has stopped sufficient water flow into its country. Similarly, the Indus water treaty with Pakistan too has come into focus in recent times. New Delhi complain about the inability of Nepal to augment its water resources as the cause of floods every year in India.

The shortage of power is another issue commonly being felt in the region. India-Nepal collaboration for power generation has created some acrimony. The idea of sharing Pakistan's surplus power by India has not yet taken off. India, now, is leaning on Bhutan for its power needs. A regional approach is needed to tackle the issue of power for the development of South Asia.

Similarly, the region shares common environmental problems. During winters, dense fog that envelops parts of Pakistan, India, Nepal and Bangladesh, is a cause of regional concern. The Maldives faces the problem of global warming and fears some of its islands may disappear over a period of time. The felling of trees in Nepal has been the cause of floods in Indian states of Bihar and UP. The environmental degradation in Nepal has repercussions on Bangladesh too. A combined approach to tackle the environmental concerns is increasingly felt in South Asia.

Healthcare is another area where the region commonly suffers. While the cities and metropolis are well covered by medical facilities, the large number of villages and hamlets in the region remain bereft of healthcare facilities. A regional approach to address the healthcare needs is increasingly felt in South Asia.

The communication network is a handy tool to buttress the progress of the region. The stark realities of underdevelopment unveiled by communication network are forcing the countries to contemplate on the alternatives to strife and conflict. However, the free flow of information is also leading to political mobilization of ethnic, religious and nationalistic groups that needs to be tackled by reaching a broad consensus over the issue.

The region shares a common cultural heritage, which remains an inherent cushion that binds it together. Agriculture related activities interlinks the predominantly rural population in South Asia. The whole region celebrates sowing and harvesting festivals at the same time. They dance in joy over the early arrival of the monsoon and pray together when the rains gods fail or delay. The wedding celebrations among all South Asian communities takes place after the harvest season.

Then, there is a linguistic interlinking of the region. Common lingual groups across the border speak the Punjabi, Bengali, Tamil and Nepali languages. Others can criss-cross the subcontinent speaking English or Hindustani.

Through the establishment of SAARC, an attempt is being made to improve the well being of the people in the region. Since 1985, SAARC has been focusing on economic and other nonpolitical issues and has been instrumental in creating a climate to promote regionalism. As the scope of SAARC widens, it is realized that this forum alone can serve as a vehicle of regional integration.

In sum, the opposing forces of conflict and cooperation are unevenly balanced in the region. At the moment, the forces of division have gained an upper hand and those of cooperation are lying low. Notwithstanding this cyclical reality, an added stress on the forces of cohesion, could turn the region into a dynamic partner with the rest of the world.

It is being realized slowly that the salvation of the region is possible by following the path of regional cooperation. Some positive steps have been taken through the medium of SAARC, but more substantial efforts remain to be made, if the idea of regional cooperation is to be pushed forward. The shedding of the national identity and adopting a regional personality remains a dream in South Asia.

2
Partition of India and Its Aftermath

• *Did Jinnah Want Pakistan?* • *Pakistan – The Unfulfilled Dream* • *Changing Profile of the Indian Muslims* • *Mohajir Imbroglio in Pakistan* • *Peace Battles in Karachi* • *Mohajirs Remote Controlled from London*

Did Jinnah Want Pakistan?

In India, it would be blasphemous to even talk what would be the shape of the country had Mohammad Ali Jinnah led the independence struggle instead of Mohandas Karamchand Gandhi. The post partition generation generally ask, whether Jinnah, the architect of Pakistan, was the real destroyer of India's unity or had any other vision of India? Was he a nationalist or a communalist? If he started as a nationalist, why did he end up becoming a communalist? Was he, a megalomaniac, who could go to any extent to destroy India's unity or did his vision of Pakistan mean something other than partition of India?

Jinnah, started his career as a lawyer, groomed in the Bentham and Mill school of thought. As a politician, he was a follower of Dadabhai Naoraji, and his approach to politics was gradual progress towards Constitutional democracy. He championed Hindu-Muslim unity and was the architect of the Lucknow pact in 1916. He lobbied for the release of Annie Besant in 1918 and made M K Gandhi the president of Home Rule League in 1920.

It was Jinnah, who opposed the formation of Muslim League in 1906 and later, the Khilafat movement in 1920 on the grounds of mixing religion with politics. He was also averse to mass based politics and frowned upon the idea of people's mobilisation on the streets.

Jinnah left the Congress in 1921 following a tiff with the party on certain issues not acceptable to him as a matter of principal. Though communal politics was anathema to him, thereafter he leaned on to Muslim League for his political survival. In 1928, Jinnah, put forward a 14 point charter of demands before the Motilal Nehru committee to redress the growing dissatisfaction of the Muslims in India. These demands, which merely sought religious and cultural safeguards of the Muslims were rebuffed by the Congress. Disgruntled, Jinnah, retired from politics to practice law in England.

Meanwhile, some significant changes were taking place in the regional political matrix in India after the Montague-Chelmsford reforms of 1919. The trend was to muster strength from the provinces to lay claim for power at the centre. The Congress with its street based political mobilisation had taken the lead but in the process vitiated the communal atmosphere of the country.

Muslims in the minority provinces of UP, CP and Bihar started feeling insecure when they realised that they would never be able to dominate the Provincial Assembly because in the game of number they could not match the non-Muslim majority. While, Muslims in provinces where they had a majority, like Punjab, Sindh and Bengal were also apprehensive that their wafer thin majorities, meticulously built on intercommunal alliances, could easily be torpedoed by the political mechanisation of the centre, which obviously would comprise non-Muslim majority.

Muslims, of both minority and majority provinces, desperately wanted someone to plead their case in the emerging political configuration in India. Jinnah, being a floating politician, having no particular base fitted the bill instantly. He was summoned from England to take the reigns of Muslim politics following the passing of the Government of India Act of 1935.

The British government through the Government of India Act, 1935, wanted an 'Indian Federation' to be set up where the representatives of Muslims, Congress and Princely states would come to a Constituent Assembly and draft the constitution of India.

As a corollary to the Act, elections were held in India in 1937, which exposed the hollow base of the Muslim League and established the predominant position of the Congress on the Indian political scene.

The UP coalition controversy, followed by the two years of Congress rule, its mass contact programme and cultural and educational programme, drove the Muslims to search an alternative strategy to combat the majority rule in India. This was initiated by Jinnah through the Lahore resolution of 23 March 1940. More euphemistically to be later called as the demand for Pakistan, the Lahore resolution built a case to challenge the majority rule.

Pakistan, with the connotation of partition of India, was not the vision of Jinnah. He wanted Pakistan to be part of united India on the model of Scotland and Wales, which are parts of Great Britain.

What Jinnah wanted was complete autonomy for the Muslim dominated provinces in the North and East of the country, to be declared as Pakistan first. Having secured a base, Jinnah then wanted to enter into an alliance with India on the matter of defence and communal safeguards. He wanted to assure sufficient safeguards to the non-Muslims in the areas to be called as Pakistan in lieu of similar assurance from India.

However, translation of Jinnah's vision into reality depended on the approval of the Congress and the British government. The Congress, the dominant political party never agreed to yield anything before complete independence of India. The British government, which had always been giving assurances about the protection of the Muslims and the Princes, seems to be in no mood to continue and were in a great deal of hurry to wind up the Raj after the end of the World War II.

Whatever may have been the cherished dream of Jinnah, it was under tremendous strain due to the political mobilisation of the Muslims on the communal lines. The crystallisation of communal identity, which took place during the course of building the movement of Pakistan, could hardly be wielded back on the secular platform. In the end, Jinnah had to be content with something, which he actually did not want and may have used only for bargaining purposes to remain in united India.

The creation of Pakistan, thus, represents a story of both triumph and despair of Jinnah. Triumph, because Jinnah was able to achieve partially what he explicitly vouched for, though in his heart of hearts he may not have cherished it. Despair because he could not keep India united – a dream which he had nursed since the beginning of his political career. This conflicting persona of Jinnah makes him one of the most enigmatic personalities of the subcontinent.

Pakistan – The Unfulfilled Dream

At the fiftieth year of India's independence in 2000, the theme – Partition of India – attracted a spate of thought provoking writings. Most of them happens to be random reflections filled with memoirs of that period. The hallmarks of these writings are the themes of common culture, language and social identity. Conspicuously, most of the writings glossed over the reasons of partition of India, a sordid drama, soaked in blood and tears in the summer of 1947.

Now, when the heat and dust have settled down and the event has been consigned to the pages of history, one would like to kick off a debate whether it was really partition of India or more appropriately a failure of the grand strategy built up by Jinnah who pleaded the case for Muslims to live with respect and dignity in Independent India.

The genesis of the demand for Pakistan was not the ideological divide or the territorial division but the power sharing between the political elites of the two communities; Hindus and Muslims of the subcontinent. In their power struggle, secular and communal ideology became a potent weapon for the mobilisation of their respective constituencies.

One side launched the struggle making secularism as its planks and invited specificities to merge their identity and share the spoils of power. The other side, apprehending being swept away by the wind of democracy wanted to circumvent their permanent minority status, mobilised themselves on communal platform for being co-opted in the emerging power structure.

The secularists were on a firm turf, since it was obvious that when democracy becomes the rule and the ballot box its arbitrator, the majority community would become the repository of power. Their position was so strong that even a powerful coalition of various specificities could no way dislodge them from their new-found place.

On the contrary, democratisation of India portrayed a bleak future for the minorities specially for the Muslims of the country. They developed an alternative strategy to overcome their minority status by regrouping themselves with the backing of their five majority provinces and inventing the euphemism of Pakistan – a catch-phrase that was the rallying point for all the Muslims of the subcontinent.

Pakistan was interpreted by the Muslims in their majority provinces of Punjab, Sindh and Bengal to free them from the clutches of the central authority, while Muslims in minority provinces of UP, CP and Bihar interpreted it to provide them protection against the majority rule in their provinces and the country.

Even though the demand for Pakistan remained undefined, it was meant for forging a quid pro quo arrangement with Hindu and Muslim majority provinces of India. The idea was to extract concessions from the non-Muslims for the Muslims living in Hindu majority areas by giving the non-Muslims the same concessions living in the Muslim majority provinces. Pakistan was never thought with the idea of the migration of religious population and was mooted to provide a shield to those Muslims who would be left in India.

The only way to drum up support for Pakistan was to harp on communal propaganda and by spreading a canard of majority domination over the minorities of India. The Pakistan bogey, though succeeded in cementing the Muslim heterogeneity to some extent, in the process it antagonised the non-Muslims beyond reparable limits. Mistrust and suspicion vitiated the political atmosphere so much so that in the end there was no room left for any reconciliation in a united India.

The anomaly in Jinnah's grand strategy was glaring further. How could five Muslim provinces equate with more than dozen Hindu dominated provinces? Apart from that, if the princely states too were democratised, Muslims majority provinces could further become unequal in any reciprocal arrangement.

In the course of the decade long political mobilisation to the run up of the independence, Congress showed overconfidence due to its inherent strength and constantly ignored the Muslim League for having a weak political standing. The British government, due to the compulsions emanating from the World War II, courted the Muslim League to keep the struggle for independence at bay. This vicious circle culminated in the building of a tornado unparalleled in Indian history.

Muslims could have been in permanent dominant position had Jinnah's plan succeeded in toto. Its failure left them to be content with dominating only the small area where they were in majority, leaving most of their peers in a hopeless minority situation in the rest of India.

The Muslim League thought that the British and the Congress might yield to their demand due to the compulsion of solving the communal puzzle. But the sudden decision of the British government to leave India dampened the Muslim cause. It further placed the Congress in a catch twenty-two situation. Accepting the Muslim League's demand would mean belying their democratic strength, rejecting them would mean severance of those territories, which were part of united India.

In the end, the die was cast to shed the Muslim load by scissoring those provinces where they were in majority. Migration was forced upon those who were caught on the wrong side of the religious divide. The limitation of geography however, could not accommodate every Muslim in the "Promised Land".

The Muslims who found themselves on the right side of the fence could be of no help for those caught on the wrong side. On the other hand, those locked in the minority situation got politically emasculated and stigmatised as a posthumous community mortgaged for the creation of Pakistan. Those Muslims who migrated to Pakistan were derogatorily called "Mohajirs" or refugees, and they confronted a new set of problems in an alien land.

Pakistan, which was intended to solve the problems of the Muslims, actually created many new hurdles for them. Muslims of the subcontinent are still grappling with this reality.

Changing Profile of the Indian Muslims

On the eve of independence, Muslims in India stood at the very apex of the society. They presided over the vast concentration of the rural wealth located in the north Indian plains. They were the landed aristocracy, the elite gentry, professionals, leaders and men who guided the destiny of the country.

The partition of India came to them as the biggest jolt and a large number who foresaw a bleak future migrated to Pakistan. Others who had immovable assets and chose to live in India, suffered complete destruction due to the land reforms in the fifties, which forced them to move to countries other than Pakistan. Frequent communal riots and constant discrimination further forced Muslim migration out of India.

Notwithstanding these facts, Muslims constitute more than 12 per cent, of which 60 per cent live in the Indo-Gangetic plains in north India. The profile of Indian Muslims has undergone a sea change since the independence of the country. Some are small land holders while other are engaged in commercial activities. Artisans, farm labourers, shopkeepers, public and private sector employees are the different facets of Indian Muslim's profile. Those who have gone to the oil-rich Gulf countries have seen a great deal of prosperity; while others who have moved to bigger Indian cities have also flourished due to the urban growth of India.

The fruits of growing trade, commerce and industrial activity in India have trickled down and affluence has once again started smiling at the Muslim homes. The north Indian social space, which was once depleted of Muslim populace due to migration to Pakistan, is again abuzz with their presence, since a new generation has come up in the last fifty years. Substantial pockets of Muslims have emerged all over north India and their wealth and status could be compared with the feudal aristocracy of yore.

Along with the changing times, Muslims have undergone a distinct transformation in their language, dress and demeanour. The pan-chewing, *sherwani*-clad Muslim stereotype is not a common sight anymore. Muslims are no longer obsessed with Urdu as their mother tongue and are quite at home with Hindi, the national language of the country.

Politically Muslims are as active as before. On the eve of every election, there is brisk political activity to garner the 'Muslim vote'. Being the most distinctive and integrated community, Muslims make an attractive segment to vie for votes by the different political parties in north India.

Unlike the Muslim community of the fifties and the sixties who suffered from an inferiority complex for having participated in the Pakistan movement, the new generation does not have any guilt of being Indian citizen. They are aware of their rights as the citizen of the country and demand their due from the government and the society. They are able to extract substantial incentive from the political parties for their uplift, which is a sign of their social and political vibrancy.

There is a seminal shift in the Muslim's participation in the political process due to their growing social transformation. The periodic election gives them the best opportunity to release their pent up frustration. Every election sees the community shedding off its inhibitions and coming out in large numbers to exercise their franchise. In some places they are in a situation, where if they cannot assure victory for a candidate, they can at least hand over a defeat due to their voting pattern.

However, there are some disturbing trends that have emerged in the way of the progress of Muslims in India. One is the communal riots which has become a common modern Indian phenomena. In order to abort the growth of the nascent Muslim community, there are some vested interests that deliberately attempt to disturb the peace in all the centres where Muslims are flourishing. The seventies and eighties saw a spate of communal riots where Muslim entrepreneurial activities were on the rise. Mention can be made of cities like Moradabad, Meerut, Aligarh, Kanpur, Varanasi, Bhagalpur, Jamshedpur, Ranchi, etc.

The diabolic manifestations of communal riots were seen at its peak following the destruction of the Babri mosque on 6 December 1992. The barbarism that followed virtually resurrected the scene of partition of India in every north Indian town. The worst followed when Muslims in Mumbai were targeted for the bomb blast in 1993. The crescendo of the communal riots reached its peak in March 2002, in Gujarat. Lakhs of Hindus were seen participating in the deliberate communal anti-Muslim pogrom, following the Godhra carnage where 28 Hindus were burnt alive in Sabarmati train compartment, alleged to be the handiwork of the Muslims. More than 2000 Muslims perished in the worst of the communal riots that continued for months together in Ahmedabad and other cities of Gujarat.

It is seen that over the years the communal brutality has increased manifold in every riot, the brunt of which is being felt by the Muslim community. With every communal riot, every little bit, that is meticulously built up gets violently destroyed. There seems to be no respite from this snake and ladder story, which has become the fate of Indian Muslims.

The other disturbing trend is the deliberate attempt by some political parties to polarise the society on religious lines. Communal passion is whipped by targeting Muslims to consolidate the Hindu votes. Come every election, Ram temple, uniform civil code, polygamy, Article 370, Madrasas, cow slaughter issues are raked up along with the spectre of Pakistan, Islamic jihad, Bangladeshi infiltration, etc, to consolidate the Hindu votes.

The politics of polarisation had its greatest manifestation during the course of Ayodhya movement, which led to the rise of the BJP and its capturing of power, first in several states, and later at the national level. The anti-Muslim politics has come to occupy space alongside a sympathetic political approach towards them in India.

Muslims' position has marginally improved since the community started establishing a sympathetic relationship with the backward caste categories of the Hindu community. As a result, a Dalit-Muslim configuration is shaping up in the Indo-Gangetic plains of India. Regional parties like Samajwadi and Bahujan Samaj in UP and Rashtriya Janata Dal in Bihar have sprung up with this combination of forces and are sympathetic towards the Muslims.

Muslims in India have acquired a sense of growing security under varying political patronage. Riots have considerably declined in the north Indian plains and any attempts to polarise the society on religious lines is frowned upon by the political groups sympathetic towards the Muslims. As a result they have stopped looking outside India to secure their future and consider their motherland not only to be their *Jnambhomi* (birthplace) but also to be their *Karmbhomi* (workplace). Muslims' future in India though may remain shrouded in uncertainty, nevertheless, it is, not lacking in hope.

Mohajir Imbroglio in Pakistan

The word Mohajir has an Arabic origin, which means someone who takes *pannah* or shelter. This expression has come to become synonymous with the Urdu speaking Indian migrants who settled in the province of Sindh of Pakistan, following India's partition in 1947. The migrants who left their homes for various reasons such as to escape the communal holocaust in India, others going to a land of opportunities, some fired by the zeal to build a new nation, found their dream being shattered after reaching the 'promised land'.

Indian Muslims who expected a privileged position in Pakistan due to the sacrifices made for its creation had the first shock when they were denied the entitlement of the evacuee property in lieu of their assets left behind in India. Since most of them could not carry any property documents in their possession, following communal upheaval, they were unable to file any legal claim.

Those who could get some property in the hinterland of Sindh were unable to manage their estate due to local resistance. A majority of them migrated back to the urban centres of Sindh with largest concentration in Karachi, Hyderabad and other places.

Initially most of the Indians were able to find good jobs in the government and non-government organisation, being better educated compared to the local population but as the education spread and development began to make its impact, their privileged position started being questioned.

The Mohajirs' deprivation came to fore when General Ayub Khan (1958-1968) shifted the capital from Karachi to Islamabad in 1960. The Mohajirs who manned the lower bureaucracy of the federal government lost their jobs as they again did not wanted to shift their location. The Mohajirs fell out of favour with General Ayub as they supported Fatima Jinnah, sister of M A Jinnah, in the 1966 elections.

The real rupture between Mohajirs and Sindhis surfaced during the seventies, when the idea of 'son of the soil' was floated and Indian migrants were denigrated as 'Mohajirs' (shelter seekers). The Pakistani Prime Minister Zulfikar Ali Bhutto is reported to have said, "We Sindhis would give begging bowls in the hand of the Mohajirs."

During Z A Bhutto's regime, the Sindh Assembly passed a resolution making Sindhi the official language of the state and turned down the demand of the Mohajirs to give Urdu the same status. It was during this time, that the domicile system was introduced in Sindh for admission in educational institutions and Mohajirs were discriminated in the issuance of such certificates. Further, the quota system was introduced for government jobs on the basis of urban-rural divide with a 40/60 ratio. Mohajirs living in urban centres could only compete within 40 per cent of the quota in Sindh.

The situation further exploded under General Zia-ul-Haq (1979-87) when the Punjabis made inroads to the urban centres of Sindh. Shortly after that Afghan refugees too poured in and brought the 'Kalashnikov culture' along with them. There has been a general chaos in Sindh since then.

It took about three decades for the Mohajirs to organise themselves as a political force in Sindh. Mohajir Quami Movement (MQM), which came into being on 18 March 1984, actually emerged from the All Pakistan Mohajir Student Organisation (APMSO) formed in 1978. Altaf Hussain, who emerged as its top leader, made MQM politically active since 1986 and the outfit swept the local-body polls of 1987 in the urban centres of Sindh.

MQM, which renamed itself in 1997 as Muttahida Quami Mahaz, released a charter of demands which included: increase in the number of seats in both the provincial and the National Assembly according to its population, abolition of the quota system in government jobs, increase in the Mohajir's quota for admission in various educational institutions, particularly in professional courses, and lastly repatriation of the Biharis staying in camps in Bangladesh since 1971.

The Mohajir's other demands were: that only the real Sindhis (Mohajir and Sindhis) should have the right to vote, nonvoters should not be given business licenses, they should have no right to buy property in Sindh, the public transport system should be taken over by the municipal corporations and all charges against MQM activists be dropped and Altaf Hussain be allowed to return from exile in London to Karachi.

In Pakistan's predominantly two party set-up, Pakistan's People's Party (PPP) and Pakistan Muslim League (PML – Nawaz), MQM has time and again proved itself as the third largest political force. It has swung between the two parties but has been unable to strike any compromise with either of them on its core or periphery demands. The MQM leader, Altaf Hussain has urged for the granting of 'complete' autonomy to smaller provinces, including Sindh for a permanent solution to the Mohajir problem. He has also demanded a new Constitution for Pakistan but all this has evoked no response from the Pakistani President Pervez Musharraf, as yet.

The Mohajir's problem revolves around the rural-urban constituencies of Sindh. The interests of both the constituencies run contrary to each other. Sindhis' discontentments is growing due to the Mohajir domination in urban areas and they want the domicile and quota system to stay to improve their social standing. The Mohajirs, on the other hand, perceive these as an impediment in their development and want them removed. The resultant grievances caused the Mohajir imbroglio to persist in Pakistan.

Peace Battles in Karachi

It may be business as usual in Karachi, but this commercial nerve centre of Pakistan, a few years ago, was the battleground for trigger-happy activists of MQM's Altaf and Haqiqi factions. They had turned the city virtually into a war zone. The scale of violence may have minimised now, but its embers still simmers beneath, needing just a spark to be ignited again.

Karachi's population is over 15 million where Mohajirs constitute more than 60 per cent. Sindhis, Afghans, Punjabis and other ethno-linguistic groups make up rest of the city's population. The city generates almost 75 per cent of the government's revenue and is the commercial hub of Pakistan. No wonder the city attracts a constant influx of people from various parts of the country. The tide has increased ever since the Gulf boom plummeted and a large number of unemployed youth started making a beeline for the city.

Karachi's population is increasing at a rate of over six per cent and unemployment is growing over three times annually. The city is not able to cope up with the pressures of population and unemployment, besides, its haphazard urban planning and paltry civic amenities have added to the woes of the city life.

Karachi in the seventies was like any other megalopolis where some sanity prevailed in the urban madness. The city was by and large peaceful, except occasional skirmishes between Mohajirs and Sindhis that was more politically orchestrated than the usual boil. There was some social equilibrium in the city even though every one was not happy living with each other.

All this changed since the Soviet invasion of Afghanistan in 1979. Large Afghan refugees poured into the city and slowly percolated into the unskilled sector dominating the transport and real estate business. The refugees also brought Kalashnikov culture and indulged in underworld activities which revolved around narcotics and arms trade.

Their illegal commercial activities generated huge money and there was covert participation of administration in the city's illegal expanding economy. The top political bosses who remained on the payrolls of the Mafia dons turned a blind eye to the steep rise in criminal activities in the city. The general development of the city took a bad beating because of the rise in illegal activities.

The rise of the MQM as a political party has often been accompanied by violence and has been responsible for the growing chaos in Karachi. MQM grew from the Karachi campus politics and its cadre, being armed to the teeth, has been involved in several acts of urban violence. Stockpiles of arms were kept in campuses where youth took to violence to seek admissions. Students carrying Kalashnikovs was common sight then in Karachi's campuses.

The conflict in the port city has been recurring prominently since the second half of the eighties. It was during this time, that the MQM was organising itself as a political force and clashed with the Sindhi activists due to their conflicting political interest. It is alleged that General Zia ul-Haq patronised the MQM to break the backbone of Sindhi nationalism, which was on the rise then.

The second bout of violence took place in 1988, when the Afghan refugees created a chaotic situation in Karachi. Their desire to control the illegal pattern of land development and their rough behaviour in running the public transport system brought them in conflict with the Mohajirs. Several bloody clashes with the MQM activists and Afghan refugees took place during this time. It was after a great deal of persuasion the two sides were restrained, and city was brought under control.

The third round was in 1989 when Benazir Bhutto was unseated from power following the breakdown of the pre-election alliance between PPP and MQM called Karachi Accord. Supporters of both the parties engaged in a fierce battle shortly after that to settle political scores.

Karachi was almost reduced to a war zone in the nineties. The Pakistani army, which controls the civilian government from behind, engineered a split in the MQM in 1991 and created a 'Haqiqi' (real) faction to break the growing clout of the MQM. Afaq Ahmed and Amir Khan, who originally belonged to the armed wing of the MQM, led the 'Haqiqi' group. Since then, the Haqiqi faction has seized control of some of the Mohajir dominated areas in Karachi and declared these as no go area for the activists of the Altaf group. The two factions of the MQM, since then, have been battling it out for the supremacy of the city.

Both Benazir Bhutto and Nawaz Sharif, as prime minister of Pakistan, had tried to address the issue but were unable to find a political settlement to the Mohajir problem. Both had called army several times in Karachi to maintain law and order. It was in 1998, after the proclamation of emergency in Sindh, that several strong measures were taken to bring violence under control in Karachi.

Another development in the nineties that gripped Karachi was the growth of the right wing extremist groups, championing the cause of militant Islam. They grew alongside the rise of Taliban in Afghanistan. It was these forces, which indulged in acts of violence against the Shias and Christians and were behind the killing of American journalist Daniel Pearl.

Karachi is witnessing conflict at various levels. In the political plane there is conflict between MQM and the Sindhi nationalists. On the economic level, MQM's interest clashes with Afghan and Punjabi communities. Moreover factional quarrel within MQM for the supremacy of the city is also being witnessed.

A siege mentality has set in Karachi and the city seems to have lost its sense of direction. Urbanisation has shrunk the space of competition with the interest of one group wanting to displace the other. The easy access to weaponry adds lethality to the city's life. The law enforcing mechanism has repeatedly failed to bring normalcy into the city. The results of these contradictions are frightening. Even the battle for peace is on. Life continues in all this madness, in Karachi!

Mohajirs Remote Controlled from London

Altaf Hussain, the exiled leader of the MQM party, addressing a gathering in 1994, of Urdu speaking Mohajir community in London, said, *"Jab watan tha to azadi mangi, jab azad hui to watan nahi hai."* (When we had a country we demanded independence, when we become free, we have no country).

Altaf goes on to say that, if a non-Muslim kills a Muslim at least, he attains *shahadat* or martyrdom, but even this prerogative is not available in Pakistan. "Where should we go ... the army is our enemy... the bureaucracy hate us ... the feudal element frowns upon ... whom should we complain ... there is no one to listen to us in Pakistan."

Altaf Hussain feels that the edifice of the two-nation theory has crumbled after the creation of Pakistan. He says, Pakistan, which was created as 'Promised land', for Muslims of the entire subcontinent, has become a country of Sindhis, Punjabis, Baluchis and Pathans – the four dominant nationalities of the country.

The MQM leader says, the Urdu speaking Muslims who migrated from India should too be given the status of a nationality like the other counterparts, since their population is over 20 million in Pakistan. He bemoans that the Mohajirs are hardly being treated like a 'Quam' and are constantly being discriminated in the matters of education and employment, representation in the local bodies and federal government, etc, in Pakistan.

Altaf Hussain who has emerged as the unquestioned leader of the Mohajirs of Pakistan was born and brought up in a moderate middle class locality of Karachi, called Azizabad. His house which bears the door number, '90', is now the headquarter of the MQM. Altaf's father hailed from Benaras and was an Eastern Railway employee before he migrated to Pakistan in the wake of India's partition.

The seeds of Mohajir movement were laid in Jamia-e-Islamia college and Karachi University where Mohajirs were subjected to severe harassment by the local youth. Regular clashes were witnessed between local boys and those whose parents had migrated from Hindi speaking areas of India. As a result, a protective squad of the Mohajir students called All Pakistan Mohajir Student Organisation (APMSO) was formed in 1978. The initial coterie of APMSO consisted of Altaf Hussain, Anjum Tariq, Ainul Huque, Salim Shazad and Farooq Sattar.

In 1981 APMSO was banned by the government but it quickly transformed itself into a political party called Mohajir Quami Movement (MQM). The organisation gained strength as the discrimination against Mohajir increased and later came to be called as Muthida Quami Movement.

Since 1987, when the MQM contested the election for the first time, the party emerged as a political force in Pakistan winning 27 seats. Altaf Hussain emerged as the unquestioned leader of the Mohajir community. His word runs like law on the entire community and a directive from him can bring life to a grinding halt in Karachi and Hyderabad, the two major cities of Pakistan. Altaf Hussain who survived an assassination attempt on 1 January 1992 moved to London and since then, MQM for all practical purposes have shifted to England.

The MQM's General Secretary, UK and Continent, Manzoor Yazdani, and late Nizam Ahmed, MQM's Treasurer, London Unit, in 1994, enlightened me about the vision MQM – to address the problems of the Muslim migrants from India living in Sindh.

The late Nizam Ahmed said that the MQM wanted total overhauling of the state structure of Pakistan which still clings to feudal age and is run by the archaic laws. Similarly, the character of the army, which is predominantly Punjabi, should also change. In jobs and admission, merit should be made the criterion and not ascription of birth or domicile. Ahmed further added that the parameters of the politics accordingly should change and the landed gentry should make way for more people's participation.

Talking about the organisational strength of the MQM in Pakistan, Ahmed said that in the 1987 provincial assembly, the MQM romped home with 27 seats at just six hours notice. He felt that if the party was properly organised, the tally could reach 35 seats. Ahmed said, if the seats in the Provincial Assembly were increased according to population ratio, then MQM should get at least 50 seats in the state.

Highlighting the problems of Mohajir in Karachi, Manzoor Yazdani, said that the city has over fifteen million populations of which over 60 per cent are Mohajirs. The city's population increases at the rate of 4.8 per cent and unemployment by about 25 per cent. The development of the city does not keep pace with the changes, which creates all sorts of problems for Karachi. Yazdani suggested creation of an administrative unit for Mohajirs. However, he categorically ruled out any idea of the creation of 'Jinnahpur' or something akin to that, to be carved out from Sindh.

Talking about the activities of the MQM London unit, Yazdani said that it came to existence in 1984, coinciding with the MQM organisational success in Karachi. The job of the London unit is to be in constant touch with the MQM office at Karachi. The London unit holds press conferences, publishes newsletters, organises protest marches, and highlights human right violation against Mohajirs in Pakistan.

Yazdani, whose parents hailed from UP and Ahmed whose parents came from Bihar, were young boys when they migrated to Pakistan. They later left for UK for studies, and settled down there, with jobs. Both advocate South Asian federation for the development of Pakistan and India and the region as a whole. They say, hunger, illiteracy and unemployment are the common problems of South Asia that have to be fought regionally. When asked if they still remember India, both become pensive; Nizam Ahmed broke down saying: "Nostalgia traps us, history embraces us, how can we forget our past!"

3
India-Pakistan

- *Breaking the Shackles of History* • *Growing International Focus* • *US Predicament in South Asia* • *Compulsions for Composite Dialogue to Begin* • *Caught in Optimism-Pessimism Syndrome*

Breaking the Shackles of History

Genuine fear, competitive diplomacy, intimidation, defiance and playing the game of poker are the hallmarks of the India-Pakistan relationship. Even after more than fifty years of independence, the ghost of the past still haunts the mindset of the leadership of both countries. Their non-resilient attitude to break the political deadlock compels one to wonder as to how many more years will it take for the two countries to synergise their energies to compete with the future.

While, looking for reasons, one may delve into history. One can rake up the issues of ideological, cultural and civilisational divides. This can well be countered by arguing that within the womb of these divides; there also nestled composite social fabrics which were cautiously built up over the centuries.

This culture was present during 1857 at the time of India's first war of independence, and continued during the formative years of the freedom struggle. It went hand in hand until 1920 but eventually got ruptured when the Congress and the Muslim League could not share the same political vision of the future India.

The unpleasantness and horrors generated during independence-partition period had a telling impact on the Indo-

Pak relations. The same rigidity that dominated the mindset of the pre-partition politics continues to dominate the Indo-Pak proceedings even today. Whenever the two sides come to the negotiating table, they have a preconceived notion not to come to any understanding with each other. As a result, all the previous talks between the two have remained the proverbial dialogue between the deaf.

The independent history of the two nations has been dogged by two and half wars, support to opposite camps during the Cold War, arms race, negative propaganda and proxy war. The two countries approach every forum with pre-convinced mindset to run down each other, whether it was at the United Nation or the SAARC.

The genesis of Pakistan was definitely not what it stands for today. It started with the idea of sharing power whose denial led the Muslim League to search for an alternative strategy, by inventing the bogey of Pakistan, so that it could exert pressure on the Congress to seek terms with it. As a matter of reconciliation, even the idea of making the subcontinent, the United States of South Asia (USSA) was floated at that point of time. However, the rigid stand by the two parties to accommodate each other's aspirations resulted in sowing the seeds of differences, which blocked the future growth of the subcontinent.

The leadership of both the countries have continued with the same mindset and have stifled all the peace processes in their independent histories. India thinks that Pakistan has come into being not because of political necessity but due to political compulsions of achieving independence. In India's thinking, Pakistan has got enough of concessions at the time of its formation and it has to accept the ground realities to come to terms with it.

Pakistan on the other hand remains unfazed by the military and economic prowess of India and would like to bend it to its own terms. Pakistan thinks that it is a matter of time before India would yields to its demands due to international pressure and to buy peace for the subcontinent.

The compulsions of the domestic politics have compounded to the vitiating of the tension between the two countries. In domestic political discourse, the spectre of military attack on each other is periodically drummed up, raising the pitch to the level of war mongering. It suits the leadership of both the countries to keep the public attention away from pressing domestic problems by inciting war hysteria and fears of an invasion from outside.

The hate campaign perpetuated by the leadership has seeped into the veins of the citizens of both the countries. Even sincere and committed efforts for peace are seen with suspicion by constituencies, which feed upon the hate campaign by their respective countries.

The rising crescendo of this hate politics was manifested when both India and Pakistan conducted nuclear tests in 1998 and declared their nuclear weapon capabilities. This has added a new dimension to the already estranged relationship between the two neighbours.

Some feel that the acquisition of the nuclear capabilities by both the countries has complicated their relationship still further. It's argued that there cannot be lasting peace in the subcontinent as long as the sword of Damocles of nuclear war hangs over the two countries. The other argument is that nuclear capabilities have reinforced the theory that fear of mutual destruction will ultimately pave the way towards normalisation of their relationship.

Off late, the leadership of India and Pakistan are realising the gravest sin their previous generations had committed—fighting the past and holding peace to ransom for over fifty years now. They are trying to break the shackles of history by honestly attempting to resolve their differences through composite dialogue. The dialogue process, which has begun, is with good intention and being conducted with a far-sighted approach. Both the countries realise that there are no quick fix solutions to the Indo-Pak tangle but its resolution alone would help to establish a lasting peace in the subcontinent.

Growing International Focus

In the recent times there has been three instances when international powers have got directly involved to persuade India-Pakistan to sort out their differences. First was after the nuclear tests in 1998, second, during Kargil skirmishes of 1999 and third when troops were deployed on the border after the attack on Indian Parliament on 13 December 2001. Indo-Pak relationship has been marked by its highs and lows since then.

International pressure on the subcontinent was felt in the summer of 1998 when India and Pakistan announced that they have become nuclear weapon states. The world community woke up to the risk of nuclear war and mounted pressure on the leadership of both the countries to sort out their differences through a meaningful dialogue. Their pressure was to develop a mechanism so that nuclear crisis does not crop up in future.

The initiative was made at the 10th SAARC summit in Colombo in 1998, when the Indian and Pakistani leadership came face to face for the first time after becoming nuclear powers. The regional leaders at the summit persuaded their Indian and Pakistani counterparts to sort out their bilateral tension for regional stability. A beeline of international leadership was seen then visiting New Delhi and Islamabad, trying to persuade the two countries to embark upon the course of dialogue.

As a result, the early 1999 saw springtime in the Indo-Pak relationship. Then Pakistani cricket team arrived in India on a highly entertaining tour, followed by the opening of the bus services between Delhi and Lahore, whereby, the then Prime Minister, Vajpayee undertook the bus ride and shook hands with his counterpart Nawaz Sharif. Both the leaders signed the Lahore declaration and then began the process of comprehensive and composite dialogue to sort out their outstanding differences. It seemed that after becoming nuclear, the two countries had decided to embark on the journey of friendship.

The Lahore initiative proved to be a flash in the pan. Kargil surfaced in May 1999. The two countries almost came to war when India made up its mind to cross the Line of Control if Pakistan did not pull back its troops. The international community once again came into the scene and stopped the crisis from further conflagration. They disengaged India and Pakistan from going to an all out war.

Indo-Pak relationship further vitiated when General Pervez Musharraf, ousted Prime Minister Nawaz Sharif in a bloodless coup on 12 October 1999. India considered General Musharraf to be the architect of the Kargil border clash and further drifted away from Pakistan.

The highjacking of the Indian Airlines plane IC814, from Kathmandu to New Delhi on the Christmas Eve of 1999, further complicated the Indo-Pak relationship. India saw Pakistan's hand in the highjacking episode. It was at pain to release some terrorists in exchange of the safe passage of its passengers at Kandahar. Much to its chagrin, the same terrorists later resurfaced in Pakistan.

The two countries indulged in posturing and counter posturing all through the year 2000. Musharraf who emerged as another army general who was in for a long haul in Pakistan started making overtures for an unconditional dialogue with India. The Indian leadership rebuffed his bait saying, for any meaningful dialogue to start Pakistan has to stop aiding and abetting terrorism in Kashmir and dismantle all the infrastructure of terror it has built in its country.

The international powers came into picture once again nudging the two countries to seek terms. It resulted in the Agra summit of 2001. The much-hyped summit could not make any headway because Pakistan insisted on maintaining the centrality of the Kashmir issue, while India's prime concern was terrorism. The blame game once again began. The truce was short-lived. Friends became foes again.

The terrorist attack on Indian Parliament on 13 December 2001 vitiated the Indo-Pak relations further. India saw Pakistan's hand in that and reacted sharply by sending troops to the forward positions on the border which remained locked in an eyeball-to-eyeball confrontation for over a year. India severed all diplomatic ties with its neighbour and asked Pakistan to stop terrorism; it also handed over a list of 20 terrorists wanted for perpetrating crimes in India.

To defuse the situation, British Prime Minister Tony Blair, US Secretary of State Colin Powell, UN Secretary General Kofi Annan besides other host of world dignitaries visited the subcontinent. Musharraf in his 12 January 2002 address promised to weed out terrorism from his country and asked India to resume dialogue. India reacted by saying that it wanted a significant change on the ground for any talks to begin, but defused the stand off by pulling back its troops.

Similarly, Pakistan also realised that after 9/11 the world no longer recognises armed struggle as a means of conflict resolution. It implies that terrorism, as an instrument of state policy has to be given up. The international community's sensitivity to the Kashmir problem also underscored the point that the only recourse is to take the route of dialogue.

The complexities of the world politics compounded with the international resolve to put pressure on India and Pakistan to sort out their differences resulted in the beginning of the composite dialogue since March 2004. One round of talk has been completed and the two countries have further agreed to continue the parleys after monitoring its progress. The seriousness with which the talks are progressing generates hope that this time the resolution of Indo-Pak differences is not far away.

US Predicament in South Asia

Washington is caught between principles and realities in handling South Asia, mainly India and Pakistan. Some issues that haunt the US policy makers are; restoration of democracy in Pakistan, resolution of the Kashmir issue, non-proliferation and unlocking of the closed Indo-Pak mindset. The ground realities of the region however make US policy makers sacrifice its accredited principles and react to the situation as it warrants.

US predicament became apparent since the end of the Cold War, when along with Pakistan, India too started courting the US as its potential ally. It became a difficult choice, as both the countries were equally important to it though for different reasons. America's problem was compounded as India and Pakistan remain at loggerheads and their nuclear capabilities continue to disturb the global peace.

The American interest in India grew since New Delhi showed its desire for transfer of technology, purchase of weapons and opening up of new trade channels. To the US, an economically liberalised India with a booming IT industry, vibrant democracy and a country governed by Macaulay's *babus* make it an attractive destination to do business.

The problem the US faces with India is that the latter is not moving forward and improving its relations with Pakistan. America also felt uneasy about India's poor human rights record, frequent caste and communal clashes and growing religious extremism. India's nuclear capability also worries the American policy makers who perceive it as an invitation to global proliferation.

With regard to Pakistan, America's accredited policies have always been flouted in dealing with Islamabad. While, the US champions democracy, Pakistan for most of its history, has remained under various military regimes. Similarly, the US attaches a very high importance to human rights issue; there has been a great degree of its abuse in Pakistan. Even after America has launched a war on global terrorism, fundamentalism with features of terrorism, remains rampant in Pakistan. To cap it all, Pakistan's nuclear programme, gives US policy makers sleepless nights, especially after A Q Khan's episode.

In spite of all its shortcomings, the US has found Pakistan to be its most trusted ally. It may be recalled that General Zia ul Huq who had usurped power from Zulfikar Ali Bhutto, became the most important person for the US establishment because of the Soviet Union's invasion of Afghanistan in 1979. Pakistan under Zia became the frontline state whose policy of nurturing Islamic extremism and gun culture then served American interests.

It is a fact that American guns have made Pakistan a violent society, the consequences of which haunt the country today. It is an irony that the same weapons that America once supplied to Pakistan to drive out the Soviets are used to perpetrate terrorism in Kashmir. America, having forged a global coalition to fight terrorism with Pakistan as its key ally, is paradoxically unable to rein in those very elements which it once carefully nurtured.

Currently, the US is torn between two favourites in Pakistan: democracy and army rule. The US policy makers apprehend that a democratic government may not serve its interest as well as an army-controlled establishment there. America feels that a nuclear Pakistan is safer in the hands of army generals than any democratically elected fundamentalist government there.

The newly evolved situation in South Asia over the Kashmir dispute has also put US into a dilemma. This revolves around democracy and terrorism. If it sides with the democratic forces and goes ahead to implement the UN charter by organising a plebiscite in Kashmir, it may antagonise India with which its relations are getting better every day. If it acts against the terrorist groups operating in Kashmir, it may antagonise Pakistan, which has proven to be its most reliable ally.

Even though there is keen American interest to resolve the Kashmir issue, the growing Indian clout makes US move cautiously on Kashmir. The new turn around in the Indo-US relations has restrained America from taking a tough stand on the resolution of Kashmir issue.

The post 9/11 global scenario has changed the context of American policy towards the nuclear non-proliferation issue in South Asia. Pokhran II by India and Pakistan's responses to it, invited a sharp reaction by the US which slapped sanctions against both the countries asking them to sign the Comprehensive Test Ban Treaty (CTBT). However, since the US Congress has turned down the ratification of the CTBT, the whole issue of global proliferation was put on the backstage. The 9/11 catapulted the lifting of the sanctions, as building a coalition against global terrorism became more important for US policy makers than denuclearising South Asia.

This has led to a tricky situation of nuclear blackmail to propel terrorism in the region. Its heat was felt after terrorists attack on Indian Parliament on 13 December 2001, when India resorted to coercive diplomacy and Pakistan responded by threats of nuclear threats. This forced the US to step in to cool the rising temperature building between the two countries.

Because of the uneasy relationship between India and Pakistan, America is finding it hard to deal with the region. The history of the last fifty years suggests that both New Delhi and Islamabad instead of making the US a partner in the development of their countries want it to be cast in the role of a referee to sort out their differences. India asks the US to pressurise Pakistan to stop cross border terrorism, and Pakistan pleads it to tell India to come to the negotiating table.

It seems the US is content playing the role of global policeman in South Asia. The credit goes to the US for having pacified both India and Pakistan, first during the Kargil skirmishes in 1999, and then, in June 2002, when spectre of war loomed large on the subcontinent. The tragedy with the US is, it cannot go beyond a certain point in mediating the Indo-Pak differences. However, along with other powers, it has made India and Pakistan to seek reasons to initiate the composite dialogue. It remains to be seen how soon the contending parties come to terms with each other.

Compulsions for Composite Dialogue to Begin

When the former Prime Minister, Atal Behari Vajpayee, left for Islamabad to attend the 12th SAARC summit in the first week of January 2004, he had ruled out any possibilities of bilateral talks with Pakistan. He gave least indications before leaving New Delhi that he would be committing to resume dialogue with its hostile neighbour. However, within hours after reaching Islamabad, Vajpayee stated that India is not shy of talking to Pakistan and is ready to resolve all the differences including that of Jammu and Kashmir. Some three days of hectic parleys followed that statement on the sidelines of the SAARC jamboree and a joint statement was released to resume the stalled talks.

The unfolding of events at Islamabad was more or less on expected lines but it definitely raised the curiosity as to what transpired between the leadership of the two countries to agree for talks. Any one who has watched the Indo-Pak developments since half a century would not pin much hope in such joint statements as this could be another pause in their never ending acrimonious relationship. To believe that India would give Kashmir on a silver platter to Pakistan or Pakistan would forfeit its claim over Jammu and Kashmir would be being naïve to the subcontinent's realities. Then what dramatic events conspired to led the two countries resume talks?

There are few pointers which made India seek a resolution of the Kashmir issue earlier than later. Its genesis could be traced from early eighties when America introduced terrorism in this part of the world to drive out the Soviets from Afghanistan. While Americans came and left and re-entered Afghanistan, the shadows of its policy continues to haunt India even after joining the war against global terrorism. India realised that even the continued US presence in the region has not brought any substantial change on the ground situation in Kashmir.

New Delhi also had to do some rethinking after US refused to set up base in India for operations in Afghanistan following 9/11 event. India's interest in providing base was that the US would help dismantle the terror infrastructure in Pakistan, which in turn would fritter away the business of terrorism in Jammu and Kashmir. However, the compulsions of geography forced the US to opt for Pakistan, which made India become defensive because it could neither isolate Pakistan nor win the US support.

Indian decision finally crystallised to resolve Kashmir issue after US invaded Iraq. The precedent set by the US to brush aside all international ethics and bulldoze its way rang alarm bells in New Delhi. The current international scenario where there is no opposition to the US hegemonic designs and where, as a superpower, it has been meddling into all global trouble spots, bothered India to seek terms with Pakistan. India realised that it's better to come to the negotiating table on its own terms rather than be dictated by some other power.

India has also exhausted all its options to go to war with Pakistan before realising that the only way is to tread the path of peace. The Kargil border skirmish in 1999 was one such incident when India had made up its mind to cross the LoC but eventually restrained from doing so. However, the most defining moment came when India pulled back its troops after keeping it in forward position for more than a year, following attack on its Parliament on 13 December 2001. Military experts, who had advocated "brass-tacks" in 1987, then cautioned the government that any military adventurism may not result in an outright victory and such conflagration may go out of hand.

Lately, India realised that it cannot continue to play the cop and robber game forever in Jammu and Kashmir. It thought it would be prudent to resolve the issue, which lies at its heart, than take casualties on daily basis, fighting with the militants. The choice of living with the militancy began to tell upon the Indian establishment. A combination of all these factors left India with no other choice than to make friends with Pakistan.

If India agreed for talks with Pakistan owing to some compulsions, Pakistan too felt that it has to break from the past if it wants to do business with India. The sectarian violence in Pakistan made it further realise that it cannot continue with the policy of fighting terrorism at one level and abet it at other. The attempts on the life of Pakistan's President Pervez Musharraf, further led to the shoring of the idea to move away from its policy to continue giving moral support to militancy in Kashmir. Pakistan eventually gave a categorical commitment to India that in future its territory would not be used for any anti- India activity.

Another important commitment Pakistan made was to shelve the demand of the implementation of UN resolution if India showed interest in resolving the Kashmir issue. The non-implementation of several UN resolutions like the one on Palestine made Pakistan realise that harping on plebiscite in Kashmir would take it nowhere and it has to give it up for any just settlement. Similarly, Pakistan also remained aware that the world community is not interested in implementing the UN resolutions and the parties themselves have to sort out their problems. This was a major concession from Pakistan as it has been trying to put pressure on India for the implementation of UN resolution at various international forums since the past fifty years.

The final commitment Pakistan made, which was a clincher for India to reciprocate by its readiness to resume talks, was to seek the solution of the Kashmir issue without the division of the territory on religious lines. India gave commitment to Pakistan that it is ready to seek solution to the Kashmir issue, which may satisfy all the parties concerned.

It would be too early to say whether the fresh round of talks would resolve all the outstanding differences between India and Pakistan but there is no doubt that both the countries have definitely made a policy shift, which they were pursuing for more than fifty years or so. The commitment by India and Pakistan to pursue the dialogue with all its seriousness reflects that the two sides want to get out of the war trap, which looms over the subcontinent. It is wished that the new-found rapprochement between the two neighbours may resolve all their outstanding differences and the two countries start living like friends and not as enemies any more.

Caught in Optimism-Pessimism Syndrome

The India-Pakistan dialogue has elements of both tragedy and comedy. Tragedy, because at the end of every round both sides agree to disagree with each other, and comedy because both show optimism to carry the dialogue process forward. In spite of the commitment to find a consensus over the vexed issues, the many rounds of talks that were so far held between the two countries, has been caught in an optimism-pessimism syndrome. The same signal continues to emerge in the latest rounds of talks that have been initiated since March 2004.

There are nine issues which have been brought up for discussion between India and Pakistan. These are: 1) CBMs (Confidence Building Measures) on Nuclearisation, 2) Kashmir, 3) Terrorism, 4) Siachin, 5) Wullar barrage-Tulbul navigational project, 6) Sir Creek Island, 7) Drug trafficking, 8) Economic cooperation and 9) Promotion of peace and friendship.

To avoid a nuclear confrontation, India and Pakistan have come up with an impressive list of CBMs. India has proposed the no first use of nuclear weapons, while Pakistan has suggested a non-aggression pact, which includes nuclear and conventional restraint measures. The establishment of communication links between political and military authorities was another CBM put on the table by the two countries. There was partially agreement on this proposal and there is likelihood of a broad consensus emerging on a series of CBMs pertaining to nuclear risk management.

On Kashmir issue, the two sides hold divergent viewpoints. Pakistan says India's claim on Kashmir is flawed and it is not a territorial dispute, but an unfinished agenda of the partition of India. Pakistan wants the Kashmir problem to be solved in accordance with the wishes of the people of Kashmir. Indian position, in the current context, is that the dispute has to be settled bilaterally in accordance with Shimla Agreement of 1972 and Lahore Declaration of 1999. India has asserted that Jammu and Kashmir (J&K) is an integral part of its union.

Pakistan remains adamant that the progress towards an amicable solution of the Kashmir issue is central to the composite dialogue process. It wants substantial progress to be made first on Kashmir issue before agreeing on any other point under discussion. India suggested moving from simpler to complex issue and not to front-load the seemingly most complicated issue first. Pakistan's view is that the nuclearisation of the subcontinent has changed the security dimension of the region and dealing with the peripheral issue would only be papering over the cracks. India sees no linkages between the nuclear capabilities and the Kashmir situation. India, however, says it is ready to discuss Kashmir along with other issues with Pakistan.

On terrorism, New Delhi says that for any meaningful dialogue to continue, Pakistan should stop sponsoring cross-border insurgency in Kashmir and elsewhere in India. Pakistan repudiates India's allegation saying that the uprising in Kashmir is indigenous and more due to repression launched by the Indian security forces there. In the fresh round of talks, Pakistan has given categorical assurance to India that it would not allow any anti-India activities from its soil. There has been a perceptible decline in militancy in Jammu and Kashmir since then, which to a large extent has strengthened the Indo-Pak dialogue process.

The Siachin glacier is another irritant between India and Pakistan. It is an un-demarcated area, 75 kilometres in length and 2.8 kilometres in width, situated at the centre of Karakoram Range, northeast of the Pakistani side of Kashmir. Pakistan accused India of trying to occupy Siachin by force in June 1984, when India claimed the glacier to be a part of its territory. In February 1985, the countries engaged themselves in fierce fighting for the barren land that lasted for more than two weeks. Since then, a strict vigil has been kept on the strategically important glacier, making Siachin world's highest battlefield.

The dispute over Wullar barrage or Tulbul navigational project is about the objection raised by Pakistan on India's attempt to construct a 439 feet high and 40 feet wide barrage on river Jhelum in 1984. Pakistan said that India could no way start construction work without its prior permission as per agreement under the Indus water treaty of 1960.

The two countries dispute the demarcation of Sir Creek Island, a 38 kilometres marshy land, along the Rann of Kutch in Gujarat and the Sindh province of Pakistan. The other issues under discussion are drug trafficking, economic cooperation and promotion of people to people contact.

It is not that India and Pakistan have not come to terms with each other. In their previous negotiations the two countries had amicably settled the land and property dispute following the partition of India. The two sides had also signed the Indus water treaty in 1960 for the sharing of water, which has survived the two wars.

During Rajiv Gandhi and Benazir Bhutto's period (1984-88), an agreement not to attack each other's nuclear installations and to establish a hotline to inform each other of troop movements was signed. The two leaders also agreed to avoid double taxation on income incurred from international air transport and develop interaction in the field of arts, culture, education, mass media and sports.

The next phase of Indo-Pak parleys began when two rounds of talks were held at Islamabad and New Delhi in 1999. Then an agreement was reached on how to approach the problem with both the countries committed to remain engaged in further negotiations. The 1999 peace initiatives were revived in 2001 at the Agra summit. This cyclical movement has again been kick started when both the countries agreed to resume the composite dialogue in March 2004.

The peace initiatives between India and Pakistan continue unhindered even after the change in government in New Delhi in July 2004. Both the countries are adhering to the agreed mechanism to carry on the dialogue process forward. The talk, which is gradually progressing, has a perceptible amount of seriousness shown this time. It gives the impression that the optimism-pessimism syndrome that is the trademark of India-Pakistan dialogue would be exorcised soon.

4
Kashmir

• *The Genesis of Kashmir Issue* • *India-Pakistan Bilateral Talks* • *Beyond the Healing Touch* • *India's Road-map to Kashmir* • *Remembering Abdul Ghani Lone*

The Genesis of Kashmir Issue

To the younger generation who are not aware of the intricacies of India's partition, it would be difficult to comprehend why India and Pakistan are so emotional over the Kashmir issue. The two countries have fought two and half wars and had held several rounds of negotiations but still no solution have been found to this vexed issue that has been dogging the subcontinent for more than fifty years now.

To put it briefly, the princely state of Jammu and Kashmir (J&K) had an overwhelming Muslim population but was ruled by a Hindu ruler. During the freedom struggle anti-ruler politics was rife in most of the princely states and the state of J&K was no exception. The people in the state supported the Indian National Congress party for it's anti-feudal and anti-colonial campaign. However, in the late thirties, when the Muslim League rose like a phoenix in the Indian politics to challenge the supremacy of the Congress, the people in J&K too got divided on its support to a united India or Pakistan. A large number wanted independence for their state as well.

The picture that emerged after the failure of Cabinet Mission in 1946 was that India would be divided on the religious lines. Lord Mountbatten who came to New Delhi to preside over the liquidation of the British Empire announced that a separate state of Pakistan would be carved out from the Indian dominion. The area where Muslims were in overwhelming majority would be called as Pakistan, while those with Hindu majority population will remain as India. The princely states were given the choice to secede to either dominion, India or Pakistan.

The princely state of Hyderabad and Junagarh, which had Muslim rulers with Hindu subjects wanted to join Pakistan but India did not subscribed to the views of its rulers. These states were contagious regions of India with an overwhelming Hindu population. In case of Junagarh a plebiscite was held to ascertain the will of the people who voted in favour of India. The accession issue of Hyderabad was prolonged for almost a year and in the end was resolved through police action by India in September 1948.

In the case of J&K, its ruler also wavered over the accession issue, which prompted armed raiders from the Pakistan's side to swoop into Kashmir and forcibly wrest its control. This made the ruler of the J&K to sign the instrument of accession with India and after that the Indian army drove the enemy to the present Line of Control (LoC). Ever since then, the LoC has become the boundary between India and Pakistan that divides the territory of Kashmir.

Kashmir since then has become a disputed territory and India took the case to the United Nations (UN) to settle this dispute with Pakistan. The UN passed a resolution asking for holding a plebiscite in J&K to ascertain the will of the people as to which country they would like to be with. The UN resolution put a precondition that for such a plebiscite to be conducted Pakistan should vacate the area under its control and India must pull out its troops from the areas it holds. The prospects of the implementation of the UN resolution was jeopardised due to want of the idle situation, as constant tension between India and Pakistan demanded heavy deployment of troops on both sides of the LoC.

The issue as it stands now is Pakistan wants the Kashmir valley which has Muslim majority population to be given to it on the lines of Junagarh and Hyderabad which India accessed to its territory. India is not willing to concede this point saying the instrument of accession signed by the ruler of J&K had settled the issue in its favour. India, in turn demands from Pakistan to vacate the areas of Kashmir under its control and also get back those portions which it had given to China for the development of its infrastructure facilities.

The two countries are holding to these positions for more than fifty years now. They had been indulging in the war of attrition and brinkmanship to keep their positions afloat. There have been some suggestions to convert the LoC as the international boundary between the two countries, but Pakistan has opposed this idea. In the meantime, both the countries have fought two and half wars and had held several rounds of talks but could never reach to any conclusion. The Kashmir issue has further been complicated by emergence of terrorism in J&K and after the nuclear tests conducted by India and Pakistan.

The irony of South Asia is that by keeping the Kashmir issue alive, India and Pakistan are still engaged in fighting with the past. The two countries, by doing so, are not only stifling their own growth but also that of the subcontinent as a whole.

Fresh hope has once again been generated since India and Pakistan have committed themselves at the Islamabad SAARC summit in January 2004, to resolve the Kashmir issue through a sustained dialogue process. This time, given the complexities of the international relations, the talks are expected to lead towards a peaceful solution of the Kashmir problem.

India-Pakistan Bilateral Talks

There has been a long history of bilateral negotiations between India and Pakistan to solve the Kashmir issue but unfortunately all of them have remained a nonstarter. This seesaw of bilateral negotiation now has entered its sixth decades and the emerging pattern suggest that even before the two sides could start discussing the core issue, something or the other crops up leading to the suspension of their talks. The fresh round of negotiations that has being kick-started since March 2004 too has been shrouded in such uncertainties.

The dialogue between India and Pakistan can be divided into three phases – 1948-1971, 1971-1998 and 1998-till date. During the fifties and sixties India remained committed to recognise

Kashmir as a dispute and adhered to the UN resolution which wanted it to be solved in accordance with the wishes of the people of Kashmir. Several rounds of talks were held during that time but the plebiscite could never be implemented due to the unstable condition in J&K. As the time rolled by the implementation of the UN resolution become more difficult than before.

The prolonged delay of UN resolution on Kashmir prompted the 1965 war but that too could not throw any solution. The war led to the Tashkent pact, which was signed in the Uzbek capital between Pakistan's President General Ayub Khan and Indian Prime Minister Lal Bahadur Shastri to find a solution to the Kashmir problem through peaceful means. However, after that the dialogue process never took off between the two countries.

The second phase of bilateral negotiations began after the 1971 war and precisely since the Shimla conference of 1972. The two countries agreed in Shimla that they would resolve the Kashmir issue through their bilateral negotiations.

Some interesting developments took place in this phase (1971-98) when India started talking about Kashmir as the core to its nationhood and asking Pakistan to vacate the areas under its control. India started saying that the integration of Kashmir with its union had become final and the numerous elections held in the J&K are testimony to that fact. India announced that in such context the relevant UN resolution on Kashmir has become redundant.

This led Pakistan to internalise the Kashmir issue alleging that the elections held in the J&K had no relevance to the core issue, which in any case were humbug and held under the duress of the Indian bayonet. India rebutted Pakistan's charges saying, Islamabad is violating the terms of Shimla agreement, which seeks bilateral negotiations to discuss the Kashmir issue. Since then the two countries have engaged themselves in the game of brinkmanship where Pakistan at every international forum had been raising the Kashmir issue and India blunting all such charges through its diplomatic skills.

There was some thaw in Indo-Pak relations when Rajiv Gandhi and Benazir Bhutto made attempts to get around the Kashmir problem. However, before they could make any serious attempts to resume the dialogue process there was change in regimes and the talks were scuttled even before they could begin.

The Kashmir problem accentuated since 1989, when militancy began to surface in the state. This was partly due to the growing discontentment in the state and partly due to Pakistan's aggressive policy to catch international attention on Kashmir. Pakistan, though professed to give moral and political support to the Kashmir cause, started fomenting insurgency in the Indian state of J&K on certain pretexts.

India since then started saying that root cause of the Kashmir issue is not the territorial dispute with Pakistan but the militancy, which is being perpetrated from across the border. The Kashmir agenda since then started revolving around terrorism with India saying that it is ready for dialogue with Pakistan but before that to happen it must stop fomenting terrorism in J&K.

The Indo-Pak relationship changed for better when I K Gujral made moves to conceptualise the differences by holding several meetings with Pakistani Prime Minister Nawaz Sharif. The two premiers worked out the modalities under which a sustained dialogue process could begin to resolve all their differences including Kashmir. However, as it happened in the previous occasions, this time too even before the dialogue process could take off, there was a change of regime in India.

The third phase of India-Pakistan dialogue began after India and Pakistan conducted nuclear tests in 1998. This made the international community become alive to the dangers that could emanate from the Kashmir dispute. The international powers coaxed both the prime ministers of India and Pakistan, A B Vajpayee and Nawaz Sharif to seek terms. This resulted in the Lahore Declaration of 1999 and the beginning of the comprehensive and composite dialogue between the two countries. India and Pakistan identified nine issues for discussion and held two rounds of negotiations, one in New Delhi and other in Islamabad. The talks could not be sustained as 'Kargil' border clashes took place, leading to its suspension.

The Agra summit in 2001 again tried to pickup threads from 1999 but nothing substantial flowed out of it due to the rigid stand taken by the two countries on Kashmir and terrorism. The attack on Indian Parliament on 13 September 2001 led India to adopt coercive diplomacy asking Pakistan to rein in terrorism for the dialogue process to begin.

India-Pakistan relationship once again started showing signs of improvement since 2003 and breakthrough was made in January 2004, when the then Prime Minister Vajpayee agreed to resume the composite dialogue again with Pakistan. The dialogue process, which began in March, faced minor hiccup when there was a regime change in India in July 2004 but the new Prime Minister Manmohan Singh, gave the clearest indication that his government was serious about the peace initiatives with Pakistan.

Manmohan Singh shortly after being sworn in commented on the question of Kashmir and Pakistan saying that the "Indian establishment can live with anything short of secession and short of redrawing boundaries." The PM advocated that 'soft borders' might hold the key to the solution, as it is the people and not the borders that are so important. He desired that people on both sides of the border should be able to 'move freely'.

Manmohan Singh did not subscribed to the idea of plebiscite. He said, "It would take place on a religious lines which would unsettle everything and no government in India could survive that." On autonomy, the prime minister said, "India is prepared to consider such idea and it can be negotiated." He however ruled out independence of Kashmir saying, "it would become a hotbed of fundamentalism."

The prime minister's main thrust was to find a way to stop talking about going to war with Pakistan. He said that the two nuclear armed powers living in such close proximity is a big problem, and there is an obligation to solve the differences. He further said that the constant tension with Pakistan is emasculating India from realising its true economic potential.

The history of India-Pakistan dialogue suggests that even when the two rivals could settled down for talks something or other happens which leads to its suspension. Again the game of brinkmanship starts between the two countries and its takes a long time to make a fresh beginning to resume the dialogue process.

The fresh rounds of talks, which had begun in March 2004 carries a heavy baggage of history of such failed talks. Nevertheless the two countries have again made a new beginning to solve their differences again. They are aware that they would reach nowhere if they stick to their maximist positions. The only way out for them is to climb down and explore where they can find a meeting ground. The hopes this time are pinned on the talks between India and Pakistan and expectations are high that they may lead to the eventual resolution of the Kashmir issue.

Beyond the Healing Touch

The state of J&K, which has traversed over five decades of chaos, has yet to be emotionally integrated to the Indian union even though it has been its physical part for more than half a century now. India's naive handling of the problems of this bordering state which are a queer mix of political, economic, ethnic, cultural and regional factors has further resulted in distancing the state from New Delhi.

It is a common perception that Jammu and Kashmir and the Union government have always worked at cross-purpose to each other. The allegations are rife that the puppets of the 'Delhi Durbar', which have ruled the state since the beginning has been responsible for siphoning off large amount of funds meant for the development of the state. The failure of the leadership to address the developmental issues has aggravated the discontentment of the people. Their resultant anger has been let out against the 'Indian rule', which they perceive is responsible for their woes.

What initially was a socio-economic issue gradually deteriorated to militancy as disgruntled youth took shelter in violence to give vent to their pent up frustration. The local people supported such acts being anguished by the lack of developmental facilities in their state. The internal situation and dissidence in J&K was fully exploited by Pakistan being the bordering state. India, instead of putting its house in order, blamed Islamabad-backed militancy as reasons for all the ills in J&K. By making Kashmir a Pakistan centric issue, India further prompted the people of the state to distance themselves from New Delhi.

India perceived militancy in J&K as law and order problem and deployed a large number of security forces to restore peace. It also promulgated draconian laws, which curbed the civil liberties of the people and impinged upon their fundamental rights. The men in uniform at times misused these special powers and behaved inhumanly leading to gross human rights abuse. This resulted in an unending saga of violence and counter violence in the state. It is believed that these measures were widely responsible for most of the present day ills of the state and has contributed to fuel the anger of the people against the Indian rule.

It goes without saying that the key to the restoration of normalcy in J&K lies in providing good governance, which alone could scale down the act of militancy, if not completely wipe it out. That, however, is not the end of the story.

The other issues which lies at the heart of the problem is the restoration of the people's faith in the true federal character of the Indian polity. Since 1950, India has shown scant regard in this direction and took away the entire special privileges, which the state enjoyed before 1952. Further, the quashing up of Article 370 of the Indian constitution, which gives special powers to J&K, comes up during every parliamentary election in India. Then the summary rejection of the bill by the union government seeking autonomy for the state passed by the National Conference government in 2002, further reflected upon the federal character of the Indian state.

The resultant centre-state tension has led to the erosion of the people's faith in India being a true federal state. The people of J&K perceive India as a monolithic state, which is more interested in establishing its rule rather than strengthening its federal character. This has led to the growing discontentment among the people and has further accentuated the emotional integration of J&K with India.

Then, Kashmiri people also perceive the Indian government's commitment to secularism as a charade. The periodic communal clashes and the targeting of minorities in different parts of country have ominous repercussions in Kashmir. By not bringing to justice those responsible for perpetrating communal riots, which has been a periodic feature in India, New Delhi has given a handle to similar elements in Kashmir to carry out mayhem against the Hindu minority. The purging of 'Kashmiri Pandits' from the Kashmir valley is seen as a reaction to the anti-minority politics being played in the Indian heartland.

The other factor of the growing discontentment among the Kashmiris has been the tendency of the Indian politicians to use Kashmir as a handy tool to whip up anti-Pakistan hysteria in the Hindi heartland to gain political mileage. Come every election and Indian politicians threaten Pakistan with dire consequences to dare not brooking into Kashmir and thus obliquely telling the Kashmir people to bow down in submission before it, as they have no other option than to resign to their fates. More than any thing else, it is the Indian attitude to treat Kashmiris as pariah that is consolidating the voices of dissent in the state.

If India has to mend bridges with Kashmir then it has to raise itself from the parochial interests and change the perception of being a monolithic state. India's argument that Kashmir is a symbol of its secularism will have no meaning until Indian heartland politics is cleansed of religious chauvinism. If at all the people's faith has to be restored, India could do so only by practicing true federalism in the country. Indian government's assurance to the people of Kashmir that their future is best secured in India may go a long way in healing their wounded psyche that has remained bruised since over half a century now.

India's Road-map to Kashmir

The most telling development on the Kashmir front under the Vajpayee government was India outlining a road-map to restore peace in J&K. The union government in early 2001 announced a unilateral cease-fire on the LoC and Pakistan too reciprocated by pulling back its extra troops. So did the militants, who scaled down their activities in the state.

The Union Home Ministry then entered into a dialogue with the Hizbul Mujahideen, the dominant Kashmiri militant group in the valley. The talks, which were held for several days, could not be sustained due to the unacceptable demands made by the militants, but it underscored the point that India was serious about bringing peace in its troubled torn state.

The Vajpayee government then went ahead to constitute a Kashmir Committee to be headed by the then Deputy Chairman of Planning Commission, K C Pant. The government interlocutor's brief was to hold talks with various groups in the state and ascertain their views on how to ease the growing tension between the centre and the state. Pant made several visits to the J&K and held parleys with leaders of the National Conference. He tried to hold talks with the 24-parties Hurriyat Conference but the amalgam cold-shouldered his offers. Since K C Pant's powers were limited, his efforts could not go beyond an exercise in public relations.

Vajpayee government then constituted another Kashmir committee to be headed by the then Law Minister, Arun Jaitely to look into giving some degree of exclusive identity to J&K. This was done so after the union government had summarily rejected the autonomy proposal passed by the National Conference in the state assembly in 2001. The indication was that the BJP led NDA government wanted to appease its ally, the National Conference, and was considering going back to Shiekh Abdullah-Indira Gandhi Accord of 1975. The Kashmir Committee under Jaitely too in the end could not deliver anything substantial and became redundant after the defeat of National Conference in 2002 elections.

In the meantime, another unofficial Kashmir Committee was constituted under renowned lawyer, Ram Jethmalani with purpose to convince the separatist parties to contest the assembly elections. Jethmalani after making several rounds into the valley, recommended the Union government to directly hold talks with the separatists' leaders and consider giving assurances that their demands would be taken up for the discussion in near future. He also recommended that the Assembly polls be postponed so that the separatists' leaders could get enough time to think about joining the electoral battle. His third recommendation was to hold the elections under the Governor's rule in order to give more credibility to the polls.

New Delhi rejected all these recommendations of Ram Jethmalani, which made the separatists' leaders to distance from the 2003 assembly elections. Jethmalani's Kashmir Committee lost its relevance soon after the conclusion of the 2002 J&K polls.

Vajpayee government then constituted a fourth Kashmir committee, this time under the retired bureaucrat, N N Vohra, to hold talks with the political parties and groups in the various regions of the state. Vohra held wide ranging discussions with a cross section of the people of the state and submitted his report to the then Home Minister L K Advani. Vohra's efforts eventually crystallised when the union home ministry made a departure from its previous stand and called the 24 parties conglomerate, the Hurriyat Conference, for talks to New Delhi. Two rounds of discussions were held between the representatives of the Hurriyat Conference and the then Home Minister L K Advani on January 22 and March 27, 2004. After that the union government announced that the third round of talks would take place in June 2004 during which "substitutive issues" would be discussed.

The fledging talks between the separatists' amalgam and the union government generated a great deal of optimism among the people of the J&K and also among the Kashmir watchers. It was the indication of the fact that New Delhi for the first time since independence was serious about its Kashmir problem. The talks gave the impression that India has finally recognised the people of Kashmir to be the principal party whose will would eventually remain supreme in any settlement of the Kashmir issue. The other signal that emerged from New Delhi's action was that by taking Hurriyat Conference into confidence, India was showing a great deal of political acumen towards restoring peace in its trouble torn state.

The parliamentary election in India, in June-July 2004 voted out the BJP led NDA government and brought in the Congress led United Progressive Alliance (UPA) government under the leadership of Manmohan Singh. The new Union Home Minister Shivraj Patil retained N N Vohra as Special Representative for Jammu and Kashmir and made it clear that the talks with the Hurriyat Conference would be sustained. He however made a slight change in the stance from its predecessors when he announced that the UPA government is ready to hold talks with the Hurriyat

Conference but it would be 'officials' and not him who would carry forward the dialogue. He also announced that such talks would be held only within the framework of the Indian Constitution.

The Hurriyat Conference rejected this 'new line of thought' by the UPA government saying that they are willing to come forward for the negotiations but only after the centre makes its policies clear and spell out the guidelines that would govern the talks. The Hurriyat Conference said they had initiated the dialogue with the previous government only when it was made clear to them that the talks would be held at an 'appropriate level' and will be Kashmir centric in nature.

The resultant differences between the union government and the Hurriyat Conference has stalled the peace talks once again. It is giving the impression that India is going back to its preconceived assumptions about the Kashmir issue.

If at all India is interested in making a breakthrough to resolve the Kashmir deadlock, then it has to make a lot more effort to remain engaged with all the parties concerned, including the Hurriyat Conference. Peace in Kashmir can only be brokered through negotiations and accommodation, and the earliest it is done the better it is for the peaceful solution of the problem. Further delay will only lead to festering wounds getting putrefied.

Remembering Abdul Ghani Lone

Kashmir problem is a living example of how human tragedy could manifest itself in this world. Unlike the Berlin wall, which was a legacy of the Cold War and was erased in 1989 to unite the divided families of the East and West Germany, the partition of India which divides the Kashmiri people living on either side of the India-Pakistan divide show no sign of unification. A whole generation has grown up on both sides living with the lore that some day when India and Pakistan resolve their differences, they may be meeting their relatives who live just across the line of control. Their wait has become like the play *Waiting for Godot*.

One such person who could articulate the Kashmiri point of view very candidly was the senior Hurriyat Conference leader, late Abdul Ghani Lone. He was a moderate voice in the divided political spectrum of the Hurriyat Conference. Unfortunately, his assassination in 2002 was a setback to the peace efforts in Kashmir.

Just few weeks before his assassination at a political rally in Kashmir, I met him in Chennai along with another senior Hurriyat leader, Umer Farooq and discussed with them the separatists' viewpoint on Kashmir threadbare.

My first question to Lone was to react on India's position that Kashmir is the core of Indian nationhood and Pakistan's contention that Kashmir is an unfinished agenda of partition of India. Lone rebuked at both India and Pakistan saying, the two countries are unlawful claimants of Kashmir. He said Kashmir is for the Kashmiris alone and the two countries are playing politics over its territory with scant regard towards its people. He prophesied that the areas that are now under the control of India and Pakistan one day might become part of a united Kashmir.

Lone said that Kashmiris are the principal party in this dispute between India and Pakistan and all the three should sit together and discuss their differences to the satisfaction of every one. He made it clear that there cannot be any solution, till the involvement of a broad spectrum of Kashmiri leadership in the dialogue process between India and Pakistan.

Lone was critical about Indian policy towards Kashmir, saying, so far New Delhi has been riding the high horse of arrogance thinking that it could wish away its solution by 'hedging and dodging' the Kashmir problem. He narrated his experience of how as part of various Indian governments he tried to discuss the Kashmir issue with different political parties and toyed the idea of its solution with various leaders. Lone was candid in saying that all the political parties had the same ostrich like approach when it came to address the Kashmir issue and the leaders, except for paying lip service, had nothing more to offer. "No one wanted to take the bull by the horn," he lamented.

Lone said, if India thinks that it can solve the Kashmir problem without taking into account the will of its people then it is living in an ivory tower. He added that, the earlier New Delhi recognises the ground realities the better it is for India, the people of Kashmir and Pakistan.

Lone held the view that BJP led NDA government in India and Pervez Musharraf led government in Pakistan are the right leadership that can attempt for a solution to the Kashmir problem. He said that BJP being a Hindu nationalist party has more leverage than any other political party in India and any solution through them would have high degree of credibility in the country. The same applies to General Pervez Musharraf who too enjoys the support of the army and the large civilian population in Pakistan.

Talking about the possible solutions, Lone said since this problem pertains to the people of Kashmir it is they who understand it better than others, and therefore this job should be entrusted to them. He suggested that holding intra-Kashmiri consultations on both sides of Kashmir along the Line of Control could be a first step in this direction. In the process of consultation even the view of the militants could be entertained, he said. Lone was optimistic that once the responsibility of building a consensus was given to the Kashmiris, the onus would lie on their shoulders to come up with a solution. He said, in such an arrangement, neither India nor Pakistan would feel victor or vanquished and the will of the people of Kashmir would remain supreme.

Lone opposed the idea of the trifurcation of Kashmir on religious lines. He said that this was not feasible because there are six districts in Hindu majority Jammu division, which have predominant Muslim population and in the case of trifurcation, they would be lumped with Jammu division, which would be not correct.

Lone was pensive about the growing militancy in Kashmir and said that militants who have no roots in the valley are fast infesting the state. He laughed at the naivety of the Indian government to hold talks with the militant group Hizbul Mujahideen, saying that by opening up negotiations with the militants, the government not only hinted seeking a solution to the Kashmir problem through them but in the process had also given them legitimacy in the state. He reiterated that the problem of militancy is basically political in nature and it has to be resolved through the large political dialogue involving state's leadership in the negotiation process with India and Pakistan.

When asked to comment on the representative character of the Hurriyat Conference, Lone shot back, asking which are the other credible political groups in Kashmir and what is their locus standi. He said, India has been trying to engage the National Conference for more than fifty years now, but so far has not been able to solve the Kashmir problem!

Lone said that the Hurriyat's strength has been demonstrated time and again with overwhelming people's support to its agitation calls in the valley. The amalgam is not averse to the electoral process, he said adding that such elections have to be held under the supervision of the international monitoring body. He was of the opinion that the foremost thing is to solve the problems of Kashmir between India and Pakistan and not wish them away by holding sham elections and installing puppet regimes in the state.

Lone concluded his hard talk saying, "The people's struggle is kindled in every Kashmiri's heart; its flame would be carried on by our children to their generations. I may not be there to see the realisation of the dream, but the struggle would remain alive till the objective of a united Kashmir is realised."*

The assassination of Abdul Ghani Lone was a big blow to those who favoured peaceful means for the settlement of the Kashmir problem. His killing meant that the extremists in the Kashmir valley were slowly marginalising moderate voices. The greatest tribute to Lone would be to give due consideration to his vision to address the Kashmir issue, objectively and dispassionately.

---

* This interview was done in February 2002 when late Abdul Ghani Lone and Mirwaiz Umer Farooq were in Chennai.

5
Sri Lanka

• *Nuances of Sri Lanka's Ethnic Problem* • *Peace Gets Past War in Sri Lanka* • *Assessment of Chandrika's Rule* • *Bargaining for Two Nations* • *The Muslim Factor in Sri Lanka* • *India-Sri Lanka Relations* • *Tamil Fishermen's Problem* • *Sri Lankan Refugees in Tamil Nadu*

Nuances of Sri Lanka's Ethnic Problem
It is one of the ironies of the post-colonial societies that different ethnic groups come together in the struggle against the colonial rule, but differences start cropping up soon after they gain independence. This is because the post-colonial governments are unable to evolve a framework, which could ensure fair growth of its specificities within the national framework. This is what has happened in Sri Lanka, where 15 per cent Hindu Tamils inhabiting in the northeast region are at loggerhead with 70 per cent Buddhist Sinhala population in the country.

Tamil ethnic group were pervasive in every sphere of activity during colonial rule in Sri Lanka. However, soon after independence they found themselves in hopeless minority when parliamentary democracy was introduced in the country. Even being a majority in the northeastern region, the Tamils found themselves being marginalised in the national politics. The Sinhala groups, taking advantage of their majority position, too started sidelining the Tamils through systematic state policies.

Tamils first experienced discrimination when Sinhala was made the official language and Buddhism the state religion of Sri Lanka.

Their discontentment increased during the successive governments and the 1983 anti-Tamil riot in Colombo was the breaking point in the Tamil-Sinhala relationship. The Liberation of Tamil Tigers Eelam (LTTE) thereafter became their front organisation, which started waging an armed struggle against the Sinhala domination.

The ethnic problem in Sri Lanka is of a complex nature; the Tamils resists Sinhala domination of the northeast region, which is traditionally their homeland. They demand that the north and east provinces should be merged together and Tamils be given complete autonomy to manage their own state of affairs. The Sri Lankan government fears that if such demand were to be conceded, it would create a regional incongruity, and threaten the unity and integrity of the country.

The problem gets more complex in the eastern province where Sinhalas, Muslims and Tamil population are juxtaposed. Muslims and Sinhalas fear that a Tamil dominated northeast state would be detrimental to their interest and they in turn demand some micro level autonomy for their own safety. It is the failure of the national leadership to evolve a framework, which could satisfy the ethnic aspirations of the northeast region that has led to the conflagration of the ethnic problem in Sri Lanka.

History suggests that there have been various attempts to resolve the ethnic tangle in the island nation. The Sri Lankan Prime Minister S W R D Bandaranaike and Tamil leader Chelvanayakam signed an agreement called the 'BC Pact' on the 26 July 1957, for the creation of the regional councils – one for the north and two for the eastern provinces. It also agreed that two or more regions could be amalgamated even beyond their provincial boundaries that could collaborate for the specific purposes. The Sinhala hardliners did not appreciate the ideas and there was a Sinhala backlash, following which, a Buddhist monk assassinated Bandaranaike.

Then the UNP leader Dudley Senanayake signed another pact with Chelvanayakam on 24 March 1965, which provided the establishment of district councils in the two provinces. The pact formalised an agreement with the Tamils on land settlement, concerning Sinhala people in the area which was traditionally part of the Tamil inhabitants, and recognised the official use of Tamil language in the north and eastern provinces.

The essence of both the pacts comprised the recognition of the federal principle of Sri Lanka and establishment of one or more provinces where Tamils are in a majority. Further, the Tamil language was to acquire parity with Sinhala as an official language in these provinces.

Moving forward to 1987, when the Indo-Sri Lankan accord was signed to resolve the ethnic problem, a provision was made for the formation of a provincial council by clubbing the north and eastern provinces together. The Tamil groups resisted the idea because they said such council did not satisfy the aspiration of their complete domination. The hardline Sinhalas also rejected the provincial council on the ground that it did not adequately represent the multi ethnic northeastern provinces. The concept of provincial council however collapsed immediately after the IPKF pulled out of Sri Lanka.

There was some consensus between the United National Party (UNP) and the Sri Lanka Freedom Party (SLFP) after the assassination of President Premadasa in 1991. The two competing parties agreed to de-link the east from the northern province and form two administrative councils for the eastern province. The Sri Lankan Muslim Congress (SLMC) and the left parties also endorsed this proposal. However, this was turned down by the majority of the Tamil groups, including the EPRLF, which formed the interim government during IPKF presence in Sri Lanka. The Tamils were of the opinion that the de-linking provision ignores their basic demand of an autonomous single unit of governance for the northeast.

Things started looking up again after Chandrika Kumaratunga came to power in 1994. The president envisaged Sri Lanka as a union of regions and wanted to give administrative autonomy to the north and east to the extent that all the powers of the centre would rest with the chief minister and its council of ministers. The federal government would only control international airports, harbor, and other national establishments. In her scheme of things, she called for the creation of the regional councils, one for the north and two for the eastern provinces, and proposed 30 per cent reservation for the Muslims in the council dominated by the Tamils.

Chandrika's devolution package gathered dust due to lack of consensus within the Sinhala parties and also due to opposition from the Buddhist clergy. The Tamil moderates and extremists groups too turned down her proposal calling it unsatisfactory.

The ethnic problem in Sri Lanka took a new turn in 2002 when LTTE and Sri Lankan government relinquished the warpath and got engaged in a negotiation to settle their differences. At the beginning, the LTTE moved ahead cautiously during several rounds of talks but after a year they came out with a proposal demanding an Interim Self Governing Authority (ISGA) for the northeast region of the country. The proposal, a virtual blue print for a separate homeland for the Tamils, put the Sri Lankan government in quandary and halted the peace talks since October 2003.

The peace negotiations could also not be carried forward due to differences within the Sinhala political parties over the handling of the peace negotiation. The general election in 2004 voted out UNP and brought the SLFP and Janatha Vimukti Peramuna (JVP) led coalition to power.

Now the onus is on Chandrika Kumaratunga who has promised to reopen the stalled talks with the LTTE. The challenge before her is to satisfy the aspirations of Tamil, Muslim and Sinhala population in the northeast within the federal set up of Sri Lanka. Every one knows she does not have any magic wand to solve the ethnic jigsaw puzzle of Sri Lanka.

Peace Gets Past War in Sri Lanka

It's a great moment in contemporary history of Sri Lanka, the current cease-fire is the longest period of peace in the past three decades in the country. Gone are the days when people used to be worried about military check points, curfews, suicide bombings, and sudden news of the death of their loved ones. The hope now is that worst has been left behind and peace trap, which has been created due to the cease-fire, would be sustained in the days ahead to come.

However, behind the lull of peace there is a sanguine history of bloody war that has so far claimed more than 60,000 lives and rendered over a million homeless. The story of war comes in waves in Sri Lanka; first there is a militant offensive and then retaliation by the army. Even as the army is in an offensive mode, a truce is brokered and the peace talks begin. During the breathing space, the rebels and the army regroup themselves, then the negotiations fail and the war rages again. This pattern has been the hallmark of war and peace in the last two decades in this country.

Ever since the ethnic problem flared up in the island nation in mid eighties, the Sri Lankan government has been waging an unsuccessful war against the Tamil rebels. There have been four rounds of war since then, the latest being from 1996 to 2000. The army had an upper hand in 1996 when it took over Jaffna city and few other areas from the LTTE's control. Their victory was significant because the tigers were then pushed out of the mainland peninsula and had to retreat to the Wanni region.

However, the army's successes were short lived and had to face a series of defeats—first in Puliyankulam, and then at the Killinochchi areas. The LTTE wrested the 'Elephant Pass', the strategic point that controlled the Jaffna city in 1999 from the army. Since then the LTTE's influence has increased in the north and the eastern provinces. The Sri Lankan army, with the help of high security, controls major parts of the Jaffna Peninsula and also about two-third of the area in the east. The history of the war suggests that neither the army nor the LTTE could achieve an outright victory over each other.

The battle between the LTTE and the Sri Lankan army has taken a heavy toll on the civil population living in the northeastern part of Sri Lanka. There was mass migration of the civil population from the war zone. Those staying behind had to live in a war ravaged surroundings with all the hardships of the wartime. They faced curbings on free movement, shortage of essential commodities, power, and they had to grapple with the appalling civic infrastructure. Then the extortion by the rebels to fund the war added to their woes. They have been asked to voluntarily allow their children to join the militant ranks or have to face their abduction. Even girl child were not spared from being blooded into the war.

With cyanide capsules hanging from their neck, the juvenile cadres of the LTTE were romanticised about the war. The two decades of ethnic strife has taken the life of a whole generation of Tamil youth in Sri Lanka.

The Sri Lankan army too has been seriously affected by the war. More than 15,000 soldiers have lost their life, and over 25,000 had been demobilised in the last phase of the war alone. There were reports of desertions from the army camps and even general amnesty could not lure them back to their jobs. The army is finding it hard to get fresh recruits as not many Sinhala youth are coming forward to join the armed forces despite many concessions offered to them.

There is a growing feeling among the army that the LTTE cannot be militarily defeated and there has to be political settlement to the ethnic problem. At the same time, the army is skeptical about the peace process because the LTTE had kicked the negotiating table at least three times before. The Sri Lankan army has cautioned the government not to let their gains fritter away while bargaining for peace with the LTTE. There have been some differences between the government and the army over the issue but peace as an option is preferred over war.

The two major parties SLFP and the UNP have played politics on the issue of war and peace in Sri Lanka. The SLFP have accused the UNP of helping the LTTE to grow into a monster during its seventeen-years rule. It also alleges them of arming the LTTE during the IPKF presence in Sri Lanka. The UNP in opposition too had targeted the SLFP for belittling the achievements of the army and not providing them with enough resources to fight the war. The UNP say that the wrong policies of the SLFP have made the LTTE so powerful that it is hard to negotiate with them on their own terms.

The same mindset was reflected by the SLFP towards the peace talks carried out by the Ranil Wickremesinghe led UNP government in 2002-2003. The SLFP accused the UNP of mishandling the peace process and charged him of giving too much of concessions to the rebels. The general election in 2004 was fought on this issue and it brought the SLFP led coalition to power. It would be interesting to watch what position the UNP takes on the dialogue between the LTTE and the SLFP, if and when they resume.

In the meantime, some new developments surfaced in the northeast region of Sri Lanka, when LTTE's eastern commander, Murlithran alias Colonel Karuna openly revolted against the Vani leadership in March 2004. The LTTE's renegade commander accused northern leadership of sidelining the interests of the eastern provinces. An imminent internecine war between the north and the east factions of the LTTE was imminent when Prabhakaran send his troops to rein in the rebellion in the east. The bloody war however was avoided as Karuna fled the battle scene but vowed to continue the resistance. His revolt highlighted the differences within the LTTE's rank and brought a new twist to the ethnic quagmire in Sri Lanka.

As things stands, the LTTE and the Sri Lankan army are in no mood to demilitarise their positions. The government turned down LTTE's demand of de-escalation from the north, saying it may not wind up any army camps in high security zones till the LTTE completely disarms. The Tigers, on the other hand, maintain that arms are their bargaining chip and they cannot relinquish it till a sense of security is established in the region.

The beginning of the talks between Chandrika's government and the LTTE is eagerly awaited for a renewed spell of peace in the country; its further delay may trigger another round of bloody war in the teardrop island. There is apparently a very thin line that divides war and peace in Sri Lanka.

Assessment of Chandrika's Rule

"From the deep abyss of unknown darkness, I have just managed to latch on to the threshold of life, a life that is very special and portentous gift of God to serve the people of this land"... these were the words of Sri Lankan President Chandrika Kumaratunga who was voted back to power after surviving an assassination attempt barely forty-eight hours before the presidential elections of 1998.

Making an assessment of Chandrika Kumaratunga as the president of Sri Lanka, many things that has taken place during her rule, spanning nearly close to one decade now, comes under scrutiny. When Kumaratunga came to power in 1994, she almost single-handedly took the challenge to put an end to the ethnic conflict. Riding on the crest of her political mandate, she held out an olive branch to the LTTE, pledging respect to the Tamil dignity. She assured both the moderate and militant Tamil groups that she is committed to bring early peace to the northeast region of the country.

The LTTE also responded positively to her proposal and the peace talks began on a highly optimistic note. Chandrika Kumaratunga's government relaxed ceilings on several items meant for northeastern provinces and the LTTE reciprocated her gesture by releasing many political prisoners. However, after four rounds of talks there was no semblance of understanding between the contending parties. Chandrika was beset with the problem to evolve a consensus among the Sinhala parties on the quantum of the devolution of power to be given to the Tamil dominated regions of the country. She then started dilly-dallying tactics to keep the LTTE engaged. This gave enough pretexts to the LTTE to kick the negotiating table and resort to warpath. As a result, after eight months of lull, war raged again in Sri Lanka.

Chandrika's government then embarked on a two-pronged policy: one was to launch a full-scale war against the LTTE and second, was to isolate them by taking into confidence the moderates Tamils by talking to them about her peace plans. Initially, Kumaratunga succeeded in both her policies. Her government was able to put military pressure on the LTTE and the Sri Lankan army was successful in capturing Jaffna city in 1996.

The moderate Tamils who were fatigued by the war, asked Chandrika to spell out her peace proposal. They were in for a rude shock to discover that her much hyped peace basket was nothing more than a modified version of the 1987 Indo- Sri Lanka accord. All the moderate Tamil groups, including the EPRLF, which formed the government during IPKF presence, vehemently rejected her peace proposal.

Moreover, the opposition UNP blocked the devolution package whose support was essential to get the required parliamentary approval. Unable to overcome the constitutional requirements, Kumaratunga vouched for national referendum but this too could not move forward, due to the political wrangling among the Sinhala parties.

Chandrika's second option to militarily contain the LTTE too came a cropper. Her heavy focus on war bled the Sri Lankan economy white and country's defence spending rose to more than five per cent of its GDP during the war. A string of defeats by the Sri Lankan army during 1998-99 became a major embarrassment for Kumaratunga's government. Her failure to implement aggressive defense policy came to tell upon the Sri Lankan politics. She was almost voted out of power but destiny had scripted her another term in office. The assassination attempt generated a huge sympathy wave in her favour and she was re-elected to power for the second term.

The general election in Sri Lanka in 2000 brought the UNP government headed by Ranil Wickremesinghe to power. Thereafter, Wickremesinghe took control of the situation and made overtures to the LTTE to resume the peace talks. This time the talks were distinct compared to the negotiations held in 1985, 1989-90 and 1994-95. It was facilitated by the Norwegian peace brokers and took place in the background of several confidence building measures, including the government lifting embargo to the Tamil held territories, deproscribing the LTTE and agreeing on a cease-fire that was monitored for six months.

Since the first face-to-face discussions on 16 September 2002 at the Sattahip naval base in Thailand, the Sri Lankan government and the LTTE discussed several important issues, including resettlement of the internally displaced persons, and demining of the affected territory among others. The rebels made a fresh commitment to stop child recruitment and agreed to let UNICEF supervise a joint government-rebel programme to rehabilitate the 'baby brigade'.

The talks seems to be heading in the right direction but as it has happened in the past, the differences started surfacing between the president and the prime minister over the handling of the peace process. Kumaratunga accused the UNP government of being nontransparent about the talks and announced that she reserves the right on the settlement of the core issues with the LTTE. This made LTTE's then chief negotiator, Anton Balasingham to comment that he is 'pessimistically optimistic about the success of the talks'.

Balasingham's fears came true when the talks once again were stalled following the release of the counter proposal by the LTTE in October 2003 and sacking of several key UNP ministers shortly after that. The differences among the Sinhala parties prompted the general elections in 2004, which voted out the UNP government and brought the SLFP led coalition to power.

The change in government has brought the clock full circle in Sri Lanka. The mantel now has fallen on Chandrika Kumaratunga to reopen the negotiations with the LTTE again. The president has made it clear that she has no intention to scuttle the peace process and even announced to meet the LTTE chief V Prabhakaran face to face to resume the dialogue.

Chandrika Kumaratunga would be belittling her promise, which she had made in 1998, to serve the people, if the peace talks are delayed further. It remains to be seen what role the opposition UNP plays for the failure or success of the negotiations. Sri Lanka's ethnic crisis has hit the crossroads once again.

Bargaining for Two Nations

The LTTE virtually exploded a paper bomb in south of Sri Lanka on 31 October 2003 when they submitted their first ever proposal to the government to form an interim in the northeast till a political settlement is reached on the ethnic question within a united Sri Lanka. The LTTE's counter proposal was in response to the Sri Lankan government's proposal to set up an interim administrative mechanism in the northeast as a prelude to the final settlement of the ethnic issue in Sri Lanka. The government proposal was formulated within the framework of the existing constitution and it retained several federal subjects like police and security, land and revenue under its control.

In contrast, the LTTE for the first time came up with a six-page document outlining their demand to constitute an interim administration in the northeast region of Sri Lanka. The preamble of the proposal said that since the Tamils had not participated in the making of the 1972 and 1978 constitution, division of power enshrined in the constitution did not bind them and so a solution to the ethnic problem has to be found outside the constitution of Sri Lanka.

The highlight of the proposal are; until a final negotiated settlement is arrived, an Interim Self Governing Authority (ISGA) will be established to administer the eight districts of the northeast of Sri Lanka which include Trincomalee and Batticaloa. The LTTE, the government of Sri Lanka, and the Muslim minority will appoint the member of the ISGA. The LTTE should have absolute majority in the ISGA, the election of which has to be held at the end of five years under the international supervision by an independent election commission appointed by the ISGA.

The ISGA will have all powers relating to regional administration that are currently exercised by the central government. These powers would cover law and order, revenue and taxes, control over land, resettlement and rehabilitation. The ISGA would be vested with considerable financial powers and it will prepare annual budgets and negotiate and receive foreign funding, including loans. All government spending in the northeast will be channeled through the ISGA. It will appoint an auditor general who will audit all financial transactions.

The LTTE proposed that in case of any dispute between the centre and the ISGA, the matter should be submitted to a three-member panel. The government of Sri Lanka and the LTTE will appoint one member each and the third will be the chairperson, whose appointment should be made by mutual consent. In the event of disagreement over the appointment of the chairperson, the parties shall ask the president of the international court of justice to appoint the chairperson.

The Tigers proposed that this agreement would be in operation until a new government, pursuant to a negotiated settlement, is established in the northeast. However, if at the end of four years, no agreement is reached, the two parties shall negotiate for adding, clarifying and strengthening the terms of the agreement.

The other highlights of the LTTE's proposal were that the ISGA should have control over the marine and offshore resources and the adjacent seas and powers to regulate access thereto. It also mentions that no religion shall be given foremost place in the northeast.

There are two ways to look at the LTTE's counter proposal. One, to take it on the face value, which means that if these demands are accepted in toto, it would give legitimacy to them to administer a virtual Tamil Eelam in the northeast of Sri Lanka. It may also grant them the much-needed international legitimacy as the sole representatives of the Sri Lankan Tamils. The acceptance of their demand would also clearly define the borders of the Tamil homeland and their international prestige would boost, since they will have all the powers to negotiate the foreign aid. In short, if their demands were to be conceded it would mean creation of two nations within the Sri Lankan state.

The other way to look at the proposal is to get out of the text and read its essence, which points that the LTTE may like to negotiate the peace process but from a maximist position. They know that no Sri Lankan government would agree to such a proposal that would tantamount to signing its own death warrant. The other reason to believe that the LTTE want to negotiate is that if they wanted to continue with the dispute then what was the need for them to draft such a proposal. They, in any case, are administering a de facto Tamil Eelam in the northeast of Sri Lanka.

As such both the LTTE and the government of Sri Lanka knows well that the alternative to dialogue is war and for which no one is prepared. This has been amply demonstrated since 2001, as there has been no violation of the cease-fire agreement, barring few incidents. The uninterrupted lull of peace concludes that both the parties are serious about taking the dialogue route and shunning the warpath.

The counter proposal of the LTTE has to be seen in the context of the bargaining ploy with which Chandrika Kumaratunga has to grapple in the days ahead. It remains to be seen how the Sri Lankan president picks up the thread of the peace process and deals with the LTTE proposal. She has too much in hand to worry about the LTTE and the Tamils.

The Muslim Factor in Sri Lanka

In Sri Lanka's ethnic profile, Muslims constitute about 7 per cent of the country's 20 million population. Their largest concentration is in the eastern province, particularly in Amparai and Batticaloa districts, where they constitute about 40 per cent of the total population. Majority of them speak Tamil but would like to be identified by their religious and cultural moorings and not by their linguistic identity.

The eastern province of Sri Lanka has always witnessed localised friction between the Muslims and Tamil who are juxtaposed with each other with Tamils constituting about 42 per cent of the population. Muslims problem aggravated since mid-eighties when the LTTE emerged as the most powerful militant groups in northeast of Sri Lanka and coercively tried to subsume the Muslim identity in the linguistic basket of the Tamil 'Eelam'.

Historically, Muslims voted for the Tamil parties since independence and maintained a cordial relation with them till the early eighties when ethnic conflict started boiling in the Island. In fact, in those days, Muslims had a tenuous relations with the Sinhala parties for being close to the Tamil groups. Things started changing since the LTTE began armed struggle to espouse the cause of Tamil 'Eelam' and started threatening Muslims to fall in line with them. This made Muslims to turn to the Sinhala groups for their protection.

After the departure of the IPKF from Sri Lanka in 1989, the LTTE started targeting Muslims in much more brutal fashion and several gruesome massacres of Muslims were carried out by them. The most conspicuous was the en masse eviction of an estimated 70,000 Muslims from the northern province of Sri Lanka in October 1990. It was followed by displacement of about 350,000 Muslims from the eastern province in January 1991.

These incidents injected a fear among the Muslims and since then they started resisting living in the areas under the control of the LTTE. The Muslims, in order to protect their interests in eastern

Sri Lanka, formed Sri Lanka Muslim Congress party (SLMC) now led by Rauff Hakim. Hakim served as a minister in both Chandrika Kumaratunga and Ranil Wickremesinghe governments and also represented the government in the peace negotiations with the LTTE.

The author had an opportunity to meet SLMC leader, Rauff Hakim, in Chennai and discuss with him the ground realities of the peace talks and Muslims perception towards the settlement of the ethnic problem in Sri Lanka.

Hakim said that the peace process is irreversible and called it a peace trap, as no one wants to see the resumption of hostilities again. He says that what the peace process provides is a window of opportunity, which must be clinched in order to embark on the path of development and progress of the country.

He however was not happy with the trajectory of the peace process and pointed several flaws including non-participation of the Muslims in the talks. Hakim sounded suspicious about the intention of the LTTE and said that he doesn't know whether their mind and heart are both there in the peace process. The SLMC leader was also uncomfortable with the Norwegian peace facilitators but called them necessary evil because the LTTE had trust in them.

On Muslims' perception about the peace talks, Hakim said, there is serious erosion of confidence among them for being marginalised in the peace process. At the outset of the talks, it was clearly defined that Muslims would be represented as a separate delegation but this did not happened so far. The credibility of the peace talks has lost its sheen among the Muslims, Hakim said, making an appeal to the government and the LTTE, to call them separately if and when the talks resumes.

Commenting on the Muslim identity in Sri Lanka, the SLMC said this is well recognised in the constitution and quoted several clauses to buttress his claim. The moderate parties among the Tamil side of the divide all through its history too have recognised the separate identity of the Muslims. The LTTE, which flouted the constitutional guarantee to the Muslims, made a turn around after the current beginning of the cease-fire and LTTE chief Velupillai

Prabhakaran specifically mentioned about protecting Muslims interests, at the Kilinochi news conference on 10 April 2002. This was further cemented by an agreement signed between the LTTE and the SLMC on 30 April 2002 Hakim said.

However, these promises proved to be short lived as LTTE resumed extortion from the Muslim, which led to violent clashes in the eastern region. The tension aggravated since early 2002, when LTTE started setting up a network of 'police stations' in the Muslim dominated areas.

Hakim said, Muslims are angry with him because the LTTE has not honoured their commitment and its cadres are indulging in extortion, abduction and even killing of some them. He laments that Muslims youths are becoming restless; some of them even have started questioning as to what he was doing to stop those killings. He bemoans that his followers are dubbing him as a funeral-attending leader and he is dumbfounded about that.

The SLMC leader sounded alarmist saying eastern Sri Lanka is fast becoming a fertile ground of Muslim radicalisation due to the growing alienation among the Muslim youth from the peace process. He scotched off the rumours that Muslims are arming themselves to indulge in acts of terrorism. The SLMC leader argued that it is impossible to carry out an armed struggle by the Sri Lankan Muslims because there is no cushion of geography, no wherewithal of terrorism and there is no external support to them, all of which are essential to sustain any armed struggle. He however admitted that there were six to seven local groups engaged in the acts of extremism but have very small following and primitive firepower.

About India's role in the Sri Lankan peace process, Hakim said Muslims felt betrayed by the Indo-Sri Lankan accord of 1987 which did not recognised the separate identity of the Muslims and had no provisions for them in the interim administration set up by the IPKF. He reasoned that Muslims themselves are to be blamed then, because at that point they had no political party to represent their case.

Talking about the fall out of Rajiv Gandhi's assassination and India's interest in Sri Lanka, Hakim said, it is true that since that unfortunate incident, India has lost its edge in Sri Lanka but there are two sides of this story. One that the LTTE has come to the conclusion that no matter what happens, India would not step in Sri Lanka again, and second, India would never come to their help in future.

Notwithstanding these facts, Hakim said that India's goodwill is essential for the success of the peace talks. The SLMC leader feels that New Delhi's current position – that the de facto status should not become de jure, till it is acceptable to all the parties concerned and the interim solution should be the integral part of the final solution -- is a very balanced stand towards the peace process in Sri Lanka.

Discussing the Interim Self Governing Authority (ISGA) proposal submitted by the LTTE, Hakim said he is appalled why the LTTE has not made any specific mention about the percentage of Muslims in the composition of the ISGA. He made it clear that Muslims would not like be part of the LTTE controlled northeast territory and demanded that a separate regional administrative unit should be created in the eastern province in the areas dominated by the Muslims.

As things stands in Sri Lanka, the LTTE has submitted a proposal to the government asking for a de jure status of a separate homeland comprising northeast provinces of the island. The Sri Lanka Muslims, which dominates certain areas of the eastern province, have urged the government not to lump them with the LTTE but in turn demanded an exclusive unit to protect their own identity. Now all eyes are set on the government's responses to the LTTE's and Muslims' demands. The Muslim dominated districts in the eastern province of Sri Lanka have become the weakest link in the peace process of the island nation.

India-Sri Lanka Relations

The India-Sri Lanka relationship has come out of the wrinkles of the superpower rivalry pursued during the Cold War. It has also emerged from the shadows of regional conflict that hampered their relations well over five decades since independence. Now when most of the differences that had persisted in the past have been ironed out, the two countries are coming closer to build a new partnership in the twenty-first century.

The colonial history suggests that, the power, which holds sway over Sri Lanka, has a better grip over Indian Ocean and on the South-East Asian countries. During British rule, India attached a great deal of importance to Sri Lanka due to its geo-strategic location in the Indian Ocean. Successive Indian governments have continued the same policy since independence.

India-Sri Lanka relation in the first three decades was a conservative, albeit cautious, approach towards each other. The first United National Party (UNP) government under Prime Minister D S Senanayake (1947-52) adopted a conservative approach towards India. The next government under S W R D Bandaranaike (1956-59) of Sri Lanka Freedom Party (SLFP), adopted a friendlier attitude towards India. Bandaranaike indicated that India would find a special place in diplomatic and trade relations with Sri Lanka.

Ms Sirimavo Bandaranaike (1960-65) who succeeded her husband after his assassination, adopted neutralist policy towards India. She refrained from taking sides in the Indo-China war of 1962. She came up with an unsuccessful 'Colombo Proposal' to bring about a rapprochement between the two countries. The change of government brought the UNP back to power under Dudley Senanayake (1965-70) who again had a cautious approach towards India.

All these years Indo-Sri Lanka relation was wrapped up in Cold War logic. While Sri Lanka's foreign policy was guided by anti-communist and pro-West stance, India had pro-Moscow leanings during that time. Sri Lanka maintained a lukewarm relation with India due to New Delhi's apparent dependence on Moscow. Sri Lanka apprehended that if it develops friendly relations with India, Moscow might control Colombo via New Delhi.

The second term of Ms Sirimavo Bandaranaike in office (1970-77) saw Indo-Sri Lanka relationship plummet from better to bitter. This was due to the Indo-Soviet friendship treaty of August 1971 and India's crucial role in the creation of Bangladesh. The event created insecurity among the Sri Lankan leadership and they moved closer to China and other Western powers.

The resounding victory of UNP in 1978 brought J R Jayewardene (1978-83) to power in Sri Lanka. The period saw an unusual tilt towards India when New Delhi and Colombo agreed to work for the common good of each other. Jayewardene while expressing his warm feelings towards India commented that there were no disputes between the two countries.

However, Jayewardene's second term in office (1983-89) saw Sri Lanka to be drifting away from India, mainly because of India's role in the ethnic crisis in the country. Sri Lanka openly started accusing India for aiding and abetting Tamil separatism from its soil. Colombo, in a counter insurgency drive, started importing sophisticated weapons from various powers who were then unfriendly to India. It resumed diplomatic relations with Israel after a gap fourteen years and sought its help to train anti-terrorists military squads. Sri Lanka also opened Trincomalee and Colombo ports to western warships after a gap seventeen years for refueling purposes. All these measures were not appreciated by India. New Delhi also disapproved the UNP government's desire to involve extra regional powers, including countries hostile to India, to solve the ethnic problem in the country.

These developments prompted India to get involved in sorting out the Sri Lankan ethnic crisis. New Delhi brought the warring parties to the negotiating table first when it brokered the Thimpu talks in 1985, and then in New Delhi talks in 1987. However, both its attempts were unsuccessful due to unrelenting attitude of the Tamil groups and the Sri Lankan government.

In 1987, when Colombo launched a military offensive against the Tamil separatists and imposed food embargo in its northern region, public pressure mounted on India to intervene in Sri Lanka. India then launched operation 'Mazhai' or rice bombing, dropping rice packets through its 'Jaguar warplanes' to feed the Tamil population. The crisis was defused by the signing of an Indo-Sri Lankan accord on 29 July 1987 between Rajiv Gandhi and J R Jayewardene. Gandhi, who visited Colombo to sign the Indo-Sri Lankan accord, had a miraculous escape when he was attacked by a Sri Lankan soldier while inspecting the guard of honour ceremony there.

The Indo-Sri Lankan accord acknowledged the legitimate security concerns of India and agreed to jointly hammer out a solution to the ethnic strife in the country. Under its provisions, Indian Peace Keeping Force (IPKF) was sent to Sri Lanka to restore normalcy in the trouble torn regions of the country. IPKF had a torrid time in maintaining peace in Sri Lanka. Its job was to disarm the LTTE guerrillas whom it had trained earlier to fight the Sri Lankan army. Its second job was to put up a civilian administrative structure in the north and east regions for which there were non-cooperation from the local people. No wonder, the IPKF was unsuccessful in both the assigned jobs.

IPKF woes compounded when Ranasinghe Premadasa replaced Jayewardene in 1989 and showed his displeasure over the presence of the Indian peacekeepers on the Sri Lankan soil. The new president flouted the terms of the Indo-Sri Lankan accord and supplied arms to the LTTE to fight the IPKF. This was the most embarrassing situation for the IPKF who were caught in a bind in the Sri Lankan ethnic quagmire. It was only after a change of government in 1989 that New Delhi was ordered to pull out its troops from Sri Lanka.

The most shocking twist of the Indo-Sri Lankan relation took place when LTTE activists assassinated former Indian prime minister Rajiv Gandhi during an election campaign at Sriperumbudur in Tamil Nadu on 21 May 1991. Subsequently, Narasimha Rao, who became the prime minister, completely disassociated India from the Sri Lankan politics. Under Rao, India's official line changed to maintain neutrality in the internal developments of Sri Lanka. The downtrend in the Indo-Sri Lanka relations was arrested after the reassessment of the situation by the successive governments in the nineties.

Prime Minister I K Gujral took a lead and refined India's foreign policy towards the neighbours. His 'Gujral doctrine' envisaged that India would not allow its territory to be used against any neighbouring countries. India would not interfere in their internal affairs and respect the territorial integrity and sovereignty of the neighbouring countries. The subsequent Indian governments carried forward the same policy while dealing with Sri Lanka.

The Indo-Sri Lanka relationship in the twenty-first century has definitely become more pragmatic than before. In the changed global context, when diplomatic relationship with US and Israel has become important for India, their threat perception emanating from Sri Lanka has now become redundant. India's growing relations with China too has allayed fears that Sri Lanka is harbouring interests inimical to India. Further, the regional imperatives have also compelled New Delhi and Colombo to cooperate with each other to mitigate any ill feelings. This reassessment of the Indo-Sri Lanka relations has brought the two countries closer than before.

Tamil Fishermen's Problem

The problem of Tamil fishermen straying into the Sri Lankan waters is an age-old phenomenon. Since there is not much fish available in the Indian waters, these fishermen often venture beyond the national boundary in search of their catch. In the past, the Sri Lankan authorities use to treat such violations as aberration and allowed the Tamil fishermen to return home after giving them strict warnings.

However, the situation changed since the early eighties when the ethnic problem conflagrated in the north of Sri Lanka. The LTTE sympathisers used the Tamil fishermen as a conduit to help the Tamil cause in the island nation. The Sri Lankan naval authorities patrolling the Palk Bay, often found some Tamil fishermen to be engaged in smuggling racket of commodities banned in the northern region of their country. They also unearthed in their boats arms, ammunition and other military hardware meant for the LTTE.

The Sri Lankan navy since then started suspecting all the Tamil fishermen to be LTTE activists and resorted to open fire once these fishermen crossed the international waters. In such incidents more than hundred Tamil fishermen had lost their lives in mid sea ever since the ethnic conflict erupted in Sri Lanka.

The war and truce in the ethnic conflict in Sri Lanka have direct bearing on the Tamil fishermen. During the war period they come under severe surveillance by the Sri Lankan navy patrol and their lives are at risk after entering the international waters. In peacetime they are being rounded up and held in the government custody. Currently since the cease-fire has been brokered between the LTTE and the Sri Lankan government, the shooting incidents have totally stopped but the fishermen have no respite from being detained and being beaten up in custody.

Several Tamil Nadu leaders including chief ministers had written letters to the union government to find a permanent solution to this regular standoff between the Sri Lankan navy and the Tamil fishermen. However, the callous attitude of New Delhi has allowed this problem to fester without any solution in sight.

Related to this issue is the problem of the Kachatheevu Island. Tamil Nadu fishermen have been using this island since time immemorial for resting and drying their nets. The water around the island is known for lobsters. So usually the fishermen, after laying the nets, used to halt there and after collecting their catch sailed back to the coast. Even after the island became part of Sri Lanka by an agreement, signed between Indian Prime Minister Indira Gandhi and Sri Lankan President Sirimavo Bandaranaike in 1974, Tamil Nadu fishermen were allowed to continue with their activities at the Kachatheevu Island.

However, after 1980s Sri Lankan navy started objecting to Indian fishermen fishing around the Kachatheevu Island. They showed no mercy while rounding up and imprisoning these fishermen and were released only after New Delhi's mediation. Many political leaders from Tamil Nadu had urged the union government to get back the Kachatheevu Island, on lease in perpetuity from Sri Lanka to help the Tamil fishermen. However, New Delhi remains unfazed towards their demands.

A new dimension to the Indian fishermen's problem has been added since the cease-fire agreement has come into force between the LTTE and the Sri Lankan government. The LTTE of late have put up paraphernalia of administrative structure in the areas under its control and has also assembled a bunch of flotilla to keep a vigil on the Arabian Sea. The 'Sea Tigers', as the LTTE's navy is called, have started patrolling into the Palk Bay, and now instead of Sri

Lankan navy, it is the Sea Tigers who are detaining the Indian fishermen straying into the Sri Lankan waters.

The fishermen from Tamil Nadu, which once used to be respected and hailed by the LTTE for making sacrifices for the Tamil cause has become a pariah to them. Gone are the good old days of Tamil camaraderie as the LTTE now rebuke them as Indian fishermen.

There are reports that Tamil fishermen are not only round up by the LTTE but also beaten and fined before being handed over to the Sri Lankan authorities. One such incident took place on 19 August 2003 when two Indian trawlers and 10 fishermen were detained by the LTTE. They demanded one lakh fifty thousand rupees as price to set them free and after their demands were met, the LTTE handed them over to the Sri Lankan authorities. There is a growing feeling in Tamil Nadu that if the activities of the Sea Tigers remain unchecked, it would not be long when the Indian government has to approach the LTTE for the release of its fishermen.

The LTTE's presence in the Arabian Sea has also come to directly threat India's vital strategic interests in Sri Lanka. It is reported that the LTTE is strengthening its position in the eastern provinces particularly around the Trincomalee harbour where world war vintage oil tanks are located which India has taken on lease from Sri Lanka and is maintained by the India Oil Corporation. The reports say that the LTTE, by strengthening its position in this strategically located port, has made these oil tankers vulnerable to their sophisticated firepower.

Sri Lankan foreign minister, Laxman Kadirgamar has warned about the dangerous developments taking place in the eastern province of his country, which may have bearings on the Indian security. He had said, "If the LTTE is allowed to continue with its free run in the Arabian sea, the signs of gathering clouds is ominous in the Palk Bay."

What has been seen is that, the India-Sri Lanka relationship has remained so much focused on the peace process, that New Delhi is totally unaware of the threat perceptions that are emerging from its own backyard? India's security concerns could best be allayed if New Delhi immediately takes note of these developments and nip the problem in the bud.

Sri Lankan Refugees in Tamil Nadu

The picture of India-Sri Lanka relations cannot be complete without the description of Sri Lankan Tamil refugees sheltering in the southern Indian state of Tamil Nadu for well over a decade now. Ironically, New Delhi's mess of the Sri Lankan policy is also reflected in handling of the Sri Lankan refugees, which is devoid of any short or long term solutions. Being sea blind, the South block has left this problem for the Tamil Nadu government to manage it as best as it could.

The Tamil Nadu government on the other hand, has pinned all its hope on the final conclusion of Sri Lanka peace talks so that refugees could be repatriated back into their country. This however, is turning to be an endless wait and with no early solution in sight, the problem of Sri Lankan refugee loom large over Tamil Nadu.

The Sri Lankan Tamil refugees are racially Dravidian, linguistically Tamil and socially and culturally akin to the people of Tamil Nadu. The official figure released five years ago estimates about one lakh Sri Lankan refugees residing in the state but the unofficial figure is believe to be double that number. These include those who fled the country not only due to war but also for other reasons to take refuge in Tamil Nadu.

There are officially three types of refugees sheltering in Tamil Nadu. In the first category, are the people accommodated in 133 ordinary camps scattered all over the state. Their number is estimated to be about 70, 000. They have no resources and they survive on funds from the donor agencies of the world. In the second category, are the people living outside the camps numbering about 25,000. They are marginally better off and stay with their relatives and friends in the state. These people have to report from time to time at the local the police station about their whereabouts. In the third category are the militant types who are kept in special camps set up since 1990 all over the state. They are estimated to be about

2,500 and most of them are under trials, booked under various criminal laws of India.

The Sri Lankan refugees were once a pampered lot when there was growing influence of India in the island's ethnic crisis. They were allowed to be involved in the local politics, build powerful lobbies and make use of their temporary sanctuary to lend support for the cause of Eelam back home. Later, due to various complexities of Indo-Sri Lankan relations, the refugees fell out of patronage of both the central and the state government. The limited sympathy that they enjoyed too vaporised after the assassination of Rajiv Gandhi in 1991. Since then, New Delhi has become indifferent towards their plight and the Tamil Nadu government looks at them as potential security risk.

There are claims and counter claims about the status of the Sri Lankan refugees living in Tamil Nadu. A UN funded, non governmental organisation, Organisation for Refugees of Eelam Rehabilitation, (OFER), which is working with the refugees claim that the Sri Lankan refugees enjoy all the human rights and are treated well in the state. The life of those refugees living in ordinary camps is much better off than the average poor Indians. The children living in ordinary camps are allowed to attend school and youth are attending colleges. Those refugees who live outside the camps are also being accommodated in the expanding economy of the state. The OFER says it has launched several schemes to improve the condition of Sri Lankan refugees sheltering in Tamil Nadu.

However, another NGO called, Partners in Action for Refugees (PAR/NAC) paints a different picture about the living conditions of the Sri Lankan refugees in Tamil Nadu. It says that those refugees staying in special camps are leading a very dehumanised life. Medical assistance is virtually non-existent, and the food served to them is unpalatable. The children in the special camps are denied access to primary education. Many handicapped and disabled persons are also kept in solitary confinement in these special camps. Many detainees languish in these camps long after the courts had exonerated them of their crime.

The condition of those living in the ordinary camps is also no better. The NGO says that not every one is treated on equal basis in these camps and some refuges are victimised on the basis of social hierarchy, which has evolved in these camps. Children of ordinary camps are allowed to attend the school, but their classmates look upon them with suspicion and due to such social stigma children are not happy going to schools.

The plight of the refugees living outside the camps, particularly in the Nilgiri Hills, remains unnoticed. Some of them working in the coffee plantation farms have virtually become bonded labourers. The farm owners exploit them for being Sri Lankan refugees. These refugees living outside the camps face considerable harassment from the police officials when they report to them. The NGO says, Sri Lankan refugees have no legal protection and are a helpless lot.

The NGO complains that non governmental organisations are not allowed to work with the Sri Lankan refugees either living in the special or the ordinary camps. It laments that it cannot do much except apprising the media about the plight of these refugees.

Notwithstanding the contradictory claims, the fact remains that the Sri Lankan refugees are caught up in a game of conflicting politics between the Tamil Nadu and the union government. There is no effort being made to sort out their problems either on short or long-term basis and as such the problem is left in the lurch.

It is being felt that some short-term measures have to be taken to assuage the sufferings of Sri Lankan Tamil refugees. This includes their fresh enumeration, maintaining transparency of those detained in special camps and their speedy trial. With regard to the health care and education, special attention needs to be paid to women and children, and vocational and technical training should be provided to the youth. However, these measures are no substitute for their early repatriation into their country, which alone could bring relief to their sufferings.

As a long-term measure, all the South Asian countries need to evolve a common strategy to deal with this problem, spilling time and again over their national boundaries. However, such strategy is subject to the evolution of regional cohesion, which remains an elusive concept in South Asia.

6
The Maldives

- *The Maldives on Developmental Path* • *The Maldives' Economy Needs Diversification* • *Pragmatism Marks the Maldives' Foreign Policy* • *The Maldives Yearns for Political Reforms* • *India-Maldives Relationship*

The Maldives on Developmental Path

The Republic of Maldives is a group of small coral islands in the Indian Ocean to the south of the Minicoy Island. The total area covered by the archipelago is 90,000 square kilometres. The Maldives has 1190 islands, of which 198 islands grouped in 20 atolls are permanently inhabited. The chain of islands is 820 kilometres in length and 130 kilometres in width. This includes the Exclusive Economic Zone. The Maldives has an estimated population of 2,69,010 scattered in different islands. The greatest concentration is on the capital island, Male, where about 26 per cent of population lives.

In the past thirty years, there has been breathtaking changes taking place in the Maldives. In 1970 it was a nation of 1,15,000 people and its growth rate was 3.5 per cent. The people had sailing boats for interisland transport and relied on tuna fishing and shipping for their income.

However, by the year 2000 the Maldives recorded continuous improvements in all its social indicators buoyed by effective economic management of its rich marine resources. The country touched an average economic growth rate of 8 per cent with the help of vastly improved communication system. The basic literacy in the Maldives increased to 98 per cent and the country become a prime tourist destination, with over 4,29,666 tourists visiting the island at the close of 2000.

However, things are not hunky-dory for the Maldives. The country faces considerable challenges from different quarters. The physical and geographical situation of the low-lying coral islands with no land-based resources makes them very vulnerable. The impact of high population growth rate is a matter of serious concern, particularly on infrastructure and urbanisation, food security and employment and most importantly on the environment.

There is a growing concern about coral reef and marine life damage because of coral mining (used for jewellery making), sand dredging, and solid waste pollution. Mining of sand and coral have removed the natural coral reef that protected several important islands, making them highly susceptible to the erosive effects of the sea. In April 1987, high tides swept over the Maldives, inundating much of Male and the nearby islands. That event prompted the Maldives to take interest in global climatic changes, including the greenhouse effect.

The Maldives finds it expensive to provide social services and create employment opportunities to a population scattered over small island settlements. The country has limited economic viability and lacks proper transport facilities. The geographic conditions also limit demand for locally produced commodities that may help diversify its economy and sustain cottage industries. Export is the only viable alternative to this, which too has its own constraints.

The growing population and tourism put intensive pressure on the fragile coral reef environment. The impact of climatic changes on the low-lying archipelago is already manifesting itself in many ways. Coral bleaching in 1998 caused significant damage to the reefs across the country. There is escalating beach erosion and over 40 per cent of the inhabited islands are affected by this phenomenon.

The change in the pattern of workforce in the last two decades is having a long-term impact. Many Maldivian men have given up fishing and are now employed at tourist resorts. The Maldivian youth, even with limited education, aspire for better jobs in the tourism industry or government.

Male, the capital, presently houses an estimated 80,000 people on a mere two square kilometres space. The social system, which has so far allowed political stability and supported socio-economic development, is now struggling to satisfy the needs of large numbers of urban youth, half of which are less than 15 of age.

It is said that Maldivian women are amongst the most emancipated in the Islamic world. However, the opportunities actually available to them in rural islands are limited. The modernisation process may have freed women from the hardships of fish processing but has also exposed them to the modern forms of employment in the fish industry. Apart from jobs in the government, which are mainly in Male, women do not have many opportunities for progress.

Tourism and fishery remains the major source of income and are the major contributor to the GDP of the Maldives. However, the worldwide volatility in the tourism industry and depressed global tuna market has had an adverse impact on the Maldives economy.

The government of the Maldives have embarked on some ambitious projects to tackle some of the challenges it is confronted with. It has decided to do away with the even distribution of public investment in over the 200 inhabited islands and develop only 60 to 80 islands fully. The remaining 'primary islands' will continue to receive basic services.

Alongside, the Maldivian government has been working on an ambitious policy of population 'consolidation', at two regional growth centres in the country. It is also planning for resettlement of the population in the other less crowded islands. The government plans to give them major incentives, so that resettlement takes place on a voluntary basis.

Further, the government of the Maldives is working on enhancing interisland transportation infrastructure, especially harbours and causeways. It is also planning to enhance communication network to enable the island communities to remain informed about government's decisions and ensure their effective participation in the country's development.

The Maldives' government is aware of the limited technical expertise at their command and large investment that is required for the developmental projects in the country. It is also aware that this Herculean task cannot be accomplished without support from international financial institutions and the increased role of the private sector, which is at a nascent stage in the Maldives.

The best way for the government to go about this would be to make good use of the available resources and to have increased role of people in the development of the country. The Maldives is a beautiful country and needs to be made more developed in the times to come.

The Maldives' Economy Needs Diversification

In recent years, the Maldives has successfully marketed to the world its natural assets for tourism ... beautiful unpolluted beaches on small coral islands, diving in blue waters abundant with tropical fish and glorious sunsets.

Even though there is a global recession in tourism, the Maldives has been able to maintain its share in the pie in this segment without much difficulty. Tourism brings about 180 million dollars a year and contributes to about 18 per cent of the Maldives' GDP.

Making best use of its exotic islands, the Maldives started developing resorts way back in 1972. Ever since the first resort was established, more than 70 islands have been developed with state of art resort facilities. The number of tourists visiting the Maldives has increased manifold and an estimate number of 4,29,666 tourists visited the island by the close of 2000.

The hospitality sector in different categories of accommodation can host over 10,000 people at a given time. Their occupancy rate is about 68 per cent with the average tourist staying for eight or nine days in the country. European and American tourists are the most frequent visitors, buoyed by the cheap currency convertibility ratio in the Maldives.

The development of the Maldives has been centred upon the tourism industry and its complementary service sectors. Taxes from the tourist industry are ploughed back into infrastructure development and to improve communication with different islands in the country.

After tourism, fishing is the second most important source of economy for the Maldives. The total export proceeds from fish produce are about 40 million dollars and fishing sector contributes about 12 per cent of the GDP. The common fish found in the Maldives is skipjack tuna and its total production is about 1,04,000 metric tons.

Out of the total fish produce, 54 per cent of fresh fish is exported, about 28 per cent is dried or canned and another 5 per cent is frozen. Eighty per cent of the total fish produce is exported to Thailand, Sri Lanka, and Singapore.

The fishing sector employs about 20 per cent of the labour force. The fishing fleet consists of some 1,550 small, flat-bottomed boats called 'Dhonis' which over the years have shifted from sails to outboard motor boats. The use of net for fishing is banned in the Maldives. Most of the catch is procured through lines in the Maldives.

There is not much of agricultural activity taking place in the Maldives. There is no farming of staple crops. Agriculture is confined to a few subsistence crops. Poor soil and scarce arable land along with limitations of potable water have historically limited agricultural activities in the Maldives. On the whole, agriculture contributes about 8 per cent of the GDP.

Like agriculture, the industrial sector is also small in the Maldives. While the traditional industry consists of boat building and handicrafts, modern industry is limited to tuna canneries, garment factories, bottling plant, manufacturing of PVC pipes, soap, food products and furniture. Private entrepreneurs are doing most of these activities and their numbers are limited.

The private sector is also involved in operating international shipping to and from the Maldives. In comparison to national carrier – Maldives Shipping Management Ltd – which handles only a small fraction of the tonnage, the private vessels handles most of the country's imports and exports. The reason why agriculture and industry has limited growth in the Maldives is because there is a shortage of local skilled labour and most of the industrial labour is imported from Sri Lanka and elsewhere in the country.

The Maldives has enjoyed an average growth rate of about 10 per cent over the last decade. Its per capita income is 920 US dollars and the GDP growth rate was over 6 per cent. Since there is not much agriculture, the entire requirement of essential supplies is imported. The Maldives' total export is about 64 million US dollar and its imports is 402 million US dollars. The countries high on the Maldives' export list are, Sri Lanka, Thailand, UK and Japan, while those on the import list are, Singapore, Sri Lanka, UAE, India and Malaysia.

Indian imports from the Maldives primarily comprises cowrie shells and red corals while its exports include agriculture and poultry items, variety of engineering and industrial products and medicines. India exports about 176 million US dollars worth of goods and imports goods worth about 0.80 million US dollar from Maldives.

Over the years, Maldives has received economic assistance from multinational development organisations, including the UN Development Programme and the World Bank. Individual donors – including Japan, India, Australia, European and Arab countries – also have contributed to help its economy. In return of aid, the Maldives had leased its Gan Island to United Kingdom for twenty years in 1956. The British government, which had an air station at Gan, shut down its operations shortly after the agreement expired in 1976.

The Maldives's economy has not grown to its full potential. Tourism and fishing contributes only about 30 per cent of the country's GDP. The recession in global tourism market and decline in exports of tuna fish products has necessitated the demand for diversification of the Maldives' nascent economy. The Maldives needs to develop core competency in new areas, particularly in industrial and manufacturing sector in order to boost its economic growth

The favourable industrial climate is one of the great assets which the Maldives has to attract foreign investment. The areas of opportunity for business include tourism, construction, export-oriented manufacturing, such as garments and electrical appliances besides others. Greater awareness about the country and its people would help in a big way, giving fillip to the growth of the nascent Maldivian economy. The Maldives as a potential investment destination needs to be sold to the captains of industries of South Asia.

Pragmatism Marks the Maldives' Foreign Policy

The Maldives has conducted its foreign relations with self-confidence, dignity and equality with all nations, since its independence in 1965. In spite of being a tiny country of a cluster of islands, it has never become a satellite of the global powers in its independent history. This is the most striking fact about the Maldives' foreign policy.

The foreign policy of the Maldives is based on strengthening friendly relations with all the nations. It enjoys cordial relations with all SAARC countries, Islamic and Arab countries and with many developing countries as well as developed countries. The Maldives has actively been promoting the UN Resolution on the Security of Small States and remains committed to the principles of the UN Charter as the basis for the conduct of relations amongst nations.

The Maldives follows a non-aligned foreign policy and seeks a balanced relationship with major powers. It is a member of United Nation (UN), non aligned movement (NAM), Commonwealth (CHOGM), South Asian Association of Regional Cooperation (SAARC) and Organisation of Islamic Countries (OIC).

The Maldives has a UN Mission in New York, an embassy in Sri Lanka and trade representatives in London and Singapore. India, Pakistan, and Sri Lanka maintain resident embassies in Male. Denmark, Norway, the UK, Germany, Turkey, and Sweden have consular agencies in Male under the supervision of their embassies in Sri Lanka and India. The UNDP has a representative resident in Male, as do UNICEF and WHO. Like the US, many countries have non-resident ambassadors accredited to the Maldives and most of them are based in Sri Lanka or India.

India and the Maldives share very close ties. Most of the commodities of daily consumption in the Maldives are exported from India at very nominal tariff from the Tuticorin port in Tamil Nadu. India is involved in number of projects in the Maldives and provides training to a large number of its workforce to reinvigorate various sectors of the Maldivian economy.

The Maldives also maintains very close ties with Sri Lanka. In 2002 when Sri Lanka faced extended period of drought, the Maldives helped it with financial aid. Both governments remain committed for maintaining friendly relations and give high priority to strengthen their bilateral ties.

The Maldives being a predominantly Islamic country has strong ties with most of the West Asian countries and South East Asian countries. Over the centuries, it has been on the cross roads of the trade-route taking place between the West Asian and South East Asian countries. Cashing upon these historical ties, the Maldives in its independent history has been able to channelise these relationship to its advantage.

The state of Israel was the first country to send an ambassador to Male after the United Kingdom relinquished control over the Maldives in 1965. The ambassador of the Jewish state presented his credentials to King Mohamed Farid, which made the Maldives the first Muslim country to recognise Israel and establish diplomatic relations at ambassadorial level. However, since late 1970s the Maldives withdrew its recognition to the Jewish state.

Now, the Maldives strongly criticises Israel for its action towards Palestinian people. It has deplored the failure of Israel to abide by the United Nations resolutions and its continued occupation of the Palestine land. It has demanded immediate restoration of homeland to the people of Palestine and recognition of the state of Palestine.

The United States has friendly relations with the Republic of the Maldives. The US ambassador and some embassy staff in Sri Lanka are accredited to the Maldives and make periodic visits to that country. The United States supports the Maldives independence and its territorial integrity. It had publicly endorsed India's timely intervention in the Maldives to defuse the coup attempt in November 1988. US naval vessels have regularly berthed at Male in recent years.

US' contributions to economic development in the Maldives have been made principally though international organisation programmes. The United States has directly funded training in airport management and provided computer infrastructure for the Maldivian customs and immigration. The US is also helping the Maldives in narcotics interdiction and drug-control efforts. Some 25 US citizens are resident in the Maldives and about 2,000 Americans visit the Maldives annually. The official Maldives-US exchange rate is controlled by the United States Chase Manhattan Bank. The US also trains a small number of the Maldivian military personnel annually.

The environmental concern of the Maldives has been top on the agenda of the world leaders. British Deputy Prime Minister, John Prescott, who visited Male in 1999, said that international community could not ignore the consequences of the disappearance of many islands in the Maldives due to rising sea levels. Prescott held elaborate talks with President Abdul Gayoom on the environmental effects of global warming and on developing environmentally friendly tourism in the Maldives.

The deliberation by the Maldives at the United Nation reflects its concerns on several issues. This country of islands called on the international community to give greater consideration to the economic damage being done to the small island states, through prevailing financial and trading arrangements. It asked the UN to take into consideration the economic vulnerability of small island states and their fragile economies and to take adequate measures to redress their existing inequalities.

At the UN, the Maldives expressed concern about the failure to convene the Colombo Conference, designed to agree on ways to implement the UN resolution to declare the Indian Ocean as a Zone of Peace. The Maldives, which is surrounded on all sides by the Indian Ocean, is convinced that the demilitarisation of the Indian Ocean is essential for the progress and stability of the region.

Maintaining a neutral foreign policy, the Maldives is party to many international treaties, conventions and agreements and fully respects and observes international law and treaty obligations. It supports all efforts to promote peace and stability in South Asia and beyond. The Maldives seeks to safeguard its independence and national identity and is active in international relations in ways consistent with the protection of national interests. On the whole, pragmatism remains the guiding force for the Maldives' foreign relations.

The Maldives Yearns for Political Reforms

In 2003 election, President Maumoon Abdul Gayoom romped home to power consecutively for the sixth time. It was no small achievement for the Maldivian president who holds the distinction of celebrating silver jubilee in office. Abdul Gayoom was initially elected as president in 1978 and was subsequently re-elected in 1983, 1988, 1993, 1999 and in 2003.

Gayoom's long stay in power may reflect his immense popularity on the surface but that's not the complete picture. The subtleties in the functioning of the political system of the Maldives are not widely known to the outside world. There has been growing opposition to Gayoom's style of functioning, particularly his control over the political apparatus and he is accused of being a dictator in a democratic garb.

To put in perspective, the Maldives was governed as an independent Islamic sultanate in most part of its history and was a British protectorate from 1887 till its independence on 25 July 1965. The sultanate continued to operate for another three years and was finally abolished on 11 November 1968.

The 1968 referendum approved the constitution, which made the Maldives a republic with executive, legislative, and judicial branches of government. Ibrahim Nasir was the prime minister under the pre-1968 sultanate and was president from 1968 to 1978. Abdul Gayoom replaced him as president in 1978.

Gayoom who studied at Al-Azhar University, Egypt, initially showed a great deal of dynamism as president. He promised to transform the parliament called Majlis into a democratic set-up. He also assured to bring multi-party democracy and bicameral legislature. All this never happened; Majlis remained a unicameral legislative body, reduced to function as an advisory committee to the president.

Gayoom, in order to consolidate his power, amended the constitution and made the office of the president all-powerful. The most conspicuous feature of the Maldivian constitution is that 60 per cent of its clauses deal with the powers and immunities of the president. The remaining 40 per cent clauses deal with the responsibilities of the state and the rights of the Maldivian people.

The functioning of political system under Gayoom's rule has drawn flake from different quarters. His critics allege that Gayoom's electoral success is due to his control over the Majlis through backroom manipulations. It is alleged that Gayoom abhors democratic pluralism and has been muzzling all opposition to him. He is also accused of using authoritative powers to suppress any support for a multi-party democracy in the Maldives.

There have been few incidents that point that the need for political reforms is brewing in the Maldives. A reformer called Mohamed Nasheed, who was elected to one of the two Male seats in the Majlis, was imprisoned on fabricated charges and subsequently exiled. In another case, Ibrahim Luthfee and few others got life imprisonment for criticising Abdul Gayoom's regime. The 8 November 1988 abortive coup to overthrow the Gayoom's regime is also attributed to the growing opposition to the Maldivian president.

In spite of such criticism there is no change on the ground realities in the Maldives. The Maldives has no organised political parties and candidates for elective office run as independents on the basis of personal qualifications. Forty-two of the 50 members in the unicameral house Majlis, come through this system and the president nominates the rest. The president has a vital say even in the election of the 42 members. The Majlis, has five-year term and functions as a legislative body with limited control over the executive.

It is the office of the president, which is all-powerful in the Maldives. Constitutionally, any person can contest the presidential election but in practice it is the selected nominee of the Majlis who can alone make up to the high office of the president. The post of the president has to be confirmed by a national referendum but the so-called public's presidential vote by 'secret ballot' is only a referendum on the candidate chosen by the Majlis. The president heads the executive and appoints the cabinet, which has a five-year term.

It is against such kind of system that there has been a growing demand for political reforms in the Maldives. However, it is uncertain whether such reforms would ever be forthcoming till Gayoom is there at the helm of affairs.

Notwithstanding these facts, it would be belittling Gayoom's achievements to label him as a mean dictator. It is primarily because of his efforts that the Maldives has made great strides on the path of development. The UNDP reports say that from a country which was struggling at bare subsistence level, the Maldives is now included among the world's developing countries. In fact, what Gayoom has been able to achieve in twenty-five years of his rule, not many democracies is able to accomplish even in double that time.

However, this does not absolve Gayoom from the criticism, which has been growing in the Maldives. He needs to silence his critics by bringing in political reforms and more transparency into his governance. This may take him into the pages of history as the only statesman the Maldives has so far produced and one to be emulated in times to come.

There had been large-scale demonstrations in September 2003 in the Maldives calling for democratic reforms. President Gayoom announced measures to reform the political and judicial systems and bring the criminal justice system into conformity with fair trial standards. Tension, however, emerged in July 2004 when many MPs accused Gayoom of reneging on his September 2003 promises. This culminated in mass demonstrations on August 12-13 in Male demanding the release of political prisoners. Dozens of people were injured when the police came down heavily upon the unruly demonstrators. A national emergency was proclaimed by the government. However, on 10 October 2004 President Gayoom has ordered lifting of the emergency due to international pressure.

India-Maldives Relationship

India and the Maldives have a multidimensional relationship. The two countries share ethnic, linguistic, cultural and religious commonality, which has evolved due to commercial links steeped in antiquity. India is among the first country to recognise the Maldives' independence in 1965. It established diplomatic mission in 1972 and upgraded it to 'Resident High Commissioner' status in 1980. India's assistance in diffusing the 3 November 1988 coup and restoring Gayoom's regime within 24 hours was a further attempt to strengthen the Indo-Maldives ties.

India-Maldives relations have been nurtured and strengthened by regular ministerial level visits. Former prime ministers Rajiv Gandhi in 1986 and Narsimha Rao in 1995 made official visit to the Maldives. President Abdul Gayoom visited India on a number of occasions, including being a state guest at a Republic Day function.

During Rajiv Gandhi's visit in February 1986, a Joint Commission for Economic and Technical Cooperation was set up to identify areas for strengthening bilateral economic cooperation. During his visit it was agreed to establish a medical complex in Male with Indian assistance. The 200-bed hospital constructed with estimated cost of 42.5 crores rupees was dedicated to late Indira Gandhi and was inaugurated by former Prime Minister Narsimha Rao in 1995.

During Prime Minister Narsimha Rao's visit to Male, India agreed to set up Maldives Institute of Technical Education (MITE) at an estimated cost of 12 crores rupees as grant-in-aid. MITE was completed in 1996 and was formally inaugurated by President Gayoom in 1997.

Besides, India successfully executed the development of the present infrastructure of the Male International Airport. The construction was completed under difficult logistics and adverse climatic conditions. The extension of the airport's runway was done on reclaimed land on the coral base for which transportation of building materials and machinery was done by sea.

India's HRD (Human Resources and Development) ministry, in June 2001, agreed to train the Maldivian candidates in Indian institutions that could cater to the needs of the key sectors of the Maldivian economy. The training of the Maldivian headmasters was done under this agreement. India provided 10 seats annually to the Maldivian candidates under the ICCR scholarship scheme. Besides, India agreed to depute experts such as teachers and sports coaches to the Maldives from time to time.

The Maldivian government has taken India's help to establish Distance Education to meet the paucity of educational institutions and to cut down the infrastructure cost. Maldives and India signed an agreement in 1999, which made available distance education programmes of IGNOU (Indira Gandhi National Open University) to the Maldivian students. The agreement also envisaged the setting up of a Study Centre in Male' as part of Distance Education Project.

India and the Maldives signed a trade agreement in 1981 which provides for export of essential commodities, otherwise banned from India. In August 1995, India and the Maldives agreed to set up a subgroup to facilitate enhanced two-way trade. Indian banks help was sought by the Maldives in helping export of its marine products and in establishing its business enterprises.

Growing from a modest beginning, India-Maldives bilateral trade is showing significant growth. Indian exports to the Maldives during the year 2000 were worth Rs 168.4 crore, imports were worth Rs 1.10 crore. This is in sharp contrast to the situation about five years ago, when Indian exports to Maldives formed only 5 per cent of the Maldives' total imports as against 9 to 10 per cent now.

In March 2000, India agreed to provide heavy equipment for road construction-maintenance and waste management to the Maldives. The Confederation of Indian Industry held an exhibition of Indian products titled Made in India show in Male in 2001. About 40 Indian exhibitors participated in the exhibition, showcasing a wide variety of Indian products. The show generated considerable response in the local business circles and also among the general public.

India has been playing a vital role in the promotion of tourism in the Maldives. It has helped in establishing resorts at many islands of the country. India-Maldives have agreed to set up a subgroup to look into the possibilities of establishing close links to give a boost to the tourism industry in the Maldives.

Indians are the largest expatriate community in the Maldives with a total strength of approximately 13,000 people. They belong to various professions and are spread to various islands. The Maldives-India Friendship Association (MIFA) organises India evenings, cultural events and seminars in Male. Besides there is an India Club which regularly organises Indian community functions featuring Indian cultural shows. Hindi commercial films and Indian music are immensely popular in the Maldives. Cultural exchange programmes are regularly organised to promote people to people contact between the two countries.

The small versus big syndrome, national identity, bilateral tensions that are the hallmarks of India's relationship with its neighbours are conspicuously absent with reference to the Maldives. India-Maldives relations provides a perfect model of good neighbourly relations in South Asia.

7
Bangladesh

• *Bangladesh: Emergence and Lessons* • *Parties and Politics in Bangladesh* • *India-Bangladesh Relations* • *Bangladeshi Immigrants Issue* • *Bangladesh Health Care Scene*

Bangladesh: Emergence and Lessons

The creation of Bangladesh in 1971 is one of the epoch making events in South Asia. It was an event of rebellion and carnage for those who have been witness to the era. The myth of the two-nation theory propounded to build the movement for Pakistan was flouted when the eastern wing of Pakistan seceded following constant discrimination by its western half. Indian military intervention in December 1971 catapulted the dismemberment process of Pakistan.

Renewed interest in the creation of Bangladesh has been generated after fresh evidences have come to limelight by the declassification of the British secret documents. These papers are now available at the public record office in London. Pakistan has already produced Mahmood-ur- Rehman report on the reasons for the debacle of 1971 war. These papers and reports provide insights about the creation of Bangladesh.

Eastern Pakistan has constantly faced discrimination in terms of its budgetary allocations by the central government based in West Pakistan. The need for systematic development of East Pakistan, which being a low-lying area, plagued by natural calamities, was constantly ignored by West Pakistan. The leaders of East Pakistan were often discriminated when it came to plum position in the cabinet of the central government. The cultural and linguistic difference further divided the two halves of Pakistan. The eastern wing had been mobilizing public opinion built around their linguistic and cultural identity to demonstrate their anger and frustration against West Pakistan.

Though the demand for an independent nation may not be there in the initial stage of Bengali nationalism, which saw quite a bloodletting in the fifties and the sixties, the repeated failure of the West leadership to address their grievances resulted in the demand of autonomy for the East Pakistan.

The issue exploded in December 1970 when Pakistan held general elections, it's first since independence. The Awami League party headed by East Pakistan's popular leader Shiekh Mujibur Rahman (1920-75) won a majority of the seats in the general election. But, the then Pakistan's president, General Yahya Khan, refused to honour the democratic choice of his nation by making Shiekh Mujib the prime minister of Pakistan.

All negotiations failed to resolve the issue by the end of March 1971. Shiekh Mujib then virtually demanded independence for the east wing of Pakistan. Yahya Khan proclaimed emergency and arrested Shiekh Mujib who was flown to West Pakistan where he was incarcerated.

Pakistan sent troops under General Tika Khan, later known as butcher of Bengal, after reports of defections among the soldiers and police in East Pakistan, to launch a fierce campaign to suppress the Bengali resistance movement. Thousands of East Pakistanis died at the hands of the Pakistani army and no fewer than 90 lakh refugees fled to India in the ensuing atmosphere of violence and rebellion.

In the absence of a political solution to the East Pakistan crisis, India stepped in to assist the Bengali immigrants. India not only provided shelter to the refugees by lodging them in camps but also simultaneously organised trained, liberation force called Mukti Bahini to lead an armed struggle against West Pakistan. In this, Soviet Union provided military and diplomatic support to India under the peace, friendship treaty that was signed by the two countries in August 1970.

The final assault was made by India in mid December 1971 when the Indian army launched a three-pronged attack on East Pakistan. Indian armed forces advanced to Dhaka virtually unopposed, helped by the Mukti Bahini guerrillas. The 1971 war culminated in the surrender of 90,000 Pakistani soldiers. Zulfikar Ali Bhutto, who had taken over from Yahya Khan, released Shiekh Mujib who returned to Dhaka to a hero's welcome in January 1972. He became the first prime minister of Bangladesh. Mujib was later assassinated in a military coup in 1975.

Secret British official papers from 30 years ago shed new light on the 1971 war. The papers include secret transcripts of a summit meeting between the US President Richard Nixon and UK Prime Minister Edward Heath in December that year in Bermuda.

The papers from the Bermuda summit highlights that 'President Nixon and his foreign affairs adviser, Henry Kissinger, suspected India of planning not just the separation of East Pakistan, but also the breakup of West Pakistan with moves inside the Pakistani side of Kashmir. Nixon told the British Prime Minister Edward Heath that Mrs Gandhi was being steered by the Soviets, in response to US building ties with China and Pakistan.'

The transcript quoted Nixon saying that Kissinger had secretly contacted the Soviet leadership to seek an assurance to restrain India from breaking up West Pakistan. It added, such promise was forthcoming only after the US Seventh Fleet took up a threatening posture in Indian Ocean.

The secret British official papers talk about Mrs Gandhi seeking British help during her visit to Britain. In her conversation with Edward Heath, Mrs Gandhi said that Nixon's friendly overtures to the Chinese, and their closeness to Pakistan, had made it necessary for India to sign a treaty with the Soviet Union. She also told Heath that there was pressure on her from cabinet colleagues to take on Pakistan.

The secret paper says that, Pakistani president, Yahya Khan also sought British support. "Khan wrote to Mr Heath outlining the Indian military build-up, which included seven army divisions mobilized near West Pakistan and eight near East Pakistan. He also wrote about the deployment of Indian Air Force and Navy saying the offensive posture by India points not at the direction of peace but of conflict."

The creation of Bangladesh has several lessons to be learnt. It was the first instance, and is still by far the most important case after 1945, of one state participating with military force in the dismemberment of another. The event created a precedent that further territorial adjustments were possible for the nations that have emerged from colonial rule.

However, Indian intervention in Bangladesh draws it legitimacy from the fact that, there was an overwhelming popular support for the liberation movement in East Pakistan, which looked towards India. India also hold the view that it had no other option than to intervene after the crisis in East Pakistan showed no signs of ending and the refugees keep mounting on the India soil.

The other lesson from the creation of Bangladesh is the staying power of well-defined communities in the world. Bangladesh has established itself as a viable state with a strong identity, however poor and ill governed it remains. Bangladesh has made much more progress than in the years when it was East Pakistan. Bangladesh has made great strides in the areas of agriculture, education, health care and family planning, etc.

The relative success of ethnic nationalism in Bangladesh however has no visible negative impact on India. It shows how heterogeneous societies could be kept intact by political commitment to pluralism. Pluralism can be as much a binder of, and catalyst as it can otherwise be exploited. Bangladesh stands testimony to the former premise.

Parties and Politics in Bangladesh

The political scene in Bangladesh remains volatile as ever. The Bangladesh National Party (BNP) headed by Khaleda Zia and the Awami League Party headed by Hasina Wajid are the two main political outfits in Bangladesh. Their competitive politics have led both to cultivate their own different constituencies. Among those who support BNP are religious groups because of the party's stress to give an Islamic identity to Bangladesh. The BNP also has good support from the men in uniform due to the party founder being late General Zia-ur-Rehman, husband of Khaleda Zia. BNP's leanings for free market economy evoke support from the powerful business establishment in the country. The party's most favoured anti-India plank draws support from the voters who feel Indian hand in all the woes of Bangladesh.

The Awami League Party draws the secularists due to its pluralistic outlook. Awami League's criticism about religious extremism and pro India tilt fetches the support of 11 per cent Hindu minority in Bangladesh. The left parties support the Awami League, due to its criticism of the pro-capitalist economic policies of the BNP. The nationalists are drawn to the Awami League because of its criticism against the government's inept handling of issues like gas reserves and water sharing with India.

Hasina Wajid, the leader of the Awami League, and the BNP's leader, Khaleda Zia have many things in common. Both leaders have a firm charismatic appeal for their respective constituencies. Both draw their sustenance from close relatives, the former, from her father Shiekh Mujib-ur-Rahman, and the latter from her husband, late General Zia- ur- Rehman. Both like to dress elegantly. Begum Zia, dresses in classy French chiffon saris while, Hasina Wajid in local Jamdani saris. What comes between them is their antagonist political approach. The personal egos of the two leaders have many a time blocked a consensus on seemingly simpler issues, which at times have undermined the fragile democracy in Bangladesh.

Democracy was first strangulated in Bangladesh, when the father of the nation, Sheikh Mujib Ur Rahman was assassinated in 1975. The army General Zia-ur-Rehman who took over the reigns of power in 1975 tried to provide stability to the country. General Rehman's six year of rule saw suspension of all democratic activity which was revived by the formation of the BNP party, just before his assassination in a military coup in 1981.

Thereafter, a brief stint at democracy was attempted but its failure led to another phase of military rule in Bangladesh. General Mohmmad Ershad who ruled for most of the eighties was like any other military ruler who suppressed democracy to perpetuate his own rule. His rule was marred by charges of corruption, nepotism and immorality, which prompted massive street protest leading to his overthrow in 1990 and ushering of democracy in Bangladesh.

The BNP led by Khaleda Zia was voted to power in the first election that was held in Bangladesh in 1991. She was the first woman prime minister of Bangladesh. However, she was not able to complete her full tenure (1991-1996) and the last few months of her term were marred by violent street demonstrations against her rule.

The next election in 1996 brought the Awami League led by Shiekh Hasina Wajid to power. She was the first elected government in the history of the country to serve its full five-year term. The cycle was repeated when the BNP returned to power with a landslide victory in the October 2001 election.

The October election threw a coalition government of four parties including hardliner Jamaat-e-Islami. The rightist ideology of Jamaat-e-Islami holds considerable sway in the Muslim dominated country. The BNP, which harps on the religious moorings, while trying to placate Jamaat-e-Islami, is trying to give a rightist tilt to the country.

The growing fundamentalist influence was seen soon after the general elections in 2001 when there were widespread communal attacks on the Hindus in Bangladesh. Hundreds fled their home; some even crossed the border into India fearing for their lives. The severity of the problem could be ascertained by the fact that the then Indian prime minister's special envoy, Brajesh Mishra, made a brief trip to Dhaka to convey India's concerns.

The opposition Awami League party described the atrocities against the minorities as politically motivated. Even though the communal attacks were controlled immediately, but it's very initiation at the behest of the BNP's cadre was seen as an indication to erase the secular character of Bangladesh.

The two political parties in Bangladesh are at loggerheads regarding the handling of the export of natural gas to India. The Awami League alleges of a secret deal struck by the ruling coalition with some US companies to supply natural gas to India. In fact, Shiekh Hasina Wajid attributed her party's electoral defeat in 2001 to her refusal to export gas to India. She pledged "all-out resistance" to any move to sell the country's gas reserve, saying it undermined the national interest.

Anti-India rhetoric is another issue that plays a major part in Bangladesh's politics. The two political parties have cashed on the anti-India sentiment that runs high in Bangladesh. The curious thing was the allegations that New Delhi hatched a conspiracy to install the BNP-led coalition for the favour of gas imports from Bangladesh. The allegation gives rise to speculation that a sizable section of Bangladeshi society remains unhappy with India.

Prime Minister Khaleda Zia who had come to power on the promise to address the flagging economy and ridding the country of the lawlessness and corruption has done precarious little in terms of general development of the country. The Awami League is out on street criticising the BNP led coalition for it's all round failures.

It is felt that most of the problems in Bangladesh could well be addressed, if the two political parties bury their hatchet and evolve a consensus on the general development of the country. A healthy political climate could alone take the country on the road of peace and progress. The required political stability would go a long way; in achieving the much needed economic development of Bangladesh.

India-Bangladesh Relations

India-Bangladesh relationship remains torn between two divergent expressions. On the one hand, its Islamic and Bangla moorings demand sharpening of religious and linguistic nationalism to forge extra-regional identity, and on the other the limitation of geography forces Bangladesh to be guided by the subcontinental politics. India-Bangladesh relationship therefore remains geared to synchronise these diverse pulls and pressures.

The three-decades of India-Bangladesh relationship suggests that the foreign policy of the two countries have moved in a cyclical form. The peace and friendship treaty signed at the time of emergence of Bangladesh in 1971 guided the Indo-Bangla relations during the reign of Sheikh Mujib ur Rahman (1971-75). The treaty became outdated soon after the assassination of Bangla Bandhu in 1975.

General Zia-ur-Rehman who took over in 1975 initiated a significant shift in Indo-Bangla relations. His rule saw Bangladesh-India relationship being brought to a bilateral level. It was General Zia-ur-Rehman who pioneered the idea of a regional body called South Asian Association of Regional Cooperation (SAARC), visualizing the fear psychosis of small nations vis-à-vis India, in the region.

Bangladesh continued its stint with military rule. General Mohmmad Ershad replaced General Rehman following a military coup. During his decade long rule, General Ershad tried to reverse the hardline position taken by his predecessor and the relationship with India moved from conflict to cooperation. At that time, rumours were agog that General Ershad's regime was sustained by India.

Democracy returned to Bangladesh in 1990 and Bangladesh National Party (BNP) headed by General Rehman's widow Begum Khaleda Zia, the first woman prime minister of the country came to power. During her rule, anti-India rhetoric was found once again blaring in Bangladesh. Relation with India became acrimonious over the issue of water, illegal immigrants, land boundary and maritime delimitations and Chakma refugees.

The Awami League party, which came to power in 1996 elections, engaged in damage control exercise and relations with India was improved. Its leader, Shiekh Hasina Wajid, made it clear that all the differences with India would be sorted out through mutual dialogue. The return of BNP to power in the election of 2001 vitiated the relationship with India once again. The outlook of BNP government was characterised by unusual toughness in relationship with India.

During the successive democratic regimes, three significant developments have taken place leading to improvement in the Indo-Bangla bilateral relationship. The first was handing over of the Teen Bigha corridor, a lease in perpetuity to Bangladesh by India in early nineties. The second was the solution of repatriation of 24,000 Chakma tribal refugees sheltering in camps in Tripura. Third was Kolkata-Dhaka bus service, inaugurated in 1999.

One of the major problems that confront the two nations is sharing of the water resources. Bangladesh accuses India of not letting it have enough water for irrigational purposes during dry season and allowing excess water to drain during monsoon causing floods. The central problem is the construction of dams in India on the common rivers, which traverse between the two countries. Bangladesh has been pressing for a construction of a reservoir in Nepal to augment the water resources but India wants to construct a 320-kilometre link canal connecting the Brahmaputra river with Farakka barrage through Bangladesh to solve the problem.

Several rounds of talks have been held including summit level meeting but nothing substantial have come out of them. Bangladesh wants a regional approach to solve the problem, while India insists on the bilateral approach. The issue took an acrimonious turn in early 1990s when Khaleda Zia raised the issue in the world forums and India frowned over her remarks. Some quick fix arrangements were made during I K Gujral's regime but no permanent solution is in sight.

The other hurdles which comes in the way between India and Bangladesh is leading a joint survey for the delimitation of the maritime borders and settle the territorial claim of Talpetty or the New Moore island. The two nations also have to settle the land boundary dispute, which remain the cause of border tension between the two countries. The border dispute claimed 19 lives in 2002, prompting tighter security along the line of control.

Another issue that vitiates the Indo-Bangla relationship is the allegation that anti-India activities are being perpetuated from the Bangladeshi soil. The NDA government had accused Bangladesh of sheltering Al-Qaeda terrorists and alleged that Pakistan's High Commission in Dhaka was being used as a base by the ISI to conduct anti-India activities. The NDA government also made public a list of 99 terrorist training camps run by northeast insurgents in Bangladesh.

Bangladesh dismissed the Indian allegations as "baseless and motivated". Bangladesh foreign minister Morshed Khan commented that his country was opposed to any form of terrorism and religious fundamentalism and assured India that its territory would not be allowed to be used for any "kind of activity that is detrimental" to New Delhi's interests. Notwithstanding the foreign minister's assurances, this issue remains a major impediment in bilateral ties.

The human rights issue, particularly ill treatment of the 11 per cent Hindu minorities in Bangladesh, is another issue that has soured the bilateral relationship. The issue took an ugly turn soon after Begum Khaleda Zia was sworn in as prime minister in 2001. Many Bangladeshi Hindus fled to West Bengal, alleging intimidation and torture by the BNP activists in their homeland. The issue became so serious that Prime Minister Vajpayee had to send his security advisor Brajesh Mishra to Dhaka to convey India's concern. Bangladesh allayed Indian fears and in the wake of communal carnage in Gujarat in 2002, its security forces guarded Hindu temples and minority business establishments to maintain communal peace.

The other issues in Indo-Bangla relations are the Indian interest in buying Bangladesh's surplus gas. Some exploratory talks were done during the Awami League's regime but the matter has been on hold since the return of BNP to power. Similarly, India is interested in using Bangladesh roads to reach its northeast states. It is believed that Bangladesh is considering the proposal and has assured India that it would provide security to its vehicles transporting containers to the northeast states.

The references suggest that India and Bangladesh needs to establish long-term economic linkages in trade and investment and infrastructure and communication to cement their relationship. Diversifying trade and commerce can give a boost to bilateral relations. Trade imbalances could be rectified by joint ventures, industrial investments and technical cooperation. To begin with, the two countries may first strengthen the ties in the areas of cooperation and then move on to settle the issues of dispute. A reconciliatory attitude would only take the India-Bangladesh relationship on the path of progress and development.

Bangladeshi Immigrants Issue

In the biting winter of February 2003, Indo-Bangladesh relations touched an all time low. Tensions ran high between the two countries on the international border in Cooch Behar district of West Bengal when Indian Border Security Force (BSF) stopped the 213 snake charmers with 80 children and 90 cobra, trying to cross over to the Indian side illegally. The BSF asked them to go back, but the Bangladesh Rifles (BDR) refused to let them in saying they were Indian nationals being pushed into Bangladesh.

On either side of the border, India and Bangladesh forces took pot-shots at the poor immigrants who remained huddled for about a week in the open sky on the grassy stretch known as the 'Zero line'.

It was only after some tough talking at the highest level that the crisis was finally defused. It was under the cover of a dense fog on a chilly morning that the illegal migrants made a hasty retreat. The only visible signs left behind by them were pots and pans, toys and clothing, which reminded of a high voltage drama that took place there for about a week.

Tension between the two countries flared up further over the issue, and close on the heels of this incident, three more infiltration bid was foiled by the BSF in a span of ten days. India alleged that Bangladesh Rifles was trying to push their nationals through the porous 4,000-kilometer border, a charge denied by the BDR. India stepped up vigilance by reinforcing security forces on its borders with Bangladesh to stop such activities.

The then, Home Minister L K Advani took a tough stand on the issue in view of the threat perception towards the internal security of the country. He announced to deport an estimated 20 million Bangladeshis living illegally in the country. Discussing the issue in Parliament, Advani said that talks were held with the Awami League government and some proposals were exchanged to issue ID cards cum work permits to such persons who criss-cross the international borders regularly. He informed the house that further discussions on the subject have come to a halt since the BNP government came to power.

In a damage control exercise, Bangladesh Foreign Minister Manzur Morshed Khan visited New Delhi in the last week of February 2003. He opined that there were international norms and rules to deal with the problem of illegal migrants and added that minor irritants should not become a stumbling block in promoting bilateral ties between the two neighbours. Bangladeshi foreign minister felt that the responsibility of stopping illegal migration lay with India and urged New Delhi to resolve all contentious issues in a spirit of accommodation and mutual trust to solve the problem.

It may be recalled that India and Bangladesh signed an agreement in August 2002 for creating a Joint Working Group (JWG) to solve the problem of illegal immigration. The JWG was to meet twice every year and monitor border management, surveillance and sharing of intelligence to check illegal immigration. Both sides also discussed sharing intelligence between the security agencies to check other illegal activities. Both sides agreed to take 'visible steps' to ensure that commitments on better border security management were reflected on the ground.

However, the issue that flared in February 2003 threw overboard the agreements made a few months earlier. The situation since then has been salvaged and the agreement on JWC is again being honoured, but no one is ready to take a sympathetic view at what lay at the heart of the problem. The bottom line is, people are crossing the borders illegally because they are driven by economic necessity or due to the problem of Lebensraum, a fact that is not being publicly considered.

In India, what we have seen is that the Bangladeshi immigration issue has become an election plank to whip up national and communal hysteria. The opposition in West Bengal accuses the left front government for being soft towards Bangladeshi immigrants which is changing the demographic profile of the state. At the national level, the Vishwa Hindu Parishad, exploiting the Hindu sentiments, allege that if the illegal immigration from Bangladesh continues, Muslims would soon outnumber Hindus in India.

In the cacophony of electoral politics, the real issue is lost. Media reports suggest a pattern, where once an illegal migration attempt is foiled; a serious concern is raised by India which is diplomatically being pacified by Bangladesh, and then the usual lull follows the storm.

The issue is not as simple as that of a border management as seen by India. What is required is a deeper understanding of the problem and then to make a calibrated approach towards its solution on a permanent basis. Unfortunately, both India and Bangladesh by posturing and counter posturing attitude remain viciously trapped. The fact remains that a serious attempt by both the countries alone would solve the problem of illegal Bangladeshi immigrants that in turn may pave the way for better ties between the two neighbours.

Bangladesh Health Care Scene

One of the limitations of democracy is that it cannot do what a dictatorial regime can achieve with a single stroke of a pen. This is not to belittle the virtues of democracy or to appreciate the ills of authoritative rule, but just to make a point. It was in 1982, Bangladesh's military ruler, General Mohammad Irshad who took a landmark decision by approving the new drug policy visualised by Zafrullah Choudhary, hailed as the father of Bangladesh health care policy and owner of Ganashashtyphia, the local drug manufacturing company in the country.

Bangladesh appointed an expert committee to be headed by Professor Nurul Islam to shape up a drug policy tailoring to the health need of the country. The committee issued certain guidelines for imports and formulation policy to reduce the over dependence of the country on imports for the production of bulk drugs. The committee was guided by the idea to prevent foreign exchange being wasted by importing unnecessary drugs. It identified irresponsible prescribing, marketing and inappropriate self-use of medicines as the greatest source of wastage of the country's exchequer.

The framers of drug policy acknowledged the role of multinationals in providing medicines in view of their sophistication in machinery and technical know-how. The MNCs were left free to concentrate only on those items like injectable vitamins as single ingredient products and those drugs, which could not be produced by the smaller national companies. Licenses were stopped for manufacturing foreign drugs in the country to check wastage of money in royalties to the MNCs. Further, all existing licensing agreements were reviewed and MNCs, which did not own their own factories in Bangladesh, were not allowed to market their products.

The expert committee identified 31 most essential drugs, which were to be produced by the multinational companies. The committee also put a control on the operation of the bulk drug production by introducing the practice of floating global tenders. Sixteen guidelines were issued to the MNCs essentially catering towards reducing the prices and check profitability. There were some relaxations given to the MNCs for the manufacture of some 50 to 60 drugs.

Local companies were given protection in production of those drugs, which required low technology. As a measure of protection for the local industry, import was barred, for the same or close substitute of a drug, produced in the country. Further import of restorative products that had no therapeutic value and thrived on consumer ignorance was discontinued.

The committee identified a high wastage of financial resources on production of drugs with little therapeutic value. It barred the production of cough mixtures, throat lozenges, gripe water, alkali preparations and digestive enzymes. Similarly, manufacture of tonics, enzymes mixtures preparation, and restorative products, which flourished on consumer's ignorance and were habit forming, were discontinued. Drugs with slight difference in cognition but having similar action were prohibited for manufacturing.

The combination of two antibiotics was prohibited because it made the product costlier. Production of antibiotic in liquid form, which was harmful to children, was also stopped. The combination of analgesic in any form was disallowed as it increased toxicity. The use of codeine in any combination was prohibited as it caused infection.

The committee however made it clear that production of combination drug could only be approved if the drug company provides a definitive approval of the World Health Organisation and conclusively prove the drug would not increase toxicity or create side effects. Certain drugs having favourable risk benefit ratio were allowed production in limited quantity and were subject to prescription by the specialists. Vitamins, with the exception of B-Complex composites were allowed to be prepared as single ingredient products in tablets, capsules and injectable form.

As a result of these bold measures the drug prices in Bangladesh drastically came down. The lists of the essential drugs, which were prepared in consonance with the disease profile of the country, have been successful in decreasing the mortality rate. The country has been able to weed out irrational drugs from the market, which had assumed disproportionate scale.

Today, in Bangladesh, there is an upcoming indigenous drug industry. The bulk drug production from zero has reached to a modest figure of 25 per cent in a very short span of time in Bangladesh.

Bangladesh also made a pioneering attempt to introduce drugs into the market through its generic name. Zafrullah Choudhary, the man who anchored the Bangladesh drug policy spearheaded the campaign. However, this innovation could not succeed due to lack of co-ordination by the international drug manufacturing companies whose vested marketing interests came in the way.

In totality, the bold drug policy of Bangladesh has ensured that health care remains within the reach of the ordinary folks of the country. It provides a shining example for other developing nations to emulate its policies for providing better health care facilitates to their citizens.

8
Nepal

- *Nepal at Crossroads* • *Nepal: Monarchy Gains Strength*
- *Maoist Insurgency in Nepal* • *India-Nepal Relations*
- *India-Nepal Allay Security Concerns*

Nepal at Crossroads

All is not well in Nepal. The nascent democracy is in a quandary, since King Gyanendra, in a virtual coup in October 2002, took over the reigns of power, using the provisions of article 127 of the constitution. The caretaker prime minister, Sher Bahadur Deuba, was sacked for failing to hold elections before 13 November 2002 and seeking its postponement by a year due to fear of Maoist insurgency.

The king then appointed Lokendra Bahadur Chand and Surya Bahadur Thappa as prime ministers, but sacked them too for the same reasons. He has now reappointed Sher Bahadur Deuba, who has promised to hold elections sometime in 2005, as prime minister.

The moves by King Gyanendra sparked off a wide public debate on the prospects of democracy in Nepal. The two dominant political parties; Nepalese Congress Party and the United Marxist Leninist party of Nepal are spearheading pro democratic movement in Nepal. King Gyanendra is in no mood to be relenting, citing his role as the custodian of maintaining peace and stability in his kingdom.

Ever since restoration of democracy in May 1990, Nepal has seen very complex intra-party squabbles. The Nepalese Congress which had struggled for decades, first against oppressive Rana regime and then against the palace-controlled party less Panchayat system, came to power with the help of United Marxist Leninist (UML) party in 1990. Internal dissensions within the Congress party let it fall apart. There emerged many power centres, the Koirala and the Bhattrai factions, amongst others.

Due to internal differences, the Nepalese Congress Party was unable to continue their full term and invited midterm poll in 1994. Following the election, UML party came to power with a wafer thin majority and barely lasted nine months. It was replaced by an extremely fragile coalition headed by Sher Bahadur Deuba, whose survival too proved short lived.

Switching from being an absolute monarchy to democracy, Nepal has been riddled with political instability, having 11 governments since 1990. The last election was held in May 1999, when the Nepalese Congress won 113 of the 205 seats and formed a government. Since then, leadership power struggles within the party have led to three different prime ministers.

The political chaos has led to the rise of Maoist rebels in Nepal who have been waging a people's war since 1996 to overthrow the monarchy and establish a communist republic. They want to draft a new constitution under an interim government that is to quash the rights and authority of the monarch.

Sher Bahadur Deuba, who took office in 2001, initiated a cease-fire with the rebels which lasted for four months. Three rounds of talks failed to produce any agreement and the rebels launched a flurry of attacks on police stations and government targets, leading to the clamping of emergency on 26 November 2001. Since then, emergency was extended twice, first in February and then in May 2002.

In May 2002, differences arose within the National Congress party over the extension of the emergency for the third time. Prime Minister Sher Bahadur Deuba defied party leader Girija Prasad Koirala's instructions and recommended the king to dissolve the 205 member house and extend the period of emergency. The dissolution of the house led to the proclamation of general elections, slated for 13 November 2002, and extension of the emergency for another three months, which expired on 28 August 2002. The move led to a split in the National Congress party and Prime Minister

Sher Bahadur Deuba headed a faction called National Congress (democratic).

In a significant development in July 2002, Maoist dropped their demands for formation of a Constituent Assembly and revised their stand by expressing willingness to participate in the electoral process, provided the elections were conducted by an interim government. Most political parties welcomed this offer but Prime Minister Deuba rebuffed rebels offer saying, "No talks were possible with the followers of Pol Pot." He insisted that the Maoist should give up their arms.

The Maoist announced the disruption of the polls and warned that if their demands were not met, there would be bloodshed in the country. Amidst the deteriorating law and order situation, Deuba saw the futility of the polls, and recommended to the king to postpone the elections for a year. Deuba's inability to hold election prompted King Gyanendra to sack him from office.

King Gyanendra later appointed two more prime ministers, Lokendra Bahadur Chand and Surya Bahadur Thappa to hold consultation with the political parties, resolve issues with the Maoists, and hold elections for constituting the new parliament. However, lack of consensus among the political parties delayed any such process which in turn led to their sacking.

The reappointment of Sher Bahadur Deuba as prime minister has brought the clock full circle in Nepal. Deuba has announced that election in Nepal could be expected sometime in 2005. It remains to be seen when the prime minister re-opens the negotiations with the Maoist. It also remains to be seen whether the talks would create the desirable atmosphere to hold general election in Nepal.

The statement by Deuba has rekindled the hope of restoration of democracy in Nepal. However, till such time kingship will prevail over democracy in the Himalayan Kingdom. One has to wait and watch the developments in Nepal.

Nepal: Monarchy Gains Strength

Since the royal massacre on 1 June 2001, political uncertainty haunts Nepal. On 4 June, the slain King Birendra's brother,

Gyanendra, was hastily enthroned and later crowned as new king of Nepal. In a mark of assertion of his authority King Gyanendra dismissed the caretaker Prime Minister Sher Bahadur Deuba on 14 October 2002

Since then King Gyanendra has slowly strengthened his position taking advantage of the people's anguish over the internal bickering among the various political parties in Nepal. The new king has successfully held the eleventh SAARC summit in early January 2002 in Kathmandu. US Foreign Secretary Colin Powell's stopover in Nepal, during his Asia tour in late January 2002, further enhanced Gyanendra's stature as an accepted figurehead. King Gyanendra's visit to India and China in 2002, confirmed his complete control over the political apparatus of Nepal.

However, King Gyanendra has not yet defined his attitude towards democracy. At the moment all eyes are watching him as to whether he would conform to the present constitution and build consensus for holding the elections or he would continue to reign through the period of sustained emergency. The problem is, as long as political parties are unable to gain consensus over the proposed election, monarchy would continue to have upper hand in Nepal.

The contemporary history of monarchy in Nepal began when a democratic revolution was initiated against the Rana prime minister, who took control after the sudden flight of King Tribhuvan to India in 1950. The 'Delhi compromise' which was arranged by India led to a tripartite agreement between King Tribhuvan, the Rana prime minister, and the Nepali Congress to restore monarchy and install an interim government that would oversee elections to a constituent assembly.

King Tribhuvan's return to Nepal in 1951 started the first experiment of democracy in Nepal. The Interim Government of Nepal Act of 1951 vested executive powers on the king and his council of ministers, who could be appointed or dismissed at his will. An interim government comprising ministers from the Nepali Congress party and the Rana prime minister was set up. However, the coalition, comprising antagonistic interests, lasted less than a year and successive cabinets collapsed due to the internal strife. In between, the monarchy took a more active role, and power gradually became concentrated in the palace. By 1954 it became clear that monarchy had effectively regained absolute powers in Nepal.

Tribhuvan's son, Mahendra, who ascended the throne in 1955 retained the broad emergency powers of the king and called for a general election in 1959. However, the first democratically elected government came and went in less than two years. Its abrupt termination is alleged to have more to do with royal ambitions than the failure of democratic institutions.

Following that, King Mahendra proclaimed a state emergency and arrested the leaders of the Nepali Congress party. The Nepali Congress responded to the crackdown with a guerrilla uprising which was launched from Indian soil. The armed rebellion was initially encouraged by India but was abandoned after 1962 Sino-Indian war.

The Constitution of 1962, by new King Birendra, reinforced the traditional role of the monarch as the head of the state of Nepal. King Birendra conceived a new system of governance called the Panchayat Raj; a unique Nepali form of government, which had semblance of democracy, but here too the king held the power to veto and the right to formulate laws.

In 1980, a spontaneous anti-Panchayat agitation broke out and King Birendra conducted a referendum in 1981 in which opinion remained divided. The 1981 referendum liberalised the political climate to some extent and political parties though, officially banned, could effectively function. But this no way lessened the palace's power.

The popular discontent led political forces to join hands to launch a people's movement called 'Jana Andolan'. This was the first coordinated effort by political parties, particularly the Nepali Congress and United Left Front to end the Panchayat system. Parliamentary democracy was finally restored in Nepal in 1990 and the king was reduced to a constitutional head.

The Constitution of 1990 defines Nepal as "a multi-ethnic, multi-lingual, democratic, independent, indivisible, sovereign, Hindu, constitutional monarchical kingdom." Sovereignty was strictly vested with the people and not with the king of Nepal. Under the constitution, the king retained the title of supreme commander-in-chief of the army, broad emergency powers and control over palace-related issues, including succession.

Throughout the 1990s, King Birendra acted as a stabilizing factor. He never overstepped the bounds of his role as constitutional monarch. Even during the steady stream of minority and coalition governments, particularly in 1997 when democracy was struggling, as three coalition governments came and went in a single year, the king's role remained that of a political spectator.

However, with the ascendancy of King Gyanendra the situation has changed in Nepal. It seems the king is not interested in democracy till political parties bury their hatchet and an amicable climate is created for holding elections, ending the Maoist insurgency in Nepal. King Gyanendra knows that all through its history, monarchy is the single consistent factor that has kept Nepal united. His role is crucial at this juncture of history when Nepal is at crossroads.

Maoist Insurgency in Nepal

The rise of the Nepalese Maoists is directly connected with the fall of the absolute monarchy in 1990 and the subsequent introduction of a parliamentary democracy. The road to armed rebellion began when the powerful left-wing party Samyukta Jana Morcha (United Progressive Front – UPF) split on the eve of the 1994 election, which threw up a hung Parliament, and a minority government led by the Communist Party of Nepal (Unified Marxist-Leninists) came to power. The Communist party-led government fell after just nine months giving way to a series of fragile and implausible coalition governments.

The widespread corruption at all levels, social and political instability, political bickering and abuse of power caused frustration among large segments of the population. This further catapulted the Maoist insurgents to the forefront of Nepal's political space. Their influence also grew due to the huge disparities between rural and urban centres and within the different regions of Nepal. Appended to it is the imagined 'Indian factor' that has been drummed up to rationalise the ills of Nepal.

It is no wonder that instead of the usual 'Western imperialists' bogey, found in Maoist rhetoric, the 'Indian hand' has been shored up to mobilise the masses in Nepal.

The Maoists are led by Pushpa Kamal Dahal – also known as Comrade Prachanda – and Baburam Bhattarai, an Indian educated engineer. They launched their first campaign in Rolpa and Rukum districts of Nepal in 1995. Since then the Maoists have been able to expand their influence from the northwest to more than half of the 75 districts of Nepal. Their writ looms large, and their agitation call can anytime bring the whole country to a grinding halt.

Nepal's Maoist insurgency has strengthened during the years. The exact strength of the Maoists is not known, but its core fighting force is estimated to be anywhere between 2,000-3,500, apart from thousands of sympathisers and volunteers. Their arms are primitive, mostly snatched from the police, army and other sources.

So far there are no reports of any foreign agency supplying arms or money to the Maoists, even though some Indian groups accuse China of backing them up. Money for the movement comes from extortion in the villages and contributions from sympathisers in urban area. However, there have been some media reports of Maoists acquiring small arms from the Indian state of Bihar, notorious for illegal manufacturing of arms.

Sher Bahadur Deuba, who replaced Girija Prasad Koirala as prime minister of Nepal in mid of 2001, initiated a cease-fire with the rebels which lasted for four months. He held three rounds of talks but failed to produce any agreement. The breaking down of the talks led the rebels to launch a flurry of attacks on police stations and government targets, leading to the clamping of emergency on 26 November 2001. The state emergency was extended twice, first in February and then in May 2002.

During the period of emergency, the government was in no mood to comply with the Maoist demands and decided to fight them out. Nepal deployed army for the first time inside the country to fight the Maoists. It is estimated that 7,000 people have been killed, half of them since emergency was clamped for the first time in 2001. Even though security forces claim to have killed nearly

2,000 guerrillas, there seems no end in sight to the Maoist insurgency in Nepal.

The Maoist influence has grown due to Nepal's relatively small geographical size and also because of the acute underdevelopment of the country. The Maoist's tactics of holding mass meetings and kangaroo courts in the countryside further brought them closer to the masses. It seems there is no other way than a negotiated settlements co-opt them in the power structure of Nepal.

However, the reality is; if the Maoists are accommodated in the political structure, then the monarchy and the kingdom of Nepal would be under threat. On the other hand, if path of confrontation is trodden, the fear of anarchy looms large in Nepal.

There seems to be no meeting ground with the government if the Maoists continue on their core demand for the abolition of the kingship. The king who has tended to acquire an upper hand over the government would never subscribe to anything which would want him to sign the death warrant of the institution of kingship.

The talks with the Maoist, if and when takes place, should concentrate on convincing the rebels to join the mainstream politics as a political group and participate in the parliamentary democracy. There should also be public proclamation by King Gyanendra that he would play the role of a constitutional monarch after the establishment of elected government in Nepal.

However, the big question is whether, King Gyanendra would revert to the role of the Nepalese king as the titular head. The late King Birendra had relented for democracy only after a long and arduous people's struggle against the palace rule. The other question is whether the Maoist would give up their core demand and join the political mainstream. Uncertainty seems to plague Nepal.

India-Nepal Relations

India and Nepal are bounded by geography, share the same historical experiences, have roots in common tradition and culture, yet their relations have moved in a yo-yo pattern. Soon after independence, India and Nepal signed the peace and friendship treaty in 1950 to cement their relationship. Every thing was hunky-dory for the next two decades. Problems started cropping up since the eighties when the relations between the two countries became acrimonious.

India-Nepal relations started looking up since establishment of democracy in Nepal and particularly after Indian Prime Minister I K Gujral's regime. The 'Gujral doctrine', which did not seek reciprocity in bilateral relations with Nepal, helped a lot to iron out the differences between the two countries. However, the issues that remain to be addressed are; augmentation of natural resources, environmental degradation, transit facilities and trade related matters.

The most crucial factor in India-Nepal relation is the harnessing of the water resources from the rivers which flows from Nepal to India. Nepal has given assurances that it would give first preference to India with regard to the development of its natural resources and for industrial projects of mutual benefits to each other. The energy starved India is too heavily dependent on Nepal to overcome its power shortage. It has signed agreements to harness the water resources of the rivers Kosi, Gandak, Buri-Gandak, Karnali, Sapat, and Pancheswar. However, after the establishment of democracy in 1990, the general feeling in Nepal brewing is that India had gained disproportional benefits from all these projects and wanted them to be reviewed.

In 1992, an agreement was signed between G P Koirala and P V Narasimha Rao regarding the Tanakpur Hydel project on the river Mahakali. Under this agreement Nepal agreed to make available 205 hectares of Nepalese territory on which India would build an afflux bund for this project. In return India would give 10 million units of electricity free of cost annually, besides some water for irrigation, to Nepal.

The agreement on Tanakpur power project caused suspicion amongst the Nepali citizens who thought it was a sell out of their national interest. Nepal wanted a package to be worked out where India may double the supply of electricity. Kathmandu sought a 50 per cent share in the power generated and said that it is entitled to 20 million units of power and 1000 cusecs of water. India refused Kathmandu's claim for a large share of power and water and said it violated the 1992 agreement.

The problem has compounded because Nepal cannot sell its surplus power to any other country except India. The Tanakpur issue was a minor one, considering there are other major power projects where India is involved.

Linked to the honing of natural resources is the environmental issue that has cropped up due to felling of the trees in Nepal and which is causing water logging and floods in India during the monsoon season. In UP, Bihar and West Bengal, huge areas gets inundated every year, causing heavy loss to men and material due to unchecked flow of water from Nepal. Several times this issue had come up for discussions at the bilateral level but no substantial progress has been made to solve this problem.

The other issue between India and Nepal is the transit treaty. India and Nepal share 500 kilometres of border which is accessible from either side. The 1950 treaty mentions that "both the government may grant on the reciprocal basis in the territory of others, the same privileges to the nationals of others in matter of residence, owning property, participation in trade and commerce, movement and privileges of similar nature."

Nepal feels that this has led to a huge influx of Indian population and has even caused demographic imbalance in its country. The former Panchayat regime had introduced work permit system for the Indian nationals but the subsequent government abolished them at the behest of India. The matter was partially addressed in 1991 when a separate transit treaty was signed. The treaty was renewed after seven years and no acrimony was witnessed then between the two countries.

The porous border between India and Nepal has always remained a safe haven for the smugglers who cashed upon the illegal border trade. Of late, a new dimension has been added to it in the form of flesh trade. This has caused a great concern because of its potential of spreading AIDS, which is assuming alarming proportions in India. This matter has been taken up by several NGOs but the two governments are yet to take up the issue seriously.

The other contentious issue is trade which India wants to combine with the transit facilities. Nepal wants to diversify its trade with other countries and objects to Indian position to link it with the transit facilities. A crisis blew up in December 1989 when India sealed off all its fourteen transit points to Nepal, causing a virtual blockade of the goods to the Himalayan Kingdom. In 1990, an agreement was signed to restore the status quo of 1 April 1987 and finally the matter was resolved in 1992 when two separate trade and transit treaty was signed.

With regard to transit, there was also acrimony between India and Nepal, when Nepal wanted an overland passage from India for access to Bangladesh ports for its trade purposes. India initially provided Nepal transit facilities of its Haldia and Kandla ports, but later it conceded Nepal's demand and provided a corridor to Bangladesh to remove any irritants.

To boost bilateral trade with Nepal, India agreed to exempt basic custom duties and quantitative restrictions for all manufactured articles, containing not less than 65 per cent of Indian material. India also enhanced credit facilities from 25 to 35 crore rupees. Besides, India also agreed to identify products on which tariff could be further removed. The bilateral trade between the two countries is now conducted on most favoured nation (MFN) basis.

The United Progressive Alliance (UPA) government, headed by Manmohan Singh, gave top priority to Nepal. The External Affairs Minister, Natwar Singh, chose to visit Kathmandu as his first official visit abroad between 4-6 June, barely ten days after assuming office.

Singh extended full cooperation of India in Nepal's economic development by not only pursuing but expanding the economic cooperation between the two countries. Natwar Singh also extended India's cooperation in tackling the Maoist insurgency, saying that the left ultras pose challenge to the security of both the countries. On China factor, Natwar Singh said that at a time when India is improving relations with China and had proposed to Nepal to provide transit route for trade with China, there is no more zero-sum game between Nepal, India and China.

India-Nepal relations, instead of getting into competition and conflict syndrome, has to move onto a different plane. The principal of reciprocity is not being applied to India-Nepal relations. Through

Gujral doctrine and successive governments, India has tried to address some of the issues. Other irritants are also being ironed out with pragmatic approach. India and Nepal have realised this reality and are working towards it.

India-Nepal Allay Security Concerns

Indo-Nepal relations have been caught up in the geo-political compulsions. Compressed between India and China, Nepal acted as a buffer zone during the colonial rule. Since independence, Nepal is undergoing a painful process to develop an independent political personality of its own. As both the neighbours vie for influence over Nepal, guarding their security concern, the Himalayan state is caught up doing a balancing act between India and China.

The prime security interest of India towards Nepal is that it no way may come under the Chinese influence. India's policy was evident in the Delhi compromise reached in 1959 between King Tribhuvan, the Rana prime minister and the Nepalese Congress, which led King Tribhuvan to return to Nepal.

However, after the Delhi compromise, much to the chagrin of India, Nepal turned towards China. China made a policy statement that in case of any foreign attack on Nepal, it would side with the Himalayan Kingdom. China won contracts for many civil projects in the Terai region of Nepal. In the 1962 India-China war, Nepal remained neutral. Subsequently, the king appointed prime ministers on an alternate basis, having close links to India and China. The clash of interests between India and China, led Nepal to propose the idea to make its country 'a zone of peace' at the non align movement (NAM) summit at Algiers in 1973. Nepal further gravitated towards China when India took over the kingdom of Sikkim in 1975.

The problems between India and Nepal further accentuated, pertaining to the clause two of the peace and friendship treaty of 1950, concerning security. The clause says that Nepal would take India's prior approval before importing arms and ammunition into the country. In 1989 when Nepal imported arms from China without informing India, it became a major issue between the two countries. India sealed all its transit points from Nepal which caused great inconveniences to the common people. The matter was eventually diffused after Nepal's assurances that it would maintain transparency in its import of arms.

The details of the security clauses of 1950 treaty became public only after 1990 when Nepal converted to parliamentary democracy. Nepal felt that the clauses related to security were outdated, as the idea of keeping any one country under another's security umbrella had no relevance in the contemporary world.

After the upswing in Sino-Indian relationship since 1980s, China changed its policy towards guarding its interests in Nepal vis-a-vis India. Since then, Nepal has also given commitment to India to remove any misunderstanding, which may cause a breach in peace and friendship treaty.

The genuine security concerns of both countries emanate from anti national activities conducted from each other's soil. India has alleged that Nepal has become a hotbed of anti-India activities over the years. The porous border between India and Nepal makes its easy for terrorists to sneak into the country and indulge into acts of militancy and terrorism.

Indian security concerns were heightened in December 1999, when an Indian Airlines plane IC-184, bound for Delhi from Kathmandu, was highjacked soon after take-off from the Tribhuvan airport. Nepal's diplomatic channel worked overnight to assure India that such security lapses would never be repeated again. King Gyanendra, during his visit to New Delhi in 2002, reassured Indian leadership that Nepal's soil would not be used against Indian interests.

The Maoist insurgency in Nepal is another security concern of India. The Maoists have built close links with several Naxalite groups operating in various states of India. The Maoists Communists Centre (MCC) of Bihar and People's War Group (PWG) of Andhra Pradesh operates in India in close coordination with the Maoists of Nepal. There are media reports that the Maoists are reaching out to the various insurgent groups in the northeast region of India as well.

India does not want the Maoist insurgency to fester further and has been helping Nepal with military hardware to fight the insurgents. King Gyanendra's visit in 2002 was to procure arms and ammunition from India which were readily provided by New Delhi. India's External Affairs Minister Natwar Singh, during his visit to Nepal in June 2004, gave India's commitment to cooperate with Nepal to fight the Maoist insurgency due to its ramifications on India's internal security.

India has stakes in political stability and economic well being of Nepal. The two countries share a long and open border and there are no restrictions on the movement of citizens of either country. The fall-out of the internal problems of Nepal have obvious security implications for India. The China factor, the use of Nepali territory for anti India activity and the Maoist insurgency cast a long shadow on India-Nepal relations. Nepal's commitment that it would not do anything to vitiate the security scenario has gone a long way to cement the traditional bond with the two countries. In the changing context, Nepal-India security relations have progressed and changed for better.

9
Bhutan

- *Bhutan Faces Identity Crisis* • *Democracy Knocks Bhutan*
- *Democratisation of Bhutan* • *Bhutanese Refugees Issue*
- *India-Bhutan Relations* • *Bhutan's 'Operation All Clear'*

Bhutan Faces Identity Crisis

Bhutan is a reclusive land of ancient culture, a country with lush forest and exotic mountains, a tiny place wedged between India and China, a long lost land of romantic anachronism. For long it remained reclusive from the outside world, unpolluted by the global changes. Alas, it is no more so!

A lot of changes have been witnessed in Bhutan over the years. Bhutan became first alive to geopolitical realties when China took over the control of Tibet. The country's ruling elite who belong to the Drukpas tribe, follow Mahayana Buddhism, speak Dzongkha language and trace their origin from Tibet, became alarmed by this development. They feared Bhutan could be the next target of China's expansionism.

The second thing that happened in Bhutan was the large influx of Nepali population over the years. It accentuated since the modernisation of Bhutan took place under the third king Jigme Dorji Wangchuck (1952 – 1972). The unchecked migration created a situation where ruling Drukpa tribe felt threatened of being swamped over by the people of Nepali origin. The ruling elite in Bhutan did not want to repeat the experience of Sikkim which was fluxed by the people of Nepali origin and subsequently merged into India in 1975. They wanted to protect their separate identity in the multi-ethnic Bhutanese society.

In order to check the erosion of their identity, the ruling elite did two things; first, promulgated a code called *Driglam Nam Za* for Bhutanisation of the country and second conducted a census to identify the illegal immigrants.

The code of Bhutanisation was promulgated to give a separate identity to Bhutan, revive its culture and tradition and erode ethnic differences. As a result of it, history was rewritten and all traces of Tibetan origin were erased. Dzongkha, the language of the Drukpas was made the official language of Bhutan. People were advised to wear the national dress 'Gho' for men and 'Kira' for women and the latter were also asked to keep their hairs short as kept by the Drukpas women. The dress codes were also general Drukpas attire.

The code discouraged citizens from viewing Bangladesh or Indian television, for fear of foreign influences on them. The strictness of the government's dictates could be ascertained by the fact that television antennae's were dismantled from many housetops in Bhutan. The royal edict made it clear that failure on the part of the people to follow the code would be considered a serious crime.

The government brought a citizen's act in 1985, which gave citizenship to all those who have been living in the country on or before 1958. Basing on that it conducted a census in 1988 to identify the illegal immigrants. The census identified the percentage of Bhutanese of Nepali origin to be about 30 per cent of the population but the unofficial figure claimed about 50 per cent. The census led to the expulsion of a large number of Nepalese people from Bhutan.

These decisions by the government were also guided by economic considerations. The ruling elite through the code of Bhutanisation restricted the people of Nepali origin's mobility, land ownership and business in the western region, particularly in capital Thimpu. The ruling elite which dominated the economic scene in western Bhutan feared losing their economic monopoly in case Nepali population got rights to practice trade and commerce in all parts of the country.

The code of Bhutanisation was seen as an attempt towards ethnic homogenisation of the country. It was also seen as an attempt to force rest of the citizens to adhere to the dominant Drukpas tribe's norms and ways. The code discriminated the Bhutanese citizens of Nepalese origin. The 1988 census was further seen as an attempt to widen the ethnic divide between the Drukpas and the Nepalese citizens of Bhutan.

In response, organisations like the People's Forum for Human Rights, the Student Union of Bhutan and Bhutan's People's Party sprung up in protest against the policies of the Bhutanese government. The resistance to the authoritarian policies later developed into a struggle for constitutional monarchy and multi-party democracy.

Like any other country of South Asia, Bhutan has been trying to grapple with forces of change and continuity. It wants to break away from past but at the same time would like to retain the semblance of social and political structure that differentiates it from rest of the nations in the region. Bhutan is in no hurry to make the changes and would like to experiment with reforms. The transformations that are going on in Bhutan are thus slow but steady.

For Bhutan, the change is a question of when, not whether; to that end, it is important that pluralism be encouraged as a way of thought and harmony encouraged. Acrimony will only cause divisiveness that is destructive. A homogeneous, harmonious society united in plurality will pave the path of progress even with the withdrawal of the benevolent hand of monarchy under a constitutional democracy.

Democracy Knocks Bhutan

The wind of democracy, though it has come late, has also started blowing over the kingdom of Bhutan. The Bhutan People's Party (BPP), which is spearheading the pro-democracy movement constitutes of the Bhutanese people of Nepali origin. The BPP wants constitutional monarchy, multi-party democracy and ethnic pluralism in Bhutan.

The pro-democracy movement owes its momentum to the promulgation of Bhutanese code of conduct that irked many ethnic groups and was being seen as an effort to do away with ethnic pluralism of Bhutan. The code which was promulgated to maintain the domination of the ruling Drukpas tribe ignored the sensibilities of other ethnic groups and was seen as an attempt towards homogenisation of the Bhutanese society.

The pro-democracy movement was also triggered by the census of 1988, which set 1952 as the cut-off point to identify illegal Nepali immigrants in Bhutan. There has been serious opposition to such move. The repression that followed, had led many Bhutanese of Nepali origin to flee to India and Nepal and seek shelter in camps.

The story of the people of Nepali origin is that this group started migrating from Nepal and India's Darjeeling hills in the later half of the nineteenth century. They came to form the majority in five districts of southern Bhutan. Official figures estimate them to be 30 per cent but unofficial figures suggest them to be 50 per cent of the total Bhutanese population.

The Nepali people of the southern districts have been neglected since the modernisation of the country began in 1950s. While Buddhist dominated western Bhutan witnessed growth and development, the southern districts inhabited by Nepali speaking Hindus remained neglected. Further, the people of Nepali origin were subject to restrictions in mobility, land ownership and business in the western region particularly in capital Thimpu.

In the political institutions too the Nepalese were discriminated against. They could not find proper representation even after having electoral majority in southern districts. The same was the case in bureaucracy where their share has remained low even though being better educated than the western ethnic group.

The pro-democracy movement in Bhutan has passed through three stages. The first stage was the formation of Bhutan State Congress (BSC) in 1952. It was an association of the Bhutanese Nepalese for redressing their grievances against the royal government. The BSC struggled for broader political change but was suppressed by the government. This organisation continues to operate in exile from its headquarters at Siliguri in India till the late sixties.

The second stage was the formation of the people's forum for human rights in 1989, in the wake of promulgation of *Driglam Nam Za* or Bhutanese code of conduct meant for the homogenisation of the country and the 1988 census conducted to identify illegal immigrants. Organisations like, Peoples Forum for Human Rights, Student Union of Bhutan, etc, were formed to protest against the Bhutanese code of conduct. The resistance to the authoritarian policies of the government developed into a struggle for constitutional monarchy and multiparty democracy.

The third stage was the formation of the Bhutan's People's Party (BPP) in June 1990 which further intensified political struggle for the establishment of multiparty democracy in Bhutan. The BPP had put forward a 13-point charter of demands raging from basic freedoms such as religion, language and culture. The statements issued by the BPP leaders suggest that they want a democratic Bhutan with a constitutional monarchy. The BPP leaders have also said that their only grouse against the government is over the discriminatory treatment towards the people in southern Bhutan. They demand that the arbitrary laws against them be done away with and be given equal citizenship rights.

What is seen is that the support base for the pro-democratic movement has intensified over a period of time. In many places, the pro-democracy movement had taken a violent turn leading to clashes with the security forces and the BPP activists. Unlike the first and second stages which were peaceful, the democratic movement has become more demonstrative in the third stage

The pro-democracy movement in Bhutan has received support from various political parties and human rights groups in India and Nepal. The two dominant parties in Nepal, the Nepali Congress and the Communist Party of Nepal have supported the democratic movement in Bhutan. In India, the left parties, Congress and the BJP have also extended their support to the democratic movement in Bhutan.

The initial reaction to the pro-democracy movement by Bhutanese King Jigme Singye Wangchuck was to adopt a tough posture and dub it as anti-national activity. The king was also reluctant to hold direct talks with leaders of the pro-democracy movement. However, later he softened his stand and stressed the need for a dialogue to resolve the issue.

It seems that for the time being the storm of the pro-democracy movement has been stemmed in Bhutan. But the big question remains; how long can the storm be held back?

Democratisation of Bhutan

In one of the rare developments in Bhutan, that could usher in real democracy, the first draft of the Constitution of the country is ready. The draft which will be first reviewed by the council of ministers, and then debated in the National Assembly, would be revised or amended to become the supreme guide book to govern the country.

The emerging shade of democracy in Bhutan is perhaps unique in world. No doubt there has been some minor agitation initiated by Bhutan's People Party constituting mostly of Bhutanese citizens of Nepali origin regarding the harsh stand taken by the government on the foreigners issue but they were insignificant compared to other countries struggle for the same purpose. The drafting of the constitution has been a result of gradual evolution of political system in Bhutan.

The modern history of Bhutan started with the establishment of hereditary monarchy in 1907. Since then Bhutan has witnessed several political reforms undertaken during the reign of the third King Jigme Dorji Wangchuck (1952-72). These include the constitution of the National Assembly in 1953, formation of the royal advisory council in 1965 and formation of council of ministers in 1968. Political reforms in Bhutan continued under the successive kings.

The new political process, in fact, was initiated by King Jigme Singye Wangchuck following a series of measures taken by him. For the first time in 1981, development planning was taken to district level and some ten years later, it further devolved to the village level. In 1998, a royal decree delegated all executive authority from the 'throne' to an elected council of ministers. It was only after taking these measures that the king gave consent for the drafting of the new constitution.

The king of Bhutan, while emphasising the need to draft a constitution, had stressed the need to establish a dynamic system of governance which may uphold the true principles of democracy and safeguard the rights of the people and sovereignty of the country. The king, while appreciating the ideals of democracy, had said that if some democracies were emanating worrying signals, it was not because that the concept was flawed but the countries practising them had maligned it by mismanagement and corruption.

The work on the Bhutanese constitution begun on 31 December 2001 with a 39 member drafting committee under the leadership of the chief justice of Bhutanese supreme court. The committee completed the work in early November 2002 and the first copy was received by the king. The monarch handed over the draft copy to his prime minister, who in turn circulated it among his council of ministers for reviewing.

The details of the proposed constitution are yet to be published and whatever little is known is that there had been general agreement among the members of the drafting committee to draw maximum of its contents from the existing Bhutanese system.

There has been lot of debate about the powers of the executive, which is going to be vested in the council of ministers; the judiciary, comprising the supreme court of Bhutan; and also about the rights and privileges of the common man. All this has led to apprehension and criticism being voiced from many quarters.

The first apprehension is based on divergent interpretations and perceptions of the problems relating to the people of Nepali origin settled in the southern Bhutan. There is also uncertainty about the real extent of the devolution of power under the new system.

Next are the fears about the rights of the minorities in Bhutan. With none among the 39 members of the drafting committee belonging to the minority community, there is apprehension whether the minorities in Bhutan would be allowed to practise their own culture and traditions under the new constitution. There are also doubts raised about the political representation of the minorities, whether they would be entitled to proportional representation in the new political arrangement.

Leaving apart the uncertain part of the constitution, what is certain is that after the promulgation of the new constitution the people in Bhutan will be able to play a more active role in their country. They have to be prepared to accept new responsibilities to make the constitution truly work.

The present political metamorphosis in Bhutan has some unusual advantages. It is a small country governed by a balanced leadership which would see that the transition takes place in much smoother fashion than being witnessed in some other countries in the region. The ushering of democracy will be a new dawn in Bhutan.

Bhutanese Refugees Issue

The problems of Bhutanese refugees are the little known harsh facts of South Asia, even though the magnitude of the problem has regional dimensions. There are over one lakh people who have fled Bhutan since 1988. Of these, an estimated 75,000 live in eastern Nepal and about 35, 000 remain settled in the Indian states of West Bengal and Sikkim. Those who fled to Nepal initially were housed in camps at Jhapa and Dhankuta, but later became shelterless as international aid agencies had to wind up these camps due to lack of funds. Since both Bhutan and Nepal refuses to give them citizenship, these people remain stateless.

The actual turning point in the history of Bhutan came in 1988 when the census was undertaken to weed out the illegal immigrants in the country. It was found that the southern Bhutan which is dominated by the Lhotsampas tribe of Nepalese origin far exceeded in number the Drukpas in western Bhutan. The ruling elite felt that in the eventual democratisation of the country, the Lhotsampas tribe, if franchised, is likely to dominate the political scene.

The fear of disturbing the demographic balance led the governing class in Bhutan to launch a massive drive to evict the Nepalese out of Bhutan. This resulted in the fleeing of about one lakh Nepalese out of Bhutan. Most of them took shelter in Nepal and India where some died of malnutrition and lack of shelter when aid agencies like United Nation High Commissioner for Refugees (UNHCR) and Red Cross stepped in to house them in camps. However, with no political settlement in sight, the aid agencies, having run out of funds, decided to close these camps.

The problem is between Nepal and Bhutan. Nepal says that the refugees are Bhutanese citizens who have been ejected out of Bhutan due to fears of ruling elite there being swamped by them when Bhutan becomes a democratic state. Nepal wants the displaced people to be rehabilitated in Bhutan.

On the contrary, Bhutan argues that those people who have sheltered as refugees are not Bhutanese citizens but in fact are Nepalese who were hired as contract workers from Nepal in 1960s. These Nepalese along with their families had stayed on in Bhutan because of free education and health service and subsidised farming inputs given to them by government of Bhutan.

Bhutan says, it is genuinely committed to finding a solution to the problem but blames Nepal for being unconcerned about this issue. Bhutan says the attitude of Nepal has come in the way of the implementation of an agreed mechanism for identifying refugees as Bhutanese and non-Bhutanese.

The human right groups which have gone into the depth of the problem blame Bhutan's ruling elite in evicting the Lhotsampas from the kingdom. The recent reports by the human rights group allege that while the problem of the refugees remains unresolved, Bhutan continues its resettlement policy of shifting people from other parts of the country to land which once was inhibited by the Lhotsampas tribe. They want the refugees to be resettled in Bhutan.

In this acrimony between Nepal and Bhutan, India has become a scapegoat. The refugees accuses New Delhi of tacitly backing Bhutan on this issue by first allowing them to cross the strip of Indian land between Bhutan and Nepal and then by stopping them when they tried to march back into Bhutan. They have a special grouse because India being the largest democracy in the world seems to be working against the democratic forces by supporting the monarchial rule in Bhutan.

The spill over effects of the refugee crisis in Bhutan has serious repercussions for India. Since India holds a considerable leverage vis-à-vis both Bhutan and Nepal, it is in India's interest to bring both the contending countries to the negotiating table to find an amicable solution to the refugee problem. India may have to take into account that given the prevailing unrest in its northeast, the demobilisation of refugees can become another security concern in the region.

India-Bhutan Relations

India's policy towards Bhutan is guided by the pre-1947 British policy towards the Himalayan states, which desires stability in its buffer states. India does not want Bhutan to be politically unstable, as it would have a direct bearing on India's internal and external security. India's relation with Bhutan is governed by Indo-Bhutanese treaty of friendship signed on 8 August 1949. The treaty is a testimony of the Bhutanese dependence and India's commitment towards Bhutan. Article 2 of the treaty says that India would not interfere in the internal administration of Bhutan but with regard to external affairs, Bhutan would be guided by the government of India.

The 1949 treaty provides free trade between India and Bhutan. India guaranteed to provide its land and water facilities for the transportation of Bhutanese products and provides 13 transit routes to Bhutan. It is obligatory for Bhutan to take India's approval with regard to the import of arms, ammunition, machinery, war like material needed for the defense of Bhutan. To boost up special relationship, India sponsored Bhutan's membership of the Colombo Plan which Bhutan joined in 1963. India also lobbied for Bhutan's entry into the Universal Postal Union in 1969 and helped Bhutan to become the member of United Nations in 1971.

India has also been assisting Bhutan for proper husbanding of its natural resources. India has provided technical, material, financial help to Bhutan in the development of its hydro-electricity project, infrastructure, industries and tourism. Bhutan's share is 52 per cent of the total aid given by India to other developing countries. The king of Bhutan has acknowledged India's role in the building up of Bhutan's per capita income which is over 400 US dollars, the highest in South Asia.

But India-Bhutan relations have also been under strain on certain counts. Bhutan did not approve India's stand of going to war with Pakistan in 1971. Bhutan also asserted its independent identity in 1990 when it pleaded for an international security cover for small states implying India's hegemony in UN general assembly.

India baiters in Bhutan criticise Indian government for its alleged patronising of Nepali elements in spite of India's commitment not to interfere in the internal affairs of the country. The ruling elite apprehend that India's support to the Nepali population would be part of the same design which had resulted in the merger of Sikkim with India in 1975. The problems of Bhutanese refugees in Nepal further vitiate India-Bhutan relations.

India's stand of non interference in the problem of Bhutanese refugees has been criticised by the human rights groups. The Bhutanese refugees also feel the Indian stand to be ambiguous as going by the 1949 treaty; India has the right to intervene in the matter to broker tripartite talks to resolve the issue. The Indian stand – not to support pro-democracy movement in Bhutan – is seen quite in contrast to its policy of supporting pro-democracy movement in Sikkim in the seventies and in the late eighties in Nepal.

The reason India does not support any pro-democracy movement in Bhutan is because it fears that it may jeopardize India's interests. The pro-democracy movement in Bhutan is led by the people of Nepalese origin living in southern Bhutan and if they come on the helm of affairs it would bring them closer to Nepal. In such case, the concept of 'Greater Nepal' comprising Bhutan, Nepal, Sikkim and some parts of India would get a new lease of life. India which houses more than ten million Nepalese people in the bordering districts could easily become a flash point in such case.

The pro-democracy movement in Bhutan has connection with the several militant organisations in the northeast region of India. This includes United Liberation Front of Assam (ULFA), Gorkhaland Liberation Front (GLF) in the Darjeeling hills of West Bengal and the Maoist insurgents in Nepal. Any support to the pro-democracy movement in Bhutan would have an adverse effect on the various ethnic movements in the volatile northeast region of India.

The removal of monarchy in Bhutan may witness serious tension among the various ethnic groups within Bhutan. India fears that Bhutan may lose its character of a buffer state and the Chinese threat may come closer to Indian borders. China does not acknowledge the Indo-Bhutan treaty in 1949 and has also been inciting Bhutan to do away with it, calling it harsh and discriminatory.

India's official response to the pro-democracy movement in Bhutan is different from the stand taken by the different political parties. While the left and secular parties support the pro- democracy movement, the government of India is guided by its geo-strategic compulsions.

India had assured Bhutan that its territory would not be allowed for anti-Bhutanese activities. A similar commitment came from Bhutan's king, Jigme Singye Wangchuk during his visit to India in September 2003. He publicly threatened to launch a military crackdown if the ULFA rebels did not vacate their bases in Bhutan. The two countries remained committed to boost their economic cooperation.

New Delhi has also announced an enhanced economic assistance package of 1,614 crore rupees during Bhutan's ninth five year plan. India agreed to continue assisting Bhutan's economic development programmes, including the harnessing of its water resources. India also agreed to continue to purchase excess power generated by Bhutan's hydropower projects. An MoU was signed for the preparation of a 'Detailed Project Report' on the Punatsangchu Hydroelectric Power Project during the visit of the Bhutan's king to India.

India-Bhutan relationship has generally remained cordial all through their contemporary history. Both the countries are making extra efforts to build upon the economic relation to keep the friendly momentum going on.

Bhutan's 'Operation All Clear'

One of the most significant events that took place in the India-Bhutan relation was when the Royal Bhutan Army launched 'Operation All Clear' to crackdown anti-Indian militants operating in its soil on 15 December 2003. Bhutan's King Jigme Singye

Wangchuk himself led his troops to flush out the anti-Indian insurgents hiding in the hostile jungles of the country.

The operation which lasted over a week saw the Royal Bhutan Army smashing 30 extremist camps and killing about 150 rebels and making more than 500 of them to surrender. The aim of the operation was to bring stability and security on the India-Bhutan border and further the hands of friendship between the two countries.

India had been complaining to Bhutan that more than 3,000 militants belonging to various outfits operating in its northeast region had set up camps in the forests of south Bhutan. The rebels belonged to United Liberation Front of Assam (ULFA), National Democratic Front of Bodoland (NDFB) and Kamatapur Liberation Organisation (KLO). India alleged that the militants from the safe sanctuary in Bhutan were launching periodic attacks on its forces in the northeast region.

The build-up 'Operation All Clear' started in July 2003 when the Bhutanese National Assembly asked the government to make a final attempt to persuade the rebels to leave its territory or face military action. The Bhutan government appealed to the anti-Indian militants hiding in its territory to leave the country immediately. It warned that if they fail to do so the government will be compelled to launch military action to flush them out.

Bhutan's King Jigme Singye Wangchuk, who was on a five day state visit to India in September 2003, made public statement that his government would first try and persuade militant groups to close down their camps in his country. He said if the militants still did not respond to it, he would order military crackdown to evict them from the country.

Bhutan government since September to December 2003 made fervent appeals to the rebel outfits to leave their territory and settle their issue through talks with India. The militants however never took any appeal seriously and all attempts at a peaceful negotiation failed. The government was compelled to launch a military operation to flush them out.

As complementary exercise before the beginning of the operation all clear, thousands of Indian troops backed by helicopters sealed the border with Bhutan in Assam and West Bengal, to prevent the fleeing ultras from entering Indian territory. The Indian army has set up camps near the Bhutan border to ensure that the militants do not sneak into Indian territory.

The Royal Bhutan Army, buttressed by India's sporting action, launched the Operation All Clear with 6,000 troops to evict the insurgents from its territory. The Bhutanese operation was so severe that it completely destroyed the Central Command Headquarters of the ULFA and militants camping there suffered heavy casualties. The Bhutanese army overrun several of the militant installations, killed almost 100 ultras and arrested several of their outfit's top leaders.

The intensity of the Bhutanese army action was such that ULFA made fervent appeals for an immediate cease-fire. ULFA Chairman Arobinda Rajkhowa urged Bhutan King Jigme Singye Wangchuk to call off the operations citing historical bonds between people of the region and the Royal Kingdom.

Bhutan government rejected the cease-fire call by ULFA and said the military operation will continue till insurgents are completely flushed out of its soil. The government said that it undertook the operation after all attempts at a peaceful solution failed and the militants "never took any negotiation seriously".

In the ensuing operation Assam-Bhutan border was turned into a virtual fortress ... entry gates between the two countries were sealed and visitors are subjected to intense frisking. Both the Royal Bhutan Army and the Indian army stepped up round-the-clock patrolling and Indian troops provided logistics support to Bhutan military engaged in flushing out militants.

Feeling the heat of military pressure, ULFA chairman Arobinda Rajkhowa appeal to China to provide the fleeing militants temporary shelter. This prompted India to further tightened security along the Sino-Indian border by maintaining a strict vigil to nab the fleeing militants. China, however, maintained a neutral posture on the issue.

After more than a week of Operation All Clear, Bhutan government announced that there were no more militant camps in their territory, but added that the anti-insurgency operations would continue.

The Bhutanese operation which was able to break the backbone of the militant group ULFA was hailed in India. The then foreign minister Yashwant Sinha reported to the Parliament about the action of the Bhutan army in cracking down anti-Indian insurgents harbouring in their country. The gesture was widely applauded by the Indian parliamentarians.

The echo of Bhutan's action was felt at the 12th SAARC summit held in Islamabad in January 2004 as well. The then prime minister Vajpayee, in his speech, made special mention of this event, saying that Bhutan's gesture sets an example for other South Asian nations to emulate for maintaining peace and security in the region.

The real impact of Bhutan's Operation All Clear was felt during the April-May general elections in India. The Lok Sabha election passed off peacefully without any major incident of violence reported from the northeast region of the country. It demonstrated that the militant organisation, which till recently had operated at their free will, had lost its punch due to the operation against them by the Bhutanese army.

There were allegations at the Royal Bhutan Army that it actually provided cover for the Indian army to crack down the anti-India militants in its territory. There was also allegation on India that it used coercive method on Bhutan to agress and cross the international boundary to launch the operation. However, these allegations were widely perceived as canards perpetrated by anti-Indian forces with malicious intentions.

One may debate over the issue whether such crackdown would lead to eradication of terrorism, but the action of the Bhutan government shows that, such a gesture can help in maintaining peace and security in the region. It is also a lesson to other countries who overtly say that they would not allow the use of their territory for anti-India activities but in fact turn a blind eye towards such activities from their soil. The action by Bhutan government definitely has gone a long way in cementing India-Bhutan relations.

10
Myanmar

• *Military Rules Myanmar* • *Aung San Suu Kyi – Myanmar's Icon* • *Myanmar's Students Struggle* • *India-Myanmar Relations*

Military Rules Myanmar

Conditions in Myanmar have been far from normal since the May elections of 1990. The National League for Democracy (NLD) led by Aung San Suu Kyi, which had routed the military-backed National Union Party (NUP), could not take over the reigns of the government because Myanmar's armed forces (Tatmadow) refused to relinquish power.

Since more than a decade, the military has defied all international pressures to usher in civilian rule in Myanmar. Their track record on human rights is appalling and it looks no way shorter than the popular revolt that marked 1988-90 phase which brought a change in Myanmar. However, in the current political scenario it looks a tall order.

The 1990 electoral verdict was also not honoured by the military rulers because the democratic forces led by Aung San Suu Kyi's NLD party wanted to make Myanmar a federal state to accommodate several ethnic minority groups waging armed rebellion on the Thailand-Myanmar border. The NLD, as the best possible option, wanted them to be given autonomy in order to make them partners in the state.

The army is opposed to the idea of federalism as it may lead to the disintegration of the country. The military rulers want to draw a new constitution to make Myanmar a totalitarian state. It is ready to hold fresh elections under the new constitution where the democratic forces only have a limited role to play. But no consensus has been reached since early nineties over the drafting of one such constitution; consequently all democratic process remains standstill in Myanmar.

The military has not only muzzled the democratic verdict but also reasserted itself through repressive propaganda against any civilian government in the country. The army calls itself as the saviour of the country, reminding the people of its role in saving the country from breaking up in 1949, 1958 and 1962.

The story begins in the year 1962 when General Ne Win, in a bloodless coup toppled a democratically elected government of U Nu. The military ruler hobnobbed with socialism, which meant tight control over the economy, denial of liberty and enforced isolation from the rest of the world. General Ne Win crushed all the parties except his own – the Burma Socialist Programme Party (BSPP).

All this could hardly provide relief to the bedraggled country and there were demonstration against the oppressive regime. Henceforth, things did not move at a happy pace and the mismanagement of the economy led to nationalisation of banks and demonetisation currency. However, this could hardly improve the situation, and the summer of 1964 saw widespread demonstrations that was repeated in 1974 and 1987.

The crisis reached a threshold point in 1988 when General Ne Win had to resign. A military Junta that held the multi-party elections in 1990 replaced him. There were two main contestants in the election. The military patronised National Union Party (NUP) (successor to the BSPP) and combined opposition called National League for Democracy (NLD) led by Aung San Suu Kyi. The military Junta was taken by surprise by the landslide victory of the NLD which signaled the unpopularity of the military rule in Myanmar.

However, belying all fair play and justice, the army swung into action and declared the election null and void. It debarred Aung San Suu Kyi from holding power because of her English husband and alleged that she was conspiring with insurgents. The military rulers defended their stand saying that no individual can be given priority in the national interest. The army since then has taken full control over the country and has no intention to relinquish power.

In order to enhance its diminished political legitimacy, the military Junta started propaganda on state controlled media. It misrepresented facts by denying its role in the civilian massacre of 1988 and sought legitimacy by giving support to Buddhism, the dominant religion of Myanmar.

Meanwhile, the military led a crackdown on the dissident ethnic minority groups, concentrated on the borders of the country. Western media reporting on human rights violation described the conduct of Myanmar's military rulers towards its ethnic minorities as sheer barbarism. Even US state department had taken note of the human rights violation and demanded that the guilty men in uniform be punished. However, all this fell on the deaf ears of the military rulers of Myanmar.

The overwhelming support to multi-party opposition in the 1990 elections has demonstrated the unpopularity of the military rule. The military rulers' refusal to relinquish power has incurred the wrath of the international community. Myanmar is made an international pariah and is subjected to all kids of economic sanctions by the world bodies.

Myanmar's problem is its decimated economy which has been systematically exploited by the successive military rulers since 1962. In the absence of any financial support from outside, the depleted economy triggers popular discontent time and again. The World Bank report suggests that Myanmar needs massive financial support from the world bodies to improve its bedraggled economy. The foreign aid however is linked to the civilian rule, stopping of the human rights abuse and proper integration of the ethnic minorities.

The dilemma of the junta is that, it cannot take extensive reform due to its obvious political and social repercussions and may jeopardize its rule. It has tried doing some cosmetic changes by internally opening up its economy to the neighbouring states. It has signed economic agreements with China, Thailand, South Korea and India. The gross violation of human rights and open defiance to democratic rule has been overlooked by the neighbours due their growing economic interests in Myanmar. There seems no other way than massive popular upsurge to replace the military rule. The probability of such event however remains a distant dream in Myanmar.

Aung San Suu Kyi – Myanmar's Icon

It looks as if the movement for restoring democracy have slowed down in Myanmar. However, its icon Aung San Suu Kyi remains active, building her party since her release from house arrest in May 2002. It seems that the military junta, which rules the country since the last forty years, has finally buckled under threats of international sanctions by releasing Suu Kyi after nineteen months of house arrest.

One of the world's most celebrated political prisoners, Suu Kyi has spent more time in captivity than in freedom. When last freed from house arrest, in 1995, Suu Kyi was forbidden from travelling beyond the capital Yangon. Her two attempts to drive outside the city were marred by lengthy roadside standoffs with the military leading to her rearrest in October 2000. Her release in 2002 came as surprise when military rulers allowed her to tour the country and hold public meetings.

In spite of instructions by the government to the people not to show up for public meetings, Suu Kyi's countrywide tour attracted a large crowd. In one such gathering, police canned to disperse the crowd making Suu Kyi to comment that she was there in the name of democracy, which puts the people ahead of everything else.

The treatment meted to the 56 year old Nobel peace laureate suggests that the military junta is unwilling to let Suu Kyi's popularity increase in the countryside. They, however, are extremely careful to prevent large gatherings, for fear it may erupt into a spontaneous support for another spell of pro-democracy movement in the country. Suu Kyi's legendary personal appeal during the bloody army repression of 1988 and her campaign rallies before the 1990 elections, still cast spell on the country.

Suu Kyi, the daughter of independence leader, Aung San, was a housewife in England before returning to Burma in 1988 to care for her ailing mother. Upon her return she found the discontent against 26 years of military rule boiling on to the streets. Within months, Suu Kyi emerged as the electrifying leader of the opposition movement and she was then reported saying that as her father's daughter, she cannot remain indifferent to all that was going on.

However, the military junta stepped in and crushed the protests, killing and imprisoning thousands of people in 1988. Suu Kyi, who refused to bow down, was placed under house arrest in 1989.

In 1990, the military junta held elections; assuming that its hand picked party would win, but Suu Kyi led National League for Democracy (NLD) won 82 per cent of parliamentary seats. The generals however invalidated the election results and tried to muzzle NLD party by persecuting its members, arresting its leaders and closing most of its offices in the country.

The military government tried to reinforce their monopoly through repressive propaganda in the state controlled media against Suu Kyi. They accused Suu Kyi of being a traitor, having spent several decades living outside the country and marrying an English man. The government refused her request to visit England to see her ailing husband, Michael Aris, who was suffering from cancer at Oxford.

In the meantime, the noble prize conferred on Suu Kyi in 1991 further enhanced Suu Kyi's image as world leader. International pressure mounted on the military rulers to release Suu Kyi when eight noble laureates campaigned on the Thai border. Former Costa Rican President Oscar Sanchey, who was present at the campaign, is reported to have said, that Suu Kyi, by refusing to trade her own liberty in exchange of exile from the country, continues to inspire the people of the world.

The military rulers did relent to the world pressure and released Suu Kyi for a while but later decided to keep her under house arrest. Suu Kyi was released in 1995 but detained again in October 2000 to be released in May 2002. The release of Suu Kyi was a result of ongoing reconciliation talks with the military junta.

In a change of strategy, Suu Kyi since her release has studiously refrained from criticising the military rulers. She hinted at her willingness to compromise but insisted that the government convene the national parliament elected in 1990. She said that the NLD has realised that confrontation would not work and it has to find a way to coexist with the government.

The military rulers too have shown their interest in reconciliation, announcing that they are committed to allowing all citizens to participate freely in the political process. The release of Suu Kyi is seen as a significant step by military government toward addressing international criticism of its poor human rights record. The government has so far freed about 200 political prisoners, of an estimated 1,600 political prisoners, since the talks began with Suu Kyi in 2000.

The new strategy of Suu Kyi towards the military rulers has baffled many of her admirers. It remains to be seen how her strategy to balance her party's demands against those of the government could be synchronised. The new approach of Aung San Suu Kyi looks far more challenging than her confrontationist position against the military junta. Confrontation or conciliation, Suu Kyi has come to represent the democratic aspiration of the suppressed Burmese, who felled from the yoke of white suppression to that of the junta. She continues to inspire pro-democratic movement in Myanmar.

Myanmar's Students Struggle

'Bliss was dawn to be alive but to be young was very heaven' ... that was John Keats' comments on French Revolution of 1789. In contemporary history these lines could be dedicated to the students of Myanmar who laid down their lives for the struggle of democracy in their country. Their din and clatter, their volatility and juvenile impatience continue to inspire many such movements the world over.

The Burmese students, who were on the forefront of the political struggle during the period of 1987-90, touched the umbilical cords of the student community all over the world by their slogan 'cry freedom'. Stories of grit and determination with which they fought the military junta evoked admiration among fellow students, and had been talk of many campuses at that time in the world.

A chain of anti-government demonstrations was held in capital Yangon and other cities throughout 1988. The protests, which began in March, saw the resignation of General Ne Win after twenty-six years of authoritative rule. The student protests that continued unabated led to the resignation of two more heads of the state and storming of the Rangoon jail. The event reminded of the fall of Bastille, during the French Revolution and marks the highest point in the students' struggle in Myanmar.

The subsequent crackdown on the students and the usurpation of power by the current military junta has its own gory tale. The ferocity with which the student's protests were quelled could be ascertained by the fact that, during one of the raids 41 students were dumped into a police van and they died due to suffocation. The event evoked a deep sympathy among the general masses who subsequently joined the student's protests, indicating the growing opposition to the military rule. The widespread protests were halted only after the calling of general elections in 1990.

The first street demonstration of Myanmar, since its independence, took place in 1962, when General Ne Win toppled a democratically elected government headed by U Nu. Then in 1964, General Ne Win's mismanagement of the economy led to widespread students' demonstrations. The whole student movement was crushed with iron hand and the student union's office of the Rangoon University was blown up. More than 22 students were shot dead during the hostel raids of 1964.

The year 1974 witnessed one of the fiercest student's protests, which centered on the grave of the UN Secretary General U Thant. Even though the former secretary general was buried with full military honours, students dug open his grave and wanted to build his mausoleum. They were stopped by the military ruler, leading to widespread riots.

The issues of food shortage and devaluation of currency in 1987 tested the patience of the Myanmar youth. The disgruntled students, fuelled by deep frustration due to growing unemployment, came out on the streets to give vent to their pent-up anger. This time government handled their agitation with care, announcing early holidays and banning various student bodies.

However, the September 1987 protests provided an impetus to more violent riots in March 1988. The protest, which was sparked by the death of a student in police custody, took an anti-government turn. The riots that followed left as many as 50 students dead and more than 5,000 were arrested.

The campuses were reopened on 30 May 1988, to be closed down due to violence as authorities refused permission for the mourning of the students killed in March. The third spate of student protest occurred in June, within nine moths, and was the fiercest of all. The government cracked down the student demonstrations but they defied the orders to disperse and marched into the city centres holding placards denouncing 'Nazi government', demanding Ne Win's removal and acquittal of students jailed during the March disturbances.

Anti-government demonstrations spread throughout Myanmar almost on a daily basis, demanding democracy. The unrest led to the resignation of General Ne Win in July 1988 and was replaced by another hardliner, General Sein Lwin, accused of ruthlessly suppressing the 1962 uprising and also those of March and June 1988.

But barely 17 days in office, Sein Lwin also resigned on August 1988. As the bloody upheaval continued, military tried placating the democratic forces by appointing Maung Maung, a civilian as head of the state, but the protests continued in Myanmar.

The All Burma Students Democratic Association, which spearheaded the movement, was an emboldened lot. They stormed the Rangoon jail on 28 August 1988 to free many of their comrades.

The student's organisational skills were impeccable; some 20-30 student leaders whose identities were kept secret coordinated the entire movement. They were split into tight secret units; the information unit produced leaflets and posters; social welfare unit distributed food and water during the rallies; intelligence unit gave information about security forces movement, spot informers and interrogate them at the cells set up in their hostels.

The hallmark of the students protest was wearing of headband with an encircled golden peacock, epitomising a genre of macho madness. They marched on the streets, chanting democracy and their marching cries appealed to the spirit of nationalism and anguished yearning for change. Amidst carnage and rebellion students also constructed a Statue of Liberty in Yangon, which later was removed by the government. The heroic struggle of Myanmar's students finally led the military rulers to bow down and announce elections in 1990. The gagging of democracy thereafter is another story in Myanmar.

India-Myanmar Relations

India's Look East foreign policy was rejuvenated when Vajpayee government infused a new momentum to the country's dormant relationship with Myanmar. Since then New Delhi is anxious to improve its strategic and economic ties with its colonial cousin. There are serval reasons to it; one is to contain China, which has deeply increased its influence in the region taking advantage of the Western countries' sanctions on Myanmar. India sees geo-strategic implications for the region in China's attempt to build a naval base at Hyang Gyi island of Myanmar.

India's second objective is that a deep economic relationship with Myanmar would give a tremendous boost to the development of its northeast region, plagued by insurgency. India is building a major highway connecting India's northeast region with Thailand, through Mandalay and Yangon. Besides it is also building a port, at Sittwel on the Myanmar coast to help increase maritime trade. Both the projects would have far reaching influence on the northeast region of India.

The third objective of India is to increase its influence in Southeast Asian countries, which could be done through greater economic cooperation with Myanmar. To give it a concrete shape, the regional grouping called BIMST-EC (comprising Bangladesh, India, Myanmar, Sri Lanka and Thailand – Economic Cooperation) forum is already in place. BIMST-EC was set up more than five years ago, to promote bilateral and multilateral cooperation in trade and economic development.

India's relations with Myanmar have remained frozen since military took over the country in 1962. The military ruler's foreign policy of cocooning their country from rest of the world further kept India at a distance. In the changing global context, India-Myanmar relations have seen some major shifts. During Indira Gandhi's rule, India maintained distance from Myanmar for its suppression of democratic movement and poor human rights record. The Rajiv era was marked by all out support by India for the democratic movement in Myanmar.

However, during Narsimha Rao's rule attempts were made to cultivate relationship based on economic consideration. This was evident in the then India's foreign secretary J N Dixit's visit to Yangon and signing of a bilateral agreement for the control of drug trafficking and border trade. India reverted to old policy during Gujral period when stress was laid on the maintenance of human rights and restoration for democracy in Myanmar for improving bilateral relationship.

Under the Vajpayee government a visible shift was noticed in India's relationship with Myanmar. Jaswant Singh, who held the foreign affairs portfolio, visited Myanmar and singed number of agreements. Myanmar's military rulers assured India's foreign minister that Yangon's proximity with Beijing would not be directed against India. Later, General V P Malik, then India's chief of armed forces, also paid a visit to Myanmar.

As a sequel to the visit by the Indian dignitaries, Myanmar's foreign minister Win Aung visited India in January 2003. He was the first senior leader from his country to visit India after more than 15 years. The countries signed a protocol which establishes regular bilateral ministerial consultations and agreed to strengthen cooperation on several bilateral projects, mainly in the fields of infrastructure, energy and information technology.

One of Win Aung's main aims for the India visit was to drum up trade and investment. The two countries explored the possibilities to set up a joint Business Council to help encourage greater private Indian investment in Myanmar. India considered doubling $25 million commercial credit line to help Indian businessmen and encouraging them to establishing pilot projects in Myanmar. During his visit, Win Aung, proposed a summit level meeting of the regional group BIMST-EC to further boost regional cooperation.

There was substantial Indian interest in infrastructure projects particularly to tap Myanmar's gas fields and to seek its exploration rights. The visiting foreign minister however was keener for Indian investment in the energy sector. India assured all possible help to its neighbour's energy needs.

The most startling fact is that the value of bilateral trade between India and Myanmar has grown nearly eight-fold in recent times. India is now Myanmar's fourth most important export market for its beans, pulses and wood products. While pharmaceuticals, iron and steel are its main imports from India.

As the international community is preoccupied with the conflict in Iraq, the military junta is in no hurry to initiate political reforms in Myanmar. In the meantime it has initiated diplomatic missions to attract investment from the neighbours to bring its economy back on the rails.

India, on the other hand, has started a fresh diplomatic engagement with Myanmar to give the country's foreign policy a new direction towards its southeast neighbours.

Economic bilateral understanding is a buffer in any eventuality, which could prove beneficial either way if negotiated or agreed upon pragmatically. The pros outweighs the cons, though the delicateness cannot be eschewed.

11
Afghanistan

- *Afghanistan after Soviet Withdrawal* • *Reconstruction of Afghanistan* • *India and Afghanistan Relation* • *Islamic Resurgence in 21st Century* • *War against Global Terrorism*

Afghanistan after Soviet Withdrawal

Afghanistan remained plagued by internecine wars ever since the Soviet Union troops departed in 1989. The US abandoned Afghanistan after its objective of driving away the Soviets was achieved. It is an irony that the same set of people whom US patronised once to oust the Russians, formed a terror network whose hunt, tops the US global agenda now.

The Mujahideen fighting the Soviets represented a movement and not an organisation. They were unable to surmount their differences once they accomplished their goal. Since the fall of Najibullah, the state apparatus collapsed resulting into a power vacuum. The ethnic strife, which continued for the next twelve years, saw Afghanistan divided along sectarian lines. The country was sliced into three parts, with not less than 12 warlords maintaining sway over the country.

Abdul Rashid Dostum, a former communist general who controlled northwest Afghanistan was entrenched in Mazar-i-Sharif. Dostum representing the Uzbek ethnic group in Afghanistan was backed by Uzbekistan. One may recall that it was the differences with Dostum that hastened the fall of the Najibullah's government. It was Dostum's Zojani militia that prevented Najibullah from escaping from Kabul. Najib remained locked in the United Nation's office and was hanged by the Taliban which captured Kabul.

Ahmad Shah Masood, who was killed allegedly by Al-Qaeda group on 9/9/2001 just two days before 9/11 terror attack on US, occupied the northeast of the country. He was called lion of Panjsheer and represented the Tajik ethnic group in Afghanistan.

Gulbuddin Hekmatyar who represented the Pushtun ethnic group, dominated South Afghanistan. However, there were some other power centres within the Pushtun community like late commander Abdul Haq, Abdul Rasul Sayyaf and spiritual leader Gailani. The west was dominated by minority Shia community and represented by Hizb-e-Wahdat group, which was backed by Iran.

Afghanistan since then was mired in a whirlpool of violence and its internal dilemma was many sided; to keep the Hekmatyar in abeyance in south, there was unity among the Masood, Dostum and Najib's regimes' loyalists.

The pressure was not only due to contradictory personal ambition of the warlords but also due to contradictory ideological pulls in Afghanistan. The puritan Wahabi elements supported fundamentalism in Afghanistan. The westernised elites, who were reminiscent of King Zahir Shah's regime, favoured a moderate Afghanistan. There was tussle between Pushtun and non-Pushtun and Shias-Sunnis.

Afghanistan was also gripped by contradictory pulls from different external factors. The regional actors vie for influence in the beleaguered nation. Iran's link with Hizb-e-Wahdat in the western periphery encouraged the demand for co-federal arrangement in the power structure. Central Asia's complex mosaic of ethnic plurality resulted Uzbekistan to openly support the Dostum faction to keep the ethnic turmoil from spilling out of Afghanistan. Then there was deep involvement of Saudi Arabia in Afghanistan. Many warring factions in Afghanistan, during early nineties, made frequent trips to Saudi capital Riyadh.

Then there was deep involvement of Pakistan in Afghanistan. Its Inter-Services Intelligence, ISI, had spread its tentacles too far into that country. Pakistan had been seeking strategic depth in Afghanistan. It initially tried to carry out this through its protégé Gulbuddin Hekmatyar, but his failure made ISI to create another outfit called Taliban to serve Pakistan's interests.

The other external forces interested in Afghanistan's stability were China and India. The spillover of the Afghan imbroglio on China's Muslim dominated Xinjiang province kept Beijing occupied in watching the developments in Afghanistan. India also wanted a semblance of order restored in Afghanistan as it saw its linkage with peace in Kashmir.

The power struggle in Afghanistan, which was witnessed in the first half of the nineties, diminished after the rise of Taliban which controlled most part of the country in the second half of the decade. The term Taliban, if simply translated, means students who are believed to have risen from the obscurity of the madarsas or religious seminaries in Peshawar. They had a loose following revolving around common Pushtun identity and due to popular support ran through the war weary country. They were assisted by Pakistan till they established controlled over Kabul.

The Talibans too were no panacea for the woes of Afghanistan. Their half-baked knowledge about the art of governance, mixing religion with politics and sheer demonstration of medievalism in every walk of life made them an outcast in the international community. There was no love lost when their end came at the hands of US led international coalition in 2002.

What had been most disturbing about Afghanistan was the huge loss of life and property as the country swung from leftist government under Najibullah to the rightist rule under Taliban. In retrospect, one wonders, was that needed at all?

Reconstruction of Afghanistan

A climate of suspicion and fear lingers around Afghanistan. With the international community now busy dealing with Iraq and Saddam Hussein, there is a fear that the promises showered by the international coalition to rebuild Afghanistan may get blurred.

America had forged an international coalition against terrorism and went ahead to inflict collateral damage on Afghanistan in retaliation to the 9/11 attacks in 2001. US argued that since the Taliban regime was harbouring the Al-Qaeda mastermind Osama bin Laden, it reserve the right of pre-emptive attack on Afghanistan.

Before launching operation 'Enduring Freedom', US had promised for the reconstruction of Afghanistan.

The US campaign in Afghanistan came under serious criticism because of its failure to nab Osama bin Laden, his top aides and Mullah Omar, even after combing entire Afghanistan. The continued American presence is not welcomed by common Afghans who see them as intruders in their country.

The US pledge of reconstruction of Afghanistan too has come under a cloud. President Bush, while cobbling international coalition in the war against global terrorism, had promised that the reconstructing of Afghanistan would be a matter of time. However, in spite of US being the highest contributor of aid, Afghanistan is far short of funds that is needed for the reconstruction of a war ravaged country.

The US bombing had flattened the entire surface, which already had been in rubbles after over two decades of internecine warfare. All civic amenities have collapsed. Agriculture, industry, trade and commerce have to pick up all over again. The reconstruction work is a major task which the Karzai government is grappling with at the moment in Afghanistan.

Afghan authorities estimate that at least US $ 20 billion, while United Nations estimation is US $ 40 billion, would be required for the reconstruction of Afghanistan. The donor countries promised about US $ 5 billion aid at the summit at Tokyo for reconstruction of Afghanistan. Hamid Karzai's continued trips across the world netted another two to three billion US dollars which is well short of the required figure needed to rebuild Afghanistan.

In the reconstruction of Afghanistan India is playing a major role. India has pledged 100 million dollar aid during the International Donors Conference at Tokyo. The two countries signed a preferential trade agreement which provides free movement of specified goods with reduction of tariffs. India also gifted an Airbus aircraft along with 75 buses, specially designed for Afghan roads. Besides, it also pledged 70 million dollar aid for rebuilding Zaranj-Dilaram road, linking Herat and Kandahar. India is teaming up with Iran and Afghanistan to develop a new trade route, through Iran's Char Bahar port, to open with Central Asia.

There is no doubt that a credible job is being done by the new Afghan President Hamid Karzai. He has been able to give a semblance of political order to Afghanistan which so far had eluded the country. His broad based government very well reflects the country's ethnic diversity. It is to his credit that he has been able to accommodate the three dominant ethnic groups – the Uzbeks, the Tajiks and the Pushtuns – into his cabinet.

Hamid Karzai has been relentlessly trying to steer the country through its turbulent phase. There are however, many things that remain to be done so that Afghanistan does not fall prey to another cycle of retribution and revenge. The job of the international peace keeping forces does not end with maintaining peace in Kabul. There help is needed to build a lasting internal security arrangement for the entire country. However, there seems no international concern on building the internal security structure in Afghanistan.

Afghanistan still remains under the ambit of ethnic warlords who have carved out their area of influence in the country. The victorious commanders have a history of brutality and revenge. Their disbandment remains a major task along with the disarming of the heavily armed countryside. It is out of these fighting forces that the new Afghan army, paramilitary, police and security forces could be raised. There is no effort being made in this direction either.

It's well understood that the reconstruction of Afghanistan is not an overnight job, but what is intriguing is its slow pace. With the focus of the world now turned towards Iraq, Afghan watchers are dismayed by international community's lack of enthusiasm to rebuild Afghanistan. The global diversion raises fear that Afghanistan may yet again slip into internecine warfare again. It is indeed a crucial phase in the history of Afghanistan.

India and Afghanistan Relation

With the contours of a political apparatus being defined for Afghanistan, the parameters of India's Afghan policy are also being outlined. It is almost after a decade that the vistas to Afghanistan have opened up again for India. The parameters of India's new Afghan policy are manifold.

India's diplomatic initiatives have always been to ensure that successive Afghan regimes work as a bulwark against Pakistan's design to gain strategic depth in Afghanistan. India has very high stakes in keeping the radical ideology and the export of terrorists out of Afghanistan in check. India thinks stability in Afghanistan would ensure peace in its militancy-infested state of Jammu and Kashmir. India is committed to the reconstruction of Afghanistan and wants it to play the rightful role in the international arena.

America's war against Afghanistan has thawed the relationship of many countries that remained frozen through the decade-long internecine warfare. Tajikistan, Turkmenistan, Uzbekistan, Iran, Pakistan, India and Russia had historically played an important role in Afghanistan. While the three Central Asian countries have substantial ethnic population, Iran's interests emanate from its sectarian and linguistic linkages. Afghanistan's Hazara ethnic group practise the Shia sect of Islam, which is predominantly followed in Iran. Interestingly, Persian works as a unifying force in the multi-ethnic, multi lingual country like Afghanistan.

The Russian interest in Afghanistan dates back to the days of the Czars who had special interest in seeking the warm waters of the Indian Ocean. However, the British always checkmated their expansionist designs. Afghanistan became the battlefield for the Great Game between the Czar and the Raj. Britain made Afghanistan a buffer state and granted it independence in 1920. To protect their interests, the British bred successive Afghan rulers in India. The arrangement continued well after the British departure from the subcontinent.

King Zahir Shah's nephew Prince Daud usurped power in 1973. The next five years saw communists vying for power in Afghanistan. Renewed Soviet interests grew in the seventies through the Peoples Democratic Party of Afghanistan (PDPA). In 1978, the Communists overthrew Daud in a bloody coup spearheaded by the troika of Taraki, Karmal and Amin. This brought the Soviets directly into Afghanistan. The next ten years (1979-89) saw the worst ever manifestation of Cold War clawing in Afghanistan. The Afghan cauldron brought America and Pakistan together to drive out the Soviets. The Soviet departure left a power vacuum and various ethnic groups jockeyed for power in Afghanistan.

India's ties with Afghanistan go back to the 12th century and are entwined with successive Muslim rulers in Delhi. During the days of the Raj, the interest of His Majesty's government in Afghanistan was protected from India. India and Afghanistan maintained a cordial relationship long after the British departure. During King Zahir Shah's regime, trade, commerce, culture and people to people contact gained great momentum.

India's allegiance to the Soviets during the Cold War era made New Delhi offer its influences over Afghanistan to Moscow. This alliance almost took the form of an axis. New Delhi-Kabul-Moscow worked in tandem to control the fate of Afghanistan. During the Soviet occupation, India protected Soviet's interests, which continued even after their withdrawal in 1989. India held a tight grip over Afghanistan till the fall of Najibullah in 1992. In fact the Afghan president made several visits to India during his final phase to elicit New Delhi's support.

A decade of internecine warfare and lack of central authority diminished India's diplomatic maneuverability in Afghanistan. In the early nineties, India's influence almost stagnated, as warlords and renegade generals established their own rule in areas they controlled in Afghanistan. With the Taliban at the helm of affairs, Afghanistan remained virtually out of bounds for India. However, in 1998 India's interests found favour with Dostom, Masood, and Rabbani, who established the Northern Alliance with the help of Russia. India's Afghan policy has regained focus after the fall of Taliban and the establishment of Hamid Karzai's government.

The parameters of India's Afghan policy are very clear. It wants peace to be established in that beleaguered country. India wishes that no country make Afghanistan its surrogate, especially those whose interests are inimical to Indian interests. Being the largest democracy in the world, India prefers the establishment of a parliamentary form of government in Afghanistan. In India's view, parliamentary democracy alone can give true and impartial representation to all sections of the Afghan society.

India's interests in Afghanistan hinge on the fact that all terrorist groups get sanitised from that country. The last two decades of insurgency in the trouble torn state of Jammu and Kashmir have been a direct outcome of the instability in Afghanistan. India can no longer tolerate cross border terrorism having its origin in Afghanistan. India wants the rule of law to prevail and advocates disarming of the heavily armed people of Afghanistan.

India has based its new Afghan policy on the principle of humanitarian consideration. India looks forward for the rebuilding of Afghanistan in a massive way. It has announced 5000 crore rupees as aid for the reconstruction of Afghanistan. It has also announced the establishment of a hospital on the Afghan-Tajik border. The Indira Gandhi hospital in Kabul is being spruced up. India's new Afghan policy envisages a renewed diplomatic relationship based on mutual trust and confidence. The new parameters in Indo-Afghan relation has brought the two countries together. A dawn of new era has begun in India-Afghanistan relationship.

Islamic Resurgence in the 21st Century

At the dawn of the twenty-first century, we are standing at the crossroad of a transformed world order which is quite different from the one which had bid us good-bye. The ideological war between capitalism and communism that dominated most part of the second half of the last century has given way to a new form of struggle that is disturbing global peace. The new world order is clearly witnessing a duel between post capitalism and Islamic revivalism.

In the ongoing debate of science versus religion, popular theories of revolution and modernisation predicted the inevitable decline of religion. However, the twentieth century perspective suggests this to be nowhere in sight. This is also true about the socialist countries where systematic destruction of tradition was carried out.

While Communism snuffed spiritualism, Capitalism did not respond to the needs outside the parameters of the market economy. The arc lights of sordid materialism or soulless society generated growing insecurity urging solace beneath the wings of religion. The lesson that human kind have learnt through cognitive experience is that God is not dead. The socially cementing and culturally homogenising features of religion have come to have its own mass appeal.

As we trace the evolution of the modern society from the hunting-gathering stage to a settled mode of production, we find totem, magic, animism, maker, way for structured and organised form of beliefs and practices. It was forces of rationality that religion championed to overpower, the thoughts of obscurantism. It is no wonder that when our civilisation woke up from the slumber of dark ages, the primitive beliefs of the Orient and Occident were rattled by the organised religious faiths.

While Christianity witnessed Renaissance, Islam started stagnating ever since the Crusades. The Ottoman, the Safavids, the Uzbeks and the Mughals all basked under the glory of their gigantic empires. Whereas in Europe, enlightenment fomented reformation in Christianity and its Calvinist thoughts gave rise to capitalism. Since then the religious beliefs got delinked with the state and the capitalist ideology started dominating the global space.

Maximisation of profit and efficiency became the salient features of the capitalist thought. It was catapulted by the agricultural and industrial revolutions in Europe, ushering in an era of Imperialism. The crass materialism which formed the core of capitalism generated its own dichotomy to conceive socialism personified as communism.

The communist ideal of the withering away of the state, however, remained an unfulfiled dream. In the course of time, the states which followed the Marxian ideal became top heavy and their command economies could not keep pace with the free economies. Communism which primarily strived for a classless society slowly got riddled by its own contradictions and started paling as a global force.

The ideological war that was carried out in most part of the last century finally started weighing in favour of capitalism. This was more so since the collapse of the Soviet Union. The void produced by communism apparently started telling upon the unipolar world.

In the emerging world order, capitalism which has produced yawning inequalities started asserting through the forces of globalisation. The post capitalist societies are trying to maintain their hegemony through free market economy, treating the world as a global village. This has triggered resistance from various quarters, including the one being witnessed as Islamic resurgence.

In a world where there is a tendency to rediscover or invent some kind of symbolism for personal identification, religion has become a potent weapon to fight the perceived injustices. This becomes more so when a religious ideology has a potential global canvass and whose knitting together can produce a global impact.

Of late, the Islamic societies which had remained subjugated either under colonial rule or ideological suppression started searching its own strength. The Islamic revivalism being witnessed is in context of responding to their perceived injustices and making efforts to set their own house in order. Islam is trying to knit its global strength and is becoming instrumental in fighting political battles where it feels suffocated due to the real or imagined enemies.

If we make a global sweep, there are many spots where Islam as an ideological force is grappling with the realities. In West Asia the Palestinian question is a bleeding spot. Kashmir remains a sore point in South Asia, so is Chechnya in Russia. The issue of Cyprus remains unresolved in Greece. The Central Asian countries are in the grip of Islamic resurgence. China's Xinjiang province wants an Islamic order. There is Islamic movement at the Sulu Archipelago in southern Philippines. Islamic struggle continues in the Masrique region of North Africa. In the Balkans peninsula, there is emergence of Islamic identity in Bosnia-Herzegovina and Kosovo.

The problem with the protagonists of Islamic revivalism is that, they are pitting a religion against an ideology knowing well that it cannot be stretched beyond a point. One way to tread in the new world order is to follow the secular, democratic, and rational ideals and confine religion to the realm of spiritualism, the other is to make it a religious-political force and a power block. The latter is the goal the Islamic revivalists have set for themselves.

There is also a whole set of issues that need to be addressed, if Islam wants to compete globally as politico-religious force. The foremost is to eschew itself from the path of violence to gain general acceptance. The tension and turbulence that is being witnessed by the world surrounding Islam can no way be addressed by following the path of further extremism. Terrorism is a short sighted approach which triggers an unending chain of action and reactions. It is an accepted fact that extremism in any form can never lead to a just solution.

The other need is to make religion more contemporary in order to provide answers to the forces of modernisation. For this, the doors of interpretation of religion have to be opened up. Then the Islamic societies have to embark on the path of development on the lines of the capitalist societies to achieve its objectives.

The Islamic resurgence which is currently reeling under soul searching exercises is geared towards finding a balance between spiritualism and materialism. While undergoing revivalism it has to take cognisance of the fact that the two World Wars, nuclear holocaust, antiwar, peace and disarmament movements have given the world a new mandate. If Islamic revivalism wants to succeed, it has to follow its literal meaning, that is peace!

War against Global Terrorism

President Bush took upon himself the task of the destruction of the entire gamut of terrorist groups in the world when he announced Operation Enduring Freedom following the attack on American landmarks on 11 September 2001. It is debated whether such an operation could ever be accomplished in Afghanistan or Iraq.

US even after months of relentless bombing on Afghanistan and its combing, the objective of catching Osama bin Laden and destroying his Al-Qaeda network is far from over. US troops camping in the region searching for possible remnants of Al-Qaeda and Taliban activists had not achieved much success. The most wanted fugitive Osama bin Laden, Mullah Omar and others are alive and remain at large.

The US has not been able to achieve its primary objective even after enforcing unilateral war on Afghanistan. This raises the question as to how it can achieve the arduous task of liquidating a large numbers of terrorist organisations operating across the five continents. Has the operation on Iraq achieved anything in that direction?

If we make a global sweep then there are more than a dozen trouble spots. The commonality in all of them is the denial of the resolution of the political grievances through peaceful means which makes many groups to adopt violent means.

In South Asia, political rights of several groups remain unaddressed. This has led the LTTE to wage war for a separate homeland for Tamils in Sri Lanka. In order to address their grievances, many outfits are resorting to militancy in Kashmir. Similarly, various groups are fighting for territorial sovereignty in the northeast region of India.

There are also some groups fired by an ideology like the Maoist insurgents in Nepal. They aspire to bring their vision of rule of the law to create a just social order in that country. The Nepal Maoist are believed to have links with Maoist Communist Centre (MCC) of Bihar and People's War Group (PWG) of Andhra Pradesh and are slowly infiltrating into the northeast region of India.

Militancy revolving around religion is found in various Islamic groups. In Pakistan, groups like Laskar-e-Jhangvi, Sipah-e-Sahaba, Sipha-e-Mohammad are working for establishing a true Islamic state. The Islamic Movement of Uzbekistan is engaged in bringing Islamic regimes in five Central Asian countries. China's Xinjiang province, with dominant Muslim population, too wants a religious order. Across the Ural Mountains, in Russia, Chechnya remains another flash point. In Algeria the Islamic Salvation Front aspires for an Islamic state. Osama bin Laden's Al-Qaeda group globally networks for an Islamic resurgence.

Creation of Israel from territories inhabited by the Arabs has created a bleeding spot in West Asia. America's backing of Israel's expansionist designs has created a chain of violence and repression. The Israeli-Palestinian conflict is an unending saga of blood and tears.

The industrialised countries of Europe too have a significant number of terrorist groups. In France, Spain, Greece and Northern Ireland, there are over a dozen active militant outfits. There the fight is not for religion, but for cultural and territorial sovereignty.

In Spain, there are Basque Fatherland and Liberty, which operates primarily in the Basque autonomous regions of Northern

Spain and Southwestern France. In Greece, Revolutionary People's Struggle is operational as the issue of Cyprus remains unresolved.

In Northern Ireland, there are as many as eight groups, including the IRA, fighting for a separate territorial space. In former Yugoslavia, an uneasy calm prevails between the Serbs, the Croats and the Muslims.

In Japan there is an outfit – the Japanese Red Army – engaged in violence and militancy. The JRA's goal is to overthrow the Japanese government and monarchy. In southern Philippines, the Abu Sayyaf's group is striving for an independent Islamic state in Western Mindanao and the Sulu Archipelago areas.

The African continent is widely divided between South, Central and North Africa. Here tribal rivalry is the root cause of terrorism. In Rwanda and Sierra Leon tribes like Hutus and Tutsis continue to perpetrate acts of violence. In South Africa issues of race and apartheid are causes of violence. Religious and cultural issues form the backbone of militancy in North Africa.

In South America, Peru and Columbia witnesses armed struggle by the left forces. The Shining Path and Revolutionary Movement are active in Peru, while, Revolutionary Armed Forces of Colombia, (FARC) is active in Colombia.

Given the canvas of global terrorism, its containment is a tall order. Terrorism is a worldwide phenomenon which is equally prevalent in developed and underdeveloped, Christian and non-Christian countries. The root of militancy lies in political, social, economic and religious discontentment and issues like race, tribe, territory, region, religion, ideology and culture play a major role in breeding terrorism.

The lessons learned from Iraq and Afghan wars suggest that terrorism cannot be tackled by using brute force. The global war against terrorism can only be won by peaceful resolution of all the conflicting issues.

US Operation Enduring Freedom would make sense only if it accepts the plurality in the world order. Perhaps the best way US can help in tackling the issue of terrorism is to interact with the regional actors by facilitating dialogue and discussions for the peaceful resolution of the conflict situation.

12
South Asia I

- *Insecurity Plagues South Asia* • *India's Role in South Asia* • *South Asia after the Nuclear Tests* • *India and Nuclear Proliferation Debate* • *Nuclear Safety Standards in India*

Insecurity Plagues South Asia

In South Asia, there is a continued trend of insecurity exacerbated by removal of superpower rivalry, which served as a balancing role for regional peace and stability in the Cold War era. Since there is no credible guarantor for peace in this unipolar world, every country in the region is busy safeguarding their security as best they can. This is conspicuously reflected in the defence spending of the seven South Asian states.

About 40 million US dollars is spent by Nepal, and 4000 million US dollars by Bangladesh. Sri Lanka's defence expenditure is 500 million US dollars. Pakistan spends 4.5 billion US dollars on its defence. India spends 7.5 billion US dollars on its defence preparedness.

India further hiked defence spending by 15 per cent in 2002-03 national budgetary allocations and Pakistan too announced substantial hike for its defence. The scenario is becoming alarming as we notice that the South Asian countries are spending four times more on defence than non-defence related items in their annual budget. When this is compounded with per capita GNP, the cost of increased expenditure is staggering.

The military spending in the Indo-centric South Asian region reflects the insecurity scenario. It becomes more pronounced when

India started to redefine its security concerns after the fall of the Soviet Union. Initially, India's military hardware purchase was jeopardized by the discrepancy in the rupee-rouble trade with Russia but this was rectified when Vajpayee government reiterated its commitment by signing the peace and friendship treaty with Russia. At the same time, India showed a seminal shift towards US and Israel for the procurement of weapon systems.

As far as Pakistan is concerned, its nuclear designs led to the fall out with US on the supply of weapon system. However, after Soviet intervention in Afghanistan in 1979, Pakistan became the frontline state and US supplied enough of arms and ammunitions even without any payment. Pakistan in a bid to strengthen its security arrangement also leaned on China for the procurement of weapon systems. It is found cultivating relations with its northern and western neighbours for economic and strategic purposes.

Sri Lanka has been cultivating relationship with UK and other western countries for defence preparedness. So is Bangladesh which has been trying to depend upon some Southeast Asian countries and China. One thing that has come out clearly is that China has become main supplier of arms to many of India's neighbouring countries.

The nuclear component has increased the security concerns in South Asia. India says that its nuclear weapons are geared towards insecurity that emanate from threats outside the region. In response, Pakistan claims its nuclear weapons are primarily because of Indian threat which it would use as a tactical weapon for the survival of the Islamic state. The testing and deployment of missiles by India and Pakistan is aggravating the insecurity in the region. Some however argue that nuclear cover has acted as deterrence between the two countries.

South Asian countries are also disturbed by internal security concern. Almost all the states in the region are gripped by assertion of ethnic, religious and regional forces. In Sri Lanka there is the problem of Tamil ethnicity, Bangladesh faces problem of Chakma tribes, the Terai people forms part of Nepal's problem, and influx of Nepalese population has created foreigners problem in Bhutan.

Pakistan remains under the grip of the assertion of ethnic nationalism. Sindhis, Muhajirs, Baluchis, Pushtuns and Punjabi nationalism are on the rise in Pakistan. In India, tribal identity in the northeast region, linguistic identity in the southern states, ethnic identity in Punjab and Kashmir are on the rise. The sizeable deployment of paramilitary forces in Jammu and Kashmir and in the northeast region of India points to the gravity of the problem.

The overlapping population in the region has created majority-minority problem. Religious extremism against the minority in one country provokes reaction in the other country. Almost all the countries are facing the spillover effects of the population from the other country. This, in turn leads to the problem of migration and refugees in South Asia.

Since India's border touches almost all the neighbouring countries, there is constant inter state tension. Between India and Sri Lanka, there remains the question of the repatriation of the Tamil refugees, fishermen's problem and the proprietorship of the Kachatheevu Island. With Bangladesh, water sharing, and Talpati or New Moore Island causes security concerns. India and Pakistan are completely at the loggerhead over various issues including Kashmir.

The insecurity in South Asia does not end there as the entire region is plagued by insurgency. In India after Punjab, Jammu and Kashmir is under the grip of terrorists' menace, so is parts of its northeast region. In Nepal there is the Maoist insurgency, in Bhutan there is Nepalese insurgency and in Sri Lanka there is Tamil insurgency.

South Asia inherits a plethora of problems and their combination cast a bad spell on the regional security. The insecurity scenario demands efficient regional management to reduce the prevailing tension. What is required is for all contentious problems to be resolved within the ambit of regionalism. It is expected that by strengthening the bonds of regionalism through economic, environmental and cultural cooperation, the threat perceptions can be reduced. This in turn may pave the way for collective security of the region. The irony is, consensus for peace remains elusive in South Asia.

India's Role in South Asia

South Asia is dominated by India's size and resources. India shares seventy per cent of the South Asian land mass. It shares its land boundaries with all its neighbouring countries except the Maldives and Sri Lanka. The predominant size of India has led to many irritants with its neighbours. Some of them are of recent origin, others have colonial legacy. India has always remained keen to solve all the outstanding problems with its neighbours, but in spite of its sincere efforts, many problems still remain a-begging for solution.

In retrospect, India's foreign policy has not been on an even keel with most of its neighbours. The small versus big syndrome have dominated the foreign policy parameters. Most of the neighbours have felt suffocated in the last four decades, living under the shadow of mighty India. The unequal trade and transit treaty with Nepal, the water sharing problem with Bangladesh, dabbling in Sri Lanka's ethnic quagmire, and tit for tat diplomacy with Pakistan are all the highlights of India's foreign policy of past.

The genesis of the contemporary foreign policy of India can be traced to the Rajiv era when New Delhi started changing its postures from big bully to the big brother attitude. The successive governments accelerated this policy resulting in a great deal of thaw in relations by India and its neighbours. In recent times, there has been three major reference points in India's foreign policy. The first one is the Gujral doctrine, the second one is the post Pokhran II diplomacy and the third is the Common Minimum Programme of the United Progressive Alliance government under Manmohan Singh.

The Gujral doctrine by former Prime Minister I K Gujral (1987-89) did not insist on reciprocity with any other neighbours except Pakistan. This new Indian foreign policy paved the way in allaying the mistrusts and suspicion of its small neighbours. Indian gesture softened the anti-India attitude of the neighbours and a climate of trust and confidence was build up in the region.

India paid sympathetic attention to Dhaka's claim that the Farakka Barrage was creating water shortage and agreed to release water to save the crops being affected in Bangladesh. India was also able to persuade Bangladesh for the resettlement of Chakma refugees sheltering in camps at Tripura for a long period of time. India also accommodated the Bangladesh's plea to import its goods at the lower tariff barrier and to restore the balance of payment.

The main dispute with Nepal over the trade and transit agreement treaty of 1950 was resolved when the clause of trade and transit were separated from each other. Kathmandu was unhappy over the security clause of the treaty and New Delhi wanted the Nepalese soil not be used for anti-India activities. Both the countries ultimately accommodated each other's concerns. Major concessions were given to Nepal in the new treaty to improve the bilateral relationship.

India-Sri Lanka relations which waxed and waned over the Tamil question, improved when New Delhi made it clear that it would not tamper with the unity and integrity of Sri Lanka. On economic front, both the countries agreed to lower the trade barriers and to reduce the trade deficit.

Bhutan is the only neighbour with which India has enjoyed good relations all through. New Delhi provided financial and technical assistance to Bhutan and become partners in many turnkey projects. India also constructed the 336 M W Chuk Hydel project and decided to purchase the bulk of the power generated from this project in Bhutan.

The small versus big syndrome that characterises India's relationship with other neighbours do not haunt the littoral state of the Maldives. The reason being the fact that the Maldives is too small a country to nurse such an ambition. Besides, India has always helped the Maldives at all times and its ties with the nation of islands remain an ideal one.

The acrimonious relation that persisted between India and Pakistan were ultimately softened by Gujral doctrine as it declared that all the contentious issue had to be resolved through dialogue. The Gujral doctrine set the ball rolling for the resolution of Kashmir, terrorism, drug trafficking, Siachin, Tulbul navigational project, Sir Creek maritime disputes, among others.

The nuclear tests conducted by India under Vajpayee government in 1998 and reciprocated by Pakistan changed the entire security environment of South Asia. It appeared that an era of jingoistic nationalism has returned into the region again.

Vajpayee government quickly allayed the apprehension by showing urgency in India's approach for improving the relationship with its neighbours. In this phase of diplomacy, efforts were made to bring India and Sri lanka closer. India gave whole hearted support to the peace talks with the LTTE. It mooted free trade area with Sri Lanka and held talks for resuming ferry service between Tamil Nadu and Sri Lanka. India and Bangladesh agreed to start bus service between Kolkata and Dhaka. The relationship between Nepal, Bhutan and Bangladesh was improved considerably. The idea of sub region grouping connecting northeast region of India with Bangladesh, Nepal, Bhutan and Myanmar gained momentum.

Indo-Pak relations for the first time in the contemporary history witnessed spring season. The Colombo SAARC summit in December 1998 set the tone for improving the bilateral relations. Diplomacy at various levels made Vajpayee to undertake the bus journey to Lahore in 1999. The cricket and the hockey test matches eased the simmering tension between the two neighbours. The composite and integrated dialogue was started with much fanfare. Even as both the sides agreed to disagree with each other but still remained committed to carry the dialogue process forward.

However, soon after that came the Kargil border clashes in the summer of 1999. Indo-Pak relationship got deteriorated once again. The dialogue process was tried to kick-start again with General Pervez Musharaf visiting India for the Agra summit in 2001 but the failure of the summit further distanced the two countries.

Then the attack on the Indian Parliament on 13 December 2001. India responded by adopting coercive diplomacy and sent its troops to be positioned in combat position on the border with Pakistan. India suspended all possible diplomatic relations with Pakistan and Indo-Pak relations touched an all time low. The soured relation with Pakistan started picking up again when India recalled its troop in November 2002, after keeping it in high alert position for more than 10 months.

India-Pakistan relation was rejuvenated through people to people contact since the beginning of 2003. There was great deal of enthusiasm shown by several kinds of delegates visiting the two countries. The momentum that gathered in 2003, crystallized on the sidelines of the 12th SAARC summit in Islamabad, where India and Pakistan agreed to resolve all there outstanding issues including Kashmir through dialogue.

The 2004 election in India brought United Progressive Alliance (UPA) government headed by Manmohan Singh to power. The UPA, which released its common minimum programme of governance, agreed to carry forward the resolve of maintaining and strengthening good neighbourly relations. The UPA endorsed the commitment of the previous government to resolve all the differences with Pakistan through dialogue.

In retrospect, it is seen that, when the world is marching ahead with various regions evolving common agenda for its future development, South Asia remains trapped in its past. The region remains hostage to Indo-Pak relations, even more than fifty years after independence. Hopes lie in the new thaw emerging in Indo-Pak relations, and the region is preparing to face the future.

South Asia after the Nuclear Tests

The nuclear tests conducted by India and Pakistan in May 1998 changed the entire security scenario in South Asia. Even though India has assured that its nuclear programme is geared towards the threat perception from outside the region, Pakistan viewed it as a hegemonic attempt by India to dominate the South Asian scene. Its similar response has made the region a critical landmass.

The sequel of events suggests that soon after the Vajpayee government came to power in 1998, Pakistan test fired its intermediate range missile called 'Ghauri'. Indian media made a lot of hype about this missile test by Pakistan. The Vajpayee government took no time to retaliate to the Pakistani provocation, as if everything had been planned in advance.

India announced its entry into the elite group of nuclear weapon states by conducting Pokhran II tests in June 1998. Pakistan saw this as an attempt to subvert its territorial integrity and in a tit-for-tat move, conducted similar explosions to demonstrate its own nuclear prowess. With all this the lid which was kept over nuclear weapon programme in South Asia was lifted and the entire security environment vitiated further.

The India-Pakistan nuclear race actually began after the Bangladesh war. The Soviet Union, which came in support of India during the war, threatened US of flouting the nuclear deterrence, had the American seventh fleet came in aid of East Pakistan. A belated diplomatic dash by US Secretary of State Henry Kissinger to Moscow averted further breakup of West Pakistan, but by then Pakistan was a dismembered state.

The Pakistani president, Zulfikar Ali Bhutto in his book *The Myth of Independence* says that there cannot be any guarantee of territorial sovereignty for a country till it acquires nuclear weapon of its own. Bhutto in his famous speech said: "We will eat grass and would not sleep till we acquire nuclear capabilities."

Pakistan took the lab route to develop its nuclear weapon. It used high technology for the design of the bomb and then went ahead to conduct zero yield tests by conducting high-speed atomic explosion to get the right results. Since the early eighties, Pakistan started claiming acquisitions of nuclear capability without actually exploding the nuclear device.

India's nuclear programme started under the guidance of Dr Homi Bhabha in 1959. In the three phased programme, natural uranium was to be used as fuel to generate power. India maintained that its nuclear capabilities are for peaceful purpose and stated that it is not going to develop the weapon of mass destruction unless was forced to do so.

However, somewhere down the line, India started enriching uranium for the production of nuclear weapons. It became a nuclear threshold state after the first Pokhran test in 1974. Since then India maintained an ambiguous stand on the nuclear issue.

In the meantime, India went ahead with its missile technology programme and refused to sign the nuclear non-proliferation treaty (NPT) or the Missile Technology Control Regime (MTCR) on the grounds that they were discriminatory. Pakistan also followed suit on missile technology development programme and refused to sign the NPT and the MTCR, egging on Indian arguments in its defence.

The Pokhran II explosion and the similar explosion conducted by Pakistan changed the entire security scenario in South Asia. With the kind of antagonism that persists between the two countries since their inception, the introduction of the complete bomb and its storage risk made the region a critical landmass.

With no foolproof mechanism to avoid nuclear war, the constructs of the day after scenario were projected to be horrific. It is said that since the national infrastructure in Pakistan was concentrated in small areas they could become easy targets of Indian missiles. At the same time almost all the major Indian cities were on the push buttons of the Pakistani missiles.

The casualties in such eventuality were put on the high density of population on both the sides. The damage caused by the thermal effect of the nuclear explosion was predicted to be so huge that post attack recovery would be impossible without outside support. This was attributed to limited fire fighting capabilities possessed by both the countries in case of nuclear war.

However, there are some who argued that the introduction of nuclear weapons has acted as deterrence and the region remains peaceful for the last thirty years or so. This is true to some extent. However, the possession of nuclear weapons have also become a major destabilizing factor as war mongers openly profess to use them as a tactical weapon. It has contributed to widespread mistrust in the region. With nuclear arms, India and Pakistan in its game to checkmate each other have endangered the region as a whole. The smaller nations feel threatened by the narrow and asymmetry power equation developing in the region.

Notwithstanding these facts, it is difficult for India and Pakistan to give up the bomb after acquiring them. The only course left for them is to reach an agreement over their nuclear weapons. Some efforts have been made by spelling out the nuclear doctrine but a lot more remains to be done. The two countries are still to chalk out rules of the engagement of the nuclear weapons and threshold of their use.

The ultimate goal to de-nuclearise South Asia remains a dream. India and Pakistan are far from any agreement like Mutually Agreed Destruction (MAD) treaty or Arms Reduction Treaty as was done by USA and USSR during the Cold War. These issues would eventually become redundant, if both the countries could reach an understanding on the question of their national sovereignty, the key to establishing permanent peace in the region.

India and Nuclear Proliferation Debate

The US global agenda has witnessed a perceptible shift from that of the Clinton administration. The war against global terrorism and restructuring of regimes finds priority over the issue of nuclear proliferation championed by the Clinton administration.

American interest in the non proliferation issue has actually waned ever since the Congress rejected the ratification of the Comprehensive Test Ban Treaty (CTBT). Thereafter, it is seen that US' desire to denuclearize the world have been put into back burner, at least for the time being.

With the nuclear explosions in 1998, India and Pakistan have joined the elite club of five who possess nuclear weapons. The world including US does not recognise the new-found status of India and Pakistan nor does it have any policy to deal with other countries believed to be nuclear threshold states. The din of nuclear proliferation issue may have reduced now but it is unlikely that its growth would not continue for long.

The US attempt of global disarmament through the CTBT was preceded by a somewhat similar treaty called Non Proliferation Treaty (NPT). The most conspicuous feature about NPT was that it allowed the vertical proliferation by the nuclear weapons states but banned horizontal proliferation by nuclear threshold states. NPT is linked to safety and storage factor of the complete bomb. It is argued that since the threshold countries do not subscribe to them, they should be refrained from any such aggrandizement. There was intense lobbying in support of NPT, leading many countries to become its signatories.

India resisted signing the NPT arguing that it was discriminatory. India wanted a change in the treaty to make nuclear safeguards applicable to both weapon and no weapons states alike. It maintained that there should be a provision, making it obligatory for big nuclear states to stop further proliferation of nuclear weapons.

India proposed an alternative to the NPT with provisions such as no first use, complete test ban, and scrutiny of fissile material, no underground tests, and substantial reduction of nuclear arsenal. India also wanted a clause to be added to check nuclear thefts.

India also suggested underground explosion treaty, threshold test ban treaty and cut-off agreement to prohibit the production of fissionable material. It added that a new provision should be made including security guarantee to those nations becoming parties to the treaty. The talks over NPT however remained inconclusive.

The debate that was generated during Clinton administration regarding the NPT and CTBT gives the picture where the world stand as far as nuclear proliferation issues are concerned. The arguments put forward by India against both the treaty are substantial, which makes a case that whenever a new treaty comes it has to be evolved through honest negotiations.

During the Clinton administration the conclusion of the Comprehensive Test Ban Treaty (CTBT) became the major policy pillar of US foreign policy. The US through the CTBT divided the world into two categories; in the first category were the five permanent members of the Security Council and in the second, were the nuclear threshold countries.

The five nuclear powers conducted parallel discussions on CTBT about 'permitted and prescribed' weapon related activities. They disagreed with each other over some significant issues. US, Britain and France agreed on a common approach to give the treaty a mandate for a total ban on underground nuclear tests but Russia and China resisted this proposal. Russia disagreed to 'zero yield' proposal and did not want to fully comply with the CTBT. China also disagreed with the CTBT and wanted to continue nuclear tests for peaceful purposes.

Among the nuclear threshold countries the biggest resistance to the treaty came from India. New Delhi put forward the argument that the nuclear weapons were being monopolised by a few powers who want to retain them, but disarm the rest of the world. It argued that the strategy of the West was to keep the world under a technological bondage and wanted to stifle technological advancement of the rest of the world through CTBT.

India demanded a clear definition of the scope of the treaty and asked whether the countries in possession of nuclear weapons may not further indulge in nuclear weapon testing. It further demanded an end to nuclear weapon production and linked it to a time frame for global disarmament.

India's precondition to locate CTBT in the general context of global disarmament was rejected by the US. Even though US recognised India's security concerns, it mounted tremendous pressure on India, to cap, reduce and ultimately eliminate its nuclear capabilities. US insisted that New Delhi should not link CTBT with a time frame for gradual reduction or abolition of nuclear weapons. US warned that linkage could destroy the emerging consensus behind the CTBT.

The situation, as it stands now, is both India and Pakistan have neither signed the NPT nor the CTBT. Both in turn have flouted the proliferation issue by conducting nuclear tests and announcing themselves to be weapon state. The world however does not subscribe to their accredited position. In such case what would happen when non-proliferation issue is debated again remains to be seen.

The question also remains whether the five nuclear powers would agree to a time frame for a phased reduction of nuclear weapons, their means of delivery and their complete elimination or will it allow more threshold countries to join the nuclear club. Whatever may be the road-map ahead, it is clear that, any global nuclear policy that allows the nuclear weapon states the freedom to proliferate but prevents others from nonproliferation will not be accepted by countries like India. The ultimate goal to denuclearise the world, however, remains a hope.

Nuclear Safety Standards in India

How safe are India's nuclear power plants, is a question most often asked whenever any discussion on India's nuclear installation takes place. There are altogether 14 nuclear power reactors operating at six atomic power stations in the country. However, only three of these nuclear reactors fall under International Atomic Energy Agency (IAEA) standards. The rest – which were built with local technology – are accountable only to national standards set by the Atomic Energy Regulatory Board (AERB). This leaves a question mark on the safety of these plants.

The Union government has assured that the operational procedures are being scrupulously followed "at all the nuclear plants", but going by its own admission, six leaks had occurred at various installations in the past four years. Vajpayee government informed the Parliament that these incidents were of minor nature and had no significant impact on the public or the environment.

Even though India's Atomic Energy Commission has repeatedly asserted that it is doing what it can to ensure that the country's power plants are safe, still, leaks continue to occur. Unofficial figures estimate that 300 such incidents have occurred so far. Some of them of serious nature, where radiation leaks have caused physical damage to the workers.

Ever since India's nuclear-power programme has been launched in 1950s it has been kept behind the veil of secrecy. No one knows what is happening behind the iron curtain as the government never releases any information about the leaks or the accidents. The safety lapses are often hushed up and comes to light only when some serious incident occurs, and that too when raked up by some NGO.

The reason for the lack of information is because most of India's nuclear installations are located in thinly populated rural areas far from the hub of media activities. The rural populace living there are too ignorant to raise any voice about safety standards. In fact most of them are totally unaware as to how to react in case of a Chernobyl or Bhopal like disasters around them.

Some NGOs and the Centre for Science and Environment (CSE), have expressed concern at the increased incidence of cancer and deformities observed in some villages neighbouring the atomic power plants. They have demanded the introduction of consultative mechanisms to go into the safety status of nuclear installations and the people's right to information to be given due weight. However, these pleas have fallen on deaf ears as more nuclear energy projects are being announced by the government without any public consent.

Public safety remains neglected because India does not have a truly independent organisation to oversee safety and regulation of its civilian nuclear installations. The nearest thing India has is the Atomic Energy Regulatory Board (AERB), which is completely subservient to the Department of Atomic Energy (DAE). Several suggestions to follow the International Convention on Nuclear Safety were made to the Ministry of Atomic Energy and Space but hardly any attention to public safety has been paid so far. Even the plea to separate the Atomic Energy Regulatory Board (AERB) and Department of Atomic Energy (DAE) to make the nuclear safety concern foolproof has so far gone unheeded.

The real problem India faces is non approval by the Western countries to pursue its nuclear programme. Decades of denying nuclear technology have pushed the country to pursue its own indigenous programme. Access to technology or equipment from Western countries that follow rules set by the Nuclear Suppliers Group (NSG) is also not forthcoming because India does not accept full-scope international safeguards for its nuclear activities.

Nuclear safety was further pushed to the brink after India exploded its first peaceful nuclear device at Pokhran in 1974. It was placed under scrutiny of various technology transfer regimes by the West which further hardened due to its refusal to sign the NPT and the CTBT. The Pokhran II nuclear tests in 1998 accentuated the dangers to public safety.

More so, the new technology designed to upgrade the safety at nuclear power plants is too expensive for developing countries like India to afford. Unlike, other areas where the developed countries are considerate enough for technology transfer they have kept the nuclear safety technology beyond the reach of the developing nation to maintain their supremacy.

All this has led India to pursue the path of self reliance and bank on indigenous hardware production to build the nuclear reactors. At this stage red-tapeism and corruption comes home to roost. It is alleged that well-connected manufacturers cut deals with the politicians and bureaucrats, often selling defective parts. This bogey has pushed the country to a probable Chernobyl-type disaster, which is kept at bay not by any deliberate design but by good luck.

It is an irony that, though India has come out with elaborate nuclear doctrine, it has not made public any guidelines to be followed to maintain the safety standards of its nuclear power plants. As long as any foolproof nuclear safety mechanism is not evolved, every Indian would continue to end the day with a sleepless night. The insecurity is not from Pakistan or the terrorists, but from our own nuclear installations.

The need of the hour is to have a regulatory board which should regularly be briefing the government about the safety requirements and releasing press notes periodically for public information. The board should be equipped with the elaborate contingency plans of fire fighting and evacuation of local people in case of any disaster. The NGOs and local representation should be part of such regulatory board to have transparency in maintaining the safety standards.

The worst fear of nuclear disaster emanates from the probable safety lapses of India's own nuclear power plants. No one seems agitated about the time bomb ticking in the temples of modern India.

13
South Asia II

- *South Asia: Problem of Ethnicity Conflagrates* • *South Asia: Religion versus Reason* • *Refugees in South Asia* • *Human Rights in South Asia* • *Women Struggle in South Asia* • *Information Technology in South Asia* • *Economic Integration of South Asia*

South Asia: Problem of Ethnicity Conflagrates

One of the ironies of the freedom movement in South Asia is that during the course of struggle, different groups came together on a common platform, to wrest political power from the colonial rulers, but after independence only few ethno-religious groups control power. As a result, most countries of the region have become mono-ethnic states even as they remain multi-ethnic societies.

In Sri Lanka it is Sinhalese who are at the helm of affairs, Punjabis rule in Pakistan, India is run by upper caste Hindus from north India. All this in turn triggers dissatisfaction from the groups that have been left out of the power structure. Since their legitimate political, economic and cultural aspirations are not met, some ethnic groups demand autonomy within their national framework. Their demand includes maximum amount of cultural, political and economic autonomy in the geographical area where they constitute a majority.

In India, some of the ethnic movements that are manifest are Telengana, Bodoland and Purvanchal. In Pakistan, there are the surging Pushtuns, Baluch, Sindhi, Seraiki and Mohajir movements. In Nepal it's the Terai population which is mobilised. At the centre of political mobilisation in Bhutan there is the Nepali population. The Tamil ethnic group is classic case of such mobilisation in Sri Lanka.

In South Asia it is seen that some ethnic movements conflagrates and remains visible, while the process of political mobilisation and assertion remains latent in others. The latent groups however remain simmering below the surface waiting for an opportunity to explode any time.

Then, there are some native movements, which stem due to the influx of population that causes hardship to the sons of the soil. The native movements demand safeguards for their economic, linguistic and cultural rights against the outside population. The natives of Sindh in Pakistan are perturbed by the Mohajir influx from India in 1947. The Sindhi and Mohajir groups are competing in the same geographical space for their safeguards. The natives of Bhutan, called the Drupkas are uncomfortable with the influx of the Nepalese in south Bhutan.

In India, the Bangladeshi migrants put the natives of Assam and Arunachal Pradesh under pressure. In Maharashtra the Shiv Sena party evokes Marathi nationalism, against the influx of non Marathi population into Mumbai.

Then there are the out and out separatist movements, which do not want to live within the geographical boundary of the country and aspire to create an independent state of their own. The separatists groups in Indian Punjab demand creation of Khalistan. The Jammu and Kashmir Liberation Front (JKLF) demand an independent Kashmir. In Assam the United Liberation Front of Assam (ULFA) wants independence from India. In Pakistan Pushtun, Baluch and the Sindh movements, all have shades of separatism.

Another striking feature in South Asia is the aspiration of the cross-national ethno-political group to form a separate independent state defying the existing political boundary. In this category falls the concept of the Greater Himalayan Federation floated in 1964. This comprises Nepal, Sikkim, Bhutan and certain Nepali majority areas of India.

The pro-Azadi movement of Kashmir wants to break the barrier dividing them between India and Pakistan. The concept of an independent Pushtunistan, extending from NWFP of Pakistan to the Pushtun dominated areas of Afghanistan continues to be alive. The cry of 'Tamil Eelam' strikes an emotional chord in India's Tamil Nadu to bridge the Gulf of Mannar.

In the changing global context when there is consensus for preserving the existing boundaries, how far these transnational aspirations could be accommodated remains to be seen. The mobilisation of ethnic groups not only disturbs the internal balance of a country, but also impinges on the interstate relationship. It is a common feature among the South Asian countries to blame another country for the problem created by their own ethno-political groups.

Sri Lanka, for instance holds India responsible for the militant insurgency of the Tamil ethnic group. The Nepali elite in Kathmandu perceive that the Hindi speaking group of the Terai region is encouraged by India. Bhutan blames Nepal for abetting the separatist aspirations of its Nepalese population. India accuses Bangladesh for abetting insurgency in its northeast region. Pakistan perceives its Sindh and Mohajir movement to be encouraged by India. Similarly, India blames Pakistan for propagating Sikh and Kashmiri militancy on its soil.

These accusations are not unfounded. There remains a definite motive by a state to extend moral and material support to an ethno-political group, with the view to weaken the neighbouring country and extend its sphere of influence in the region. Its extreme manifestation was seen in the manner India helped the ethno-cultural aspirations of the Bengali separatism resulting in the creation of Bangladesh. Similarly, the way India used the Nepalese population to bring about the annexation of Sikkim in 1974. It tried the same in Sri Lanka but later back tracked. Such acts haunt India now in its northeast region and Jammu and Kashmir state.

Since every country in South Asia is under the grip of the ethno-political tensions, the problem of ethnicity looms large in the region. The genesis of ethnic conflict lies in the process of nation building, over centralisation of the state structure, failure of national integration.

The only remedy to reduce the problem of ethnic tension could be by de-centralising the power structure and percolating the concept of democracy at the root level. The nation builders should take into consideration the colourful mosaic of ethnic plurality and accommodate the aspirations of the ethnic groups in the state apparatus. Its failure would keep national cohesiveness hostage to strains of ethno-cultural and linguistic pressures. South Asian states have still not given a serious thought to it. If identity and integrity are to be maintained and further more strengthened, it needs to.

South Asia: Religion versus Reason

South Asia is the abode of three principal religions – Hinduism, Islam and Buddhism. Besides, followers of Christianity, Zoroastrians, Jews and Sikhs are also present in sizeable numbers in the region. India and Nepal are predominantly Hindu countries; Bangladesh, Pakistan and Maldives are predominantly Muslim while Sri Lanka and Bhutan are predominantly Buddhist countries. Every country is a conglomeration of religious plurality in South Asia. Any form of religious extremism provokes similar reaction in the neighbouring country.

South Asia has constantly witnessed stoking up of religious passions and consequently raising social temperatures. The high noon of Indian politics, which ended in the creation of Pakistan led to one of the bloodiest religious strife in the subcontinent. Its legacy continues to haunt social life of India and Pakistan even today.

The genesis of the creation of Pakistan was religion. The survival of the multi-national state rests on the over arching umbrella of Islamic faith. In contemporary history, during General Zia-ul-Haq, the Islamisation process began afresh in Pakistan. The military dictator interpreted everything in terms of religion, in order to seek political legitimacy of his regime. The persecution of Christians, Shias and Ahmadiyas began since about that time in Pakistan.

However, even during Zia's rule, there wasn't any great deal of support to the right wing religious parties in Pakistan. Subsequently, the political mandate given during the rules of Benazir and Nawaz Sharif also did not favour religious parties. This trend has changed during General Musharraf's rule. Fifty member of the present Parliament belongs to a conglomeration of six religious parties called Mutahida Quami Amal (MQA). Since they have come to power on a religious platform they have to keep religion and politics entwined to serve their interests.

Bangladesh, which came into existence on the basis of cultural and linguistic difference with Pakistan, finds itself overshadowed by India. In order to evolve an individual personality of its own it is harping on its religious moorings. The trend however had begun as early as in 1975 when General Zia-Ur Rehman deliberately sharpened the country's religious identity, perhaps to woo aid and assistance from the rich organisations of Islamic countries.

Religious and cultural identity has always come in clash with one another in Bangladesh. This has been reflected in the political mobilisation of the two dominant political parties Bangladesh National Party (BNP) and Awami League. The BNP, which is headed by Khalida Zia, represents the religious aspiration of the people; the Awami League, cashes upon the linguistic and cultural sentiments of Bangladeshis. Both the parties, ruling in rotation, sums up the popular mood of that country. It seems the people in Bangladesh neither favour the domination of religious parties nor can they tolerate a long spell by the party harping on cultural and linguistic moorings.

In Sri Lanka, the Sinhalese, who constitute the majority, are Buddhists by faith. The two centrist parties, the United Nationalist Party (UNP) and the Sri Lanka Freedom Party (SLFP) are directly competing for the Sinhala majority votes. The Jatiya Vimukti Perumuna party (JVP) which draws its aspiration from the 'Jatika Chintanya' translated as national thinking represent extreme right Sinhala aspiration. The JVP survives on stoking the raw religious passions of Sinhalese chauvinism. It has emerged as a political force in the April 2004 election and is a coalition partner in the SLFP led government which came to power replacing UNP.

The Tamil conflict in Sri Lanka is interpreted by some, more in religious terms. As custodians of Buddhism in the subcontinent, some Sinhalas feel that Hindu Tamils are threat to their race and religion. Muslims who constitute the third faith in Sri Lanka too do not enjoy a happy relationship with the Tamils even though they speak the same language. Their relations with Sinhalas too are far from being harmonious. Willy-nilly, religion becomes a key factor in Sri Lankan politics.

Contemporary India has been witnessing Hindu revivalism known as Hindutva, more pronounced in the Indo-Gangetic plains of the north and being spread out to rest of the country. Its roots could be traced to the politics of 1970s when Mrs Indira Gandhi, in order to perpetuate her authoritarian rule, used caste and religion as twin weapons for electoral manipulation. It had disastrous effects on the Indian politics. A series of communal riots between Hindus and Muslims was witnessed during Mrs Gandhi's rule. The culmination of divisive politics manifested in 'Operation Blue Star' in 1984 and ultimately to her killing by her Sikh guards in the same year. The anti-Sikh riots that followed Mrs Gandhi's murder created alienation amongst the Sikh community, which is being healed with Manmohan Singh becoming the prime minister of India.

The politicisation of religion continued unabated in India. Rajiv Gandhi annulled the Supreme Court judgment in the Shah Bano case. The balancing game that followed allowed the gates of the disputed Babri mosque in Ayodhya to be opened. Thereafter, a movement was built around the symbol 'Ram' and its birth place, Ayodhya, which generated a spate of Hindu revivalism in the country.

The ideological vacuum, which the Congress created due to the mismanagement of the Nehruvian secular ideals, provided avenues for the right wing communalists to move in. This manifested in the form of political mobilisation under the right wing Bharatiya Janta Party (BJP) which crept on the political ladder riding the wave of religious chauvinism.

The rise of BJP reflects the transformation India has undergone since independence. The sheer percentage of votes the BJP corners points to the nature and direction of the political change that is taking place in India. It is another story that BJP, constrained by coalition partners, have kept their religious agenda on the backburner during its term of governance.

What is being witnessed in South Asia, is that the politicisation of religion to reap a quick political harvest. The sharpening of the religious divide for a few more votes has been instrumental in the sowing seeds of divisiveness in most of the countries. To expect from a generation of people to strive for regional cohesiveness when it has been raised on the staple diet of religious hate mongers is a pipedream.

The politicisation of religion is the single factor that comes in the way of nation building and regional harmony in the region. If a harmonious social order has to be built in the region then it's high time to put a lid on the politics of religion. It would be more appropriate for logic of reason to prevail over religion in South Asia.

Refugees in South Asia

South Asian nations are often gripped by the problem of refugees. They are the people who fled their country on account of civil strife, religious persecution, and political instability. This subject assumes significance whenever a crisis situation develops between the two countries.

The refugee problem is not a recent phenomenon. The first horde of refugees came after the partition of the subcontinent. This was to be followed by the arrival of the Tibetan refugees in 1962. The Tibetan spiritual head, Dalai Lama, was given political asylum in India and other Tibetan refugees were spread out in other parts of India. There largest concentration remains in Dhramshala, Himachal Pradesh.

One may recall that refugee problem was one of the main causes of the emergence of Bangladesh. There were about 10 million refugees then taking shelter in India due to repression unleashed by the Pakistani army on its eastern wing in 1971. This made India support Bangladesh's war of liberation.

After the emergence of Bangladesh, the problem of the Chakma refugees cropped up with India. The Chakma tribes fled the Chittagong hill tracts of Bangladesh and took shelter in India's northeastern state of Tripura. After staying for more than a decade in camps, the Chakma refugees were finally repatriated back to their old habitat in Bangladesh.

Though India bore the brunt of the refugees in South Asia, the problem is not confined to this country alone. Since its inception in 1971, Bangladesh is beset with the problem of 100,000 Urdu-speaking Biharis accommodated in various camps in Dhaka who claim to be Pakistani nationals. Attempt to repatriate them evoked sharp reaction by Pakistan. In mid eighties Pakistan deported a plane load of 288 people from Karachi to Dhaka refusing them entry into the country.

Thousands of Rohinga refugees are staying in camps in Cox Bazaar of Bangladesh for the past many years after fleeing the Arakan hills due to repression by the military regime in Myanmar. Myanmar government refuses to take them back. Similarly, a large number of Bhutanese of Nepali origins have fled south Bhutan and have taken shelter in Nepal and India. The Bhutan government refuses to accept them as its citizens.

In Pakistan, thousand of Afghan refugees poured in owing to continued turmoil in their country. The tide which began since the Soviet intervention in Afghanistan in 1979 has not reversed even after a new political dispensation now in Kabul. The Afghan refugees in Pakistan have added to the slum and ghettos of the cities and are alleged to be behind much of the sectarian violence in that country.

The problem of refugees impinges heavily upon the bilateral relationship between India and Sri Lanka. The Sri Lankan ethnic conflict resulted in a large number of Tamil refugees taking shelter in camps all over Tamil Nadu. Refugees of Nepali origin who are expelled from Bhutan and sheltering in Nepal are causing a rift between Nepal and Bhutan. The Rohinga tribals living in the camps in Bangladesh are cause of tension between Myanmar and Bangladesh. The Urdu speaking Biharis living in camps in Bangladesh is the cause bilateral tension with Pakistan.

Refugees are different from illegal immigrants and there is a subtle politics linked with them. Though it may vary in nature and form, the politics of refugees continue to thrive in South Asia. Since refugees are a burden on the state's exchequer, the United Nations and some donor countries provide large amount of aid and assistance to the host countries. Several non governmental organisations championing the cause of the refugees thrive on the huge assistance they receive from various sources to provide succour to the refugees.

In Pakistan several NGOs receive million of dollars as aid in the name of Afghan refugees. The camps run in Nepal for the Bhutanese refugees also receive sizeable amount of assistance, so do the NGOs in Tamil Nadu taking care of the Sri Lankan Tamils. In New Delhi alone, there are several NGOs looking after the refugees of several nationalities.

In the name of political asylum, the refugees get a monthly stipend and many of them prefer to live in the host country. In some cases there could be vested interest involved, in others, genuine constraints due to political instability in their own country may hold them in camps.

They continue to live in squatter camps and makeshift dwellings for so long that even their next generations are born in camps. They suffer from the problem of being rootless and are never accepted by the country where they have taken shelter. Some of them are seen with suspicion and are alleged to be security risk for the host country.

It is a matter of fact, that the problem of refugees has assumed an alarming proportion in South Asia. The need for evolving some regional consensus on the issue remains unheard. Suggestions were made that there should be a commitment by the states that they would not allow their ethnic-religious specificities to spillover to another country. If at all it happens and once a particular category of people are given refugee status in a country, it should be the duty of the parent country to bear the expenses of basic necessities of their citizens along with their quick repatriation. All this seems easier said than done. The refugees' endless wait in camps in South Asia resembles the well-known play *Waiting for Godot* by Samuel Beckett.

Human Rights in South Asia
South Asian nations have commonly suffered under centuries of exploitation of man by man. The incongruity of social structure, varied religious groups, plethora of ethnic groups, sects, sub sects, tribes and clans make South Asia a very diverse society. The fragile democracy, repressive regimes, poverty, and illiteracy all add to the woes of the people of the region.

Most of the countries in South Asia are still governed by the archaic laws of the Raj. Some of the modern laws like the Prevention of Terrorism Act, POTA in India which detains a person indefinitely also have scant regard for human rights. Same is the case of Nepal where a person can be arrested up to three years under Public Security Act. With little variations, similar laws operate in other countries begging for judicial review.

Even though the periodicity of detainees may vary from country to country, all have one thing in common, to imprison a large number of people without trial. The constitutional guarantees only remain sacrosanct in the law books and common folk never have access to the same. The cumbersome judicial process and huge expenses incurred towards legal system makes undertrials languish in jails rather than approach for legal remedies.

South Asia's diverse social structure continues to witness societal tension unprecedented anywhere in the world. The number of deaths in communal and sectarian violence remains very high. If there is any place where systematic human rights violation continues then it's in this part of the world.

The brunt of the human rights violation is borne by the women folk of this subcontinent. The social and religious persecution spill over them and they are the worst sufferers of hate crimes. They are the first to be targeted in the sectarian and communal clashes. The traditional perception towards women remains unchanged despite modern advancement. Until recently the Hindu woman did not have the right to seek divorce by mutual consent. It's almost impossible for Indian Catholic women to obtain divorce under the present judicial system. The position of Muslim women is no better in India. The Shah Bano case in 1985 which sought alimony from the husband after divorce, created a national uproar in the country.

The question of political right of self-determination of nationalities and national groups too impinges upon human rights issue. The over-centralisation of the state structure creates centre-periphery problem and the periphery region suffering from the problem of maldevelopment asserts in violent forms. Their demand varies from autonomy to self-determination. The issue assumes greater complexities when we use the word people to imply religious, ethnic and linguistic groups.

India has made it clear that the right to self-determination cannot be made applicable to a section of people or a group of a sovereign independent state and all aspirations have to be met within the national framework. Notwithstanding this fact, the problem of Kashmir conflagrates around this theme and has assumed international dimension. The most ironical part amidst the conflicting claims on Kashmir human rights remain trampled in the beleaguered state.

Some other countries in South Asia are also plagued by the same problem. In Sri Lanka, Tamils in the northeast region demand the right to self determination alleging persecution by the Sinhalas. The Muslims living in the same area of Sri Lanka allege human right violation at the hands of Tamils. They too demand the same rights as demanded by the Tamils. So do the Chakma tribe living in Chitagong hills in Bangladesh. The Nepalese population in southern Bhutan too accuses its government of human rights violations.

In the name of self determination some radical elements unleash the reign of terror, indulging in wanton killing, extortion and other means of coercion. The brunt of their atrocities is borne by the civilian population. The classic cases in South Asia are the militancy perpetrated by the LTTE in Sri Lanka, ULFA in Assam and the various outfits in Kashmir.

Most of the countries in the region remain mired in insurgency related problem and their counter insurgency measures are not bereft of human rights abuse. The huge deployment of paramilitary forces and the enormous power at their command to keep the tinderbox in check at times result in human rights abuse in a very highhanded manner.

It is interesting to note that the neighbouring countries accuse each other of human rights violation. India raises the issue, of Christians, Mohajirs, Shias and Ahmedias being subjected to human rights abuse in Pakistan. Pakistan accuses India of abusing its minorities, marginalised section of society and curtailing their human rights. This blame game is played to cover up one's own human rights records and gain sympathy from domestic and international audience.

Another feature of human rights is its linkage with aid agencies. Various world bodies and donor countries have linked aid and assistance with human rights. Myanmar is one such country which has come under the cloud over its poor human rights record.

The point which the aid agencies miss is that the protection of human rights depends upon the level of economic development. Economic deprivation starts a chain of action and reaction resulting in human rights abuse. Moreover, the linking of aid with human rights is also seen as an infringement on the domestic affairs of the country.

Despite national differences at the United Nations, a beginning has been made towards containment of human rights violation by the women groups of South Asia. Their representation suggests a changing perception towards addressing the national problem in the regional context.

Similar attempts could be made to look into the complexities of the rights to self-determination. Instead of destabilising the region by accusing each other, an intra-regional commission on human rights could be mooted under the aegis of SAARC. Perhaps this could be a noble method to ensure human rights in South Asia.

Women Struggle in South Asia

South Asia has produced more women heads of states than any other regions of the world. Sirimavo Bandaranaike of Sri Lanka was the first woman prime minister of the world when she assumed office in 1959 after the assassination of her husband. Others who became head of the states are Indira Gandhi in India, Benazir Bhutto in Pakistan, Khaleda Zia, Shiekh Hasina Wajid in Bangladesh and Chandrika Kumaratunga in Sri Lanka. While Indira, Benazir, Hasina and Chandrika were all daughters of the head of states, Khaleda and Sirimavo are widows of head of states.

Apart from these big names and top families, there is complete marginalisation of women politicians and decision-makers at the grass-root level. Though there is no dearth of women activists in the region, only a few manage to climb up the political ladder. It is not the lack of talent or interests among women that has kept them away from the echelons of power. Rather there are a host of other reasons.

Many factors attribute to the low representation of women in the political sphere; social and cultural values of the women still restrain female to be confined to the households. The social esteem accorded to them is actually seen in relation to their husband and father. Women in public life are branded as unfeminine or of bad repute. The double workload of private and public life regardless of class and status, leaves women with little time and energy for sustained political activity. High level of illiteracy among female, use of money and muscle in politics, etc, are other factors that limit women's role in decision-making.

Sexual harassment and violence against women continues unabated despite all round progress being made in different direction in South Asia. At school and colleges females are subjected to eve teasing, while office going women are victim of sexual harassment by their male colleagues. Women become soft targets of sexual harassment during communal and sectarian riots.

The harassment of women continues at social level. They are frowned upon for not bearing male child and are looked down for remaining barren. Sati, dowry, divorce are other means by which women are harassed in the region. The most conspicuous harassment takes place in the rural milieu, particularly in agrarian setup where women who are landless labourers and farm workers are subjected to a great deal of exploitation.

Since these factors are common in most of the countries, it is increasingly realised that women must be given a special place in the political arena by all the governments in the region. Currently Bangladesh leads the list of women parliamentarians with 11.2 per cent. In India it is 7.2 per cent, Sri Lanka 4.8 per cent and in Pakistan it is 2.8 per cent.

Taking cognizance of the social pressure, some of the countries have taken steps to encourage women to enter politics. In Bangladesh, out of 330 parliamentary seats, 30 seats have been set aside for women. In Sri Lanka, the new constitution provides 25 per cent quota for women in provincial and local governments. In national assembly in Pakistan women representation is about 17 per cent. One third of all local councils seats in the Punjab province of Pakistan are reserved for women. In India, Tamil Nadu has become the first state to implement 33 per cent quota for women legislatures.

In India women groups have been trying to persuade political parties to back the proposal for 33 per cent reservation of seats in Parliament. Despite assurances from many political leaders no consensus has reached among the political parties. Some leaders argue that through such a quota, women belonging to upper caste and class may get higher representation. Others think that 33 per cent is very high figure for reservation of a single block in the 543 member lower house of Indian Parliament.

The irony is, the same politicians talk about having more number of women in elected bodies but when it comes to fielding them as candidates they shy away citing their inability to win election. This is an indicator of how Indian society treats its women. They are object of worship at one level, on other; they are being denied the right of social and political empowerment.

However, women have not lost the race in South Asia and continue to struggle for their social and political rights. The presence of many women politicians in their respective countries remain a source of inspiration for the entire womenfolk of the region. Their presence in politics signifies that women will continue their struggle till they acquire their rightful place in politics and society of South Asia.

Information Technology in South Asia

Today, we stand at the threshold of a transformed world, a world where distances have shrunk. So much so, that now it is possible to transcend the geographical boundaries and communicate any where without actually being present at the scene. The use of video satellite technology and computers to generate sound audio/video graphics, printed text materials, have all revolutionised the communication system in this human planet.

The cable TV boom has brought the entire world to one's doorstep through the news channels. The 9/11 attack, the Afghan war and the Iraq war were all watched by billions of viewers across the globe. With satellite networks beaming images, electronic mail transporting data, voice chat with video cam making live interaction possible, a new world has ushered in, which is quite different from the one we have witnessed a few years ago.

For the first time in the history of mankind, the new modes of communication network has brought both the developing and the developed world on one platform. The images of the developed world highlighting the progress made through industrialisation and modernisation and those of the developing world reflecting the vagaries of under development are being viewed at the same time. The pictures reflect the disparity between the developed and under develop worlds and have led to more vocal demand to bridge the gap between the two worlds.

The access to global newspapers on Internet, radio and television signals highlights the forces at work in different countries to the global audience. From Afghanistan to Iraq, Palestine to Kashmir, the world is alight through information highway. The pro-democracy movements, assertion of ethnic and sub-national identity are widely reported in today's world. In the age of information technology, every movement draws sustenance from other due to the cross flow of information from one country to the other.

As the world gets shrunk there is a general interest in issues that has created global following. The youth protest of Yangon in 1988; the pro-democracy movement at the Tiananmen square in China; the fall of the Berlin wall; the changes in Eastern Europe; the breakup of Soviet Union, all were followed by a large global audience. The images of 9/11, Afghan and Iraq wars, capture of Saddam Hussein, the tortures at Abu Ghraib prison, have left an everlasting impression on the people who are coming to terms with global realities.

In today's world, political boundaries are becoming redundant. A global generation is raised who belong to the global village. It's a large population which has grown up wearing blue jeans, reading same comics, watching same cartoons, eating same fast food. This SMS generation is not bound by national frontiers. The effect of electronic media on dress, culture, food has been phenomenal. It has ushered in a era of 'sexual revolution' that is helping to mitigate the gender inequality in the world.

The plethora of the electronic media since the early nineties in India has also created havoc on the insulated mindset of average Indians. This country is witnessing cataclysmic changes on its social and cultural scene. The advent of satellite TV has opened the flood gates that have drastically narrowed the journey from adolescence to adulthood.

Various soap operas dwell upon an entire gamut of topics that range from romance to dating, marriage to extra marital relationship. It is for the first time romance and sex are openly being debated on the small screen in India. Some of the soaps openly advocate inter-caste, inter-religion and interpersonal relationship cutting across cultural and linguistic barriers. The language and dialogues of some of them are so bold that the Indian audiences are taken aback by cultural shock.

Thanks to the various health and fitness programmes, the dress sense of the average Indian has changed in the big cities. A close look at the public places in the metros of India reflects how dress conscious the modern Indian has become, in the recent past. TV watching has made the current crop of Indian teenager more dynamic. Video jockeys and TV anchors have become their role models in terms of dress, language and style.

Many news channels in India have mushroomed in competition to BBC and CNN, to set the standards in news gathering. Never before have the images of real India etched on every Indian's mind with the TV reporters criss-crossing the entire length and breadth of the country with their camera crews. The free flow of information and communication in South Asia has highlighted its predicaments. The developments related to Kashmir, Tamils in Sri Lanka, nationalities issues in Pakistan, minorities in India all are keenly followed by the people of the entire region and globe.

The over lapping of population provoke sharp reaction in the neighbouring countries. This was seen in the reactions of Bangladesh and Pakistan to the communal riots breaking out in India. The attack on Tamils in Sri Lanka evokes similar reaction in the state of Tamil Nadu in India. The terror attack on Kashmiri Hindus inflames the passion in India against Pakistan. The media coverage aggravates the tension because the gory pictures shown on the television screens inflame emotions further.

In shaping the contours of South Asia, India has taken a lead in the field of information technology. India has forged ahead in the field of communication by establishing a countrywide network through National Information Center (NIC). The Education and Research Network (ERNET), links Indian educational infrastructures like Indian Institute of Technology (IIT), Tata Institute of Fundamental Research (TIFR), Indian Institute of Management (IIM), and others. The tele-communication infrastructure like mobile and Wireless Local Loop (WLL) phones have helped bridge the distance in India.

The Indian achievements in the communication and information technology should be replicated on the regional matrix of South Asia. The development of the region through use of modern means of communication can be mooted in addressing the common problems of hunger, poverty, illiteracy and population explosion in the region. Some peripheral beginning, through the exchange of newspapers, periodicals, journals and visual programmes has been made but more substantial networking is required in South Asia.

The high point of the communication revolution in South Asia is that private entrepreneurs operating in the region have already federated the region. They have unofficially declared South Asia as a regional entity even as officials of their countries are negotiating the nuts and bolts of this issue. Technology can put the region on a commendable position, providing economic sustenance and commercial identity. It is a tool that can be an effective equaliser in a pluralistic ambiance of South Asia. The regimes in South Asia have to take cognizance of these facts and act accordingly.

Economic Integration of South Asia

South Asia remains one of the most under developed regions in the world. The reason being that the moribund centrally administered economies have deliberately kept the growth rate in check. This was because privatisation would lead to capitalism which in turn would breed consumerism which was at one point of time considered a social taboo. However, after decades of reliance on the sluggish growth, South Asia is gingerly experimenting with the free market approach. A new sense of economic realism is percolating as the process of liberalisation and privatisation has ushered in a new confidence in the region.

The economic activities in South Asia are seen at two levels – one at the SAARC level, other between the six countries and India, which is their immediate neighbour. The volume of trade remains very low at the SAARC level due to political differences. The bilateral trade between India and its neighbours has grown over the years.

The encouraging symptom could be discerned in the India-Bangladesh trade pattern. Trade between the two countries is conducted in freely convertible currencies and in accordance with the foreign exchange regulation. India and Bangladesh have identified engineering goods, agriculture machinery, power generation, chemical drugs, plastics and allied items for trade. Besides, there are agreements for two wheelers and railway rolling stock. Indian export items to Bangladesh include plastic products, electronic machinery and fertilizers.

Bangladesh has a vast store house of natural gas, which India wants to import but Bangladesh has some reservations over this issue. It has been made public that without ascertaining its stocks of gas it would not make commitment about its exports. On the other hand, Bangladesh wants its non-traditional items like Jamdani sarees to be freed from duty in its export to India. There is an increasing trend to improve the economic relationship between the two countries.

The trade relation with Nepal and India continues with ebbs and flows. Custom regulation has been relaxed so that export and import between the two countries may get preference. There is no custom duty for all the items imported from Nepal to India. The Performa Clearance System has been done away with and Certificate of Origin is introduced for imports of Nepalese goods to India. As a result, imports from Nepal to India have picked up after falling to 50 per cent from 65 per cent.

To facilitate the volume of trade, Nepal's vehicle can freely ply from India's Haldia's port at Calcutta with regular permit to Nepal. India has also given access of its territory to Nepal to reach Chitagoan port of Bangladesh for import and exports of its goods. Beside, there are several joint ventures going on with Nepal and India. These include power projects for which funding are done by India.

The continued ethnic strife of Sri Lanka has adversely affected the economy of the island nation. Indian involvement in Sri Lankan ethnic strife in early eighties distanced the two countries from forging any economic linkages. With Chandrika Kumaratunga becoming the president, Sri Lanka launched some bold economic reforms geared to transform the island into one of the fast moving economies of the region. Several joint ventures with Indian public and private companies were kick-started to bring the island's economy back on rails.

Pakistan's economic base may be small in comparison to India but it has been pushing ahead to modernise its economy through liberalisation and privatisation. Pakistan has become the second most powerful economy in South Asia courtesy the aid and assistance it receives from outside. Even in the best of times, the volume of trade between India and Pakistan has remained very low. Some economic activities started during Rajiv Gandhi and Benazir era and continued during Narsimha Rao's and I K Gujral's time. During Nawaz Sharif regime trade and commerce picked up with India.

The political relation between India and Pakistan soured after the spate of terrorist activities sprouted, centering on Kashmir. The 13 December 2001 terror attack on the Indian Parliament led to the freezing of all bilateral relations and worst to suffer was the nascent trade between the two countries. With Manmohan Singh, who is hailed as father of India's economic reform, as prime minister, there is likelihood of improvement in economic relation between India and Pakistan.

In today's world where the dividing line between politics and economy is getting blurred and new alliances are motivated by opportunities of participation in market economy, the in South Asia remains stifled due to political differences. Even though bilaterally some countries are cooperating in terms of joint ventures there is hardly any increased attention towards regionalism.

There is no agreement among the nations about giving an economic personality to the whole region, even though there is a consensus about giving an impetus to their national economies through privatisation. Unfortunately, in an era where the governments are no longer in control of all the aspects of economy and trade, capital, labour, production and consumption, which have all gone beyond the pale of national consideration, there is no sign of economic regionalism emerging on the lines of the European Union in South Asia.

South Asia would become a much happier place to live in if the idea of giving precedence to economics over politics fructifies. South Asia as an economic block would help narrowing all political differences and make the region more peaceful and secure. The salvation of all South Asian countries thus lies in economic cooperation alone.

14
SAARC

* *Regionalism through SAARC* • *Economic Cooperation and SAARC* • *Bilateralism and SAARC* • *SAARC – Retrospect and Prospects* • *Sub-regionalism in South Asia*

Regionalism through SAARC

The latest trend in the world is to link nations into regions and the regions with rest of the world. This could be seen in the establishment of regional blocks and initiation of preferential trade policies. Be it Association of South East Asian Nation, European Union or North America Free Trade Area, no country is willing to limit their economic activities. The emergence of regional block and efforts being made to make them successful has become the order of the day.

The people of South Asian region are also attempting to share their experiences in addressing their common problem through South Asian Association of Regional Cooperation (SAARC). The seven nations that comprise SAARC are bounded by geographical contiguity, common cultural, ethnic and religious ties, but are plagued by political differences that come in the way of speedy development of SAARC.

SAARC owes its inception to the events in the early eighties when regional and global compulsions initiated Bangladesh, Bhutan, India, the Maldives, Nepal, Pakistan and Sri Lanka to join together in seeking solution to their common problem. The initiative was taken by the slained Bangladeshi President General Zia ur Rehman who was then looking for some bold foreign policy thrust to assert his shaky position. Whatever may be the reason, the concept of SAARC was lapped up by like-minded leadership who had emerged at that point of time in the region. The global power centres like the US and the UK also approved of the idea of the formation of SAARC.

Since the inception as regional body in 1985, SAARC has forged ahead and has covered a great deal of ground in the areas identified for cooperation. SAARC, by pushing ahead economic and other non-political agenda, prepared a climate for regional development. The inward looking economies of the region were given a new lease of life by the cautious process of opening up for regional cooperation.

There developed a broad agreement on peripheral economic cooperation among the South Asian states to expand and diversify intra-regional trade and commerce. The SAARC nations came to realized that the bane of underdevelopment could only be eradicated through regional cooperation. The initiatives like the South Asia Preferential Trade Agreement (SAPTA) and South Asia Free Trade Area (SAFTA) were steps in the direction of economic linkages of the region.

However, all through SAARC's history the conspicuous absence of a genuine climate of political trust is seen. The fragile nature of regimes is considered to be the single most factors that come in the way of forging a viable regional cooperation in South Asia. The political leadership, instead of endeavoring for efficient regional management, harp on factors that creates a wedge among nations for their own regime's survival.

Since the politics of many countries is guided by electoral considerations, the political leadership, find playing a jingoist national tune far more rewarding than telling their people the advantages of regional cooperation. The regimes prefer sharpening the differences to introducing reforms that could intensify regional cooperation.

The Indo-centric nature of SAARC is often considered to be the stumbling block in the promotion of regionalism. India accounts for three quarter of landmass, population and gross domestic product. Since India shares its borders with most of the countries of the region, the success of SAARC rest on the role and initiative that India takes in fostering closer ties with its neighbours. India's vast size, relative superior manpower and natural resources causes apprehension among smaller countries and India has to allay such feelings, highlighting the opportunities it has in store. India's cost effective technologies could be a great benefit to regional development.

In terms of transfer of technology, India is in a position to offer training facilities to apprentice from the neighbouring countries, at a fraction of cost given by the so called industrialised world. India's vast market provides ideal conditions for the entry of the goods by smaller neighbours, whose industrialisation process is severely limited by the size of their domestic market. India's role assumes enormous significance as the scope of SAARC widens.

In the course of various SAARC summits a great amount of economic will has been shown, despite political differences. It is being dreamt that SAARC could become a vehicle to integrate the regional economy where India's coal, Pakistan's cotton, and Bangladesh's jute can become the bedrock of economic cooperation. Bangladesh's achievement in population control and rural credit, Sri Lanka's breakthrough in education and recent economic reforms by India and Pakistan provide useful lessons in regional development.

The economic liberalisation has necessitated an increased role of private sector within the SAARC region. The formation of SAARC chamber of commerce has been a move to usher in a new era in privatisation in South Asia. The advancement in communication network started unofficial cooperation among the large pool of professionals within the region.

In terms of human resources and basic infrastructure there is every reason to turn this region into a dynamic partner with rest of the world. What is required is a coherent regional strategy to canalize interregional linkages at various other levels to strengthen the concepts of regionalism.

Some efforts have been made by the government through the formation of association of the SAARC parliamentarians. The lead initiated by the government has to be carried forward by the non-governmental organisations (NGO) by calibrating interaction at various levels. These NGO's in turn could become pressure groups and compel their governments to fall in line for the common well being of the people of the region. Unfortunately, South Asia's yearning for regionalism has a long way to go.

Economic Cooperation and SAARC

SAARC has come to acquire feets of its own, buttressed by the establishment of South Asia Free Trade Agreement (SAFTA), at the 12th SAARC summit at Islamabad in January 2004. The signing of South Asia Preferential Trade Agreement (SAPTA) in 1995 generated enough momentum at the subsequent SAARC summits that paved the way for the ratification of SAFTA. The lead was taken by the business community which indulged in continuous dialogue between the SAARC chambers of commerce to achieve the objective of SAFTA.

SAFTA was agreed to be made operational in 2003, calling for more transparent rule and regulation to facilitate free flow of goods and services in the region. With SAARC remaining a victim of bilateral wrangling between India and Pakistan, SAFTA remained sunken in cold storage. SAFTA became operational as a trade practice in the region only after India and Pakistan agreed to resume dialogue to sort out their outstanding issues at the 12th SAARC summit.

SAFTA was the result of the vehement demand to establish an equitable cooperation and mutually beneficial economic environment to push trade and commerce within the SAARC nations. The demand was also guided by the international situation which required urgency to achieve more progress towards intensification of economic cooperation to expand regional trade. SAFTA was preceded by South Asia Preferential Trade Agreement (SAPTA) which was signed in 1995 in New Delhi and became operational at Male in 1997.

The idea of SAPTA was mooted in the fourth SAARC summit at Islamabad, in 1989, where a consensus evolved for preferential trading among the countries of the region. The negotiations went on till the seventh summit at Dhaka in 1993, to decide on the items for preferential trading. Several rounds of bilateral and multilateral negotiations were made after which SAPTA was finally signed at the eighth SAARC summit at New Delhi.

It was largely Pakistan's lukewarm response that slowed down the pace of SAPTA. It had reservations since the beginning, for it feared that the introduction of preferential trading process would make Indian goods swamp the neighbouring markets and jeopardize the nascent manufacturing sector of other South Asian countries.

Pakistan wanted a sector wise approach for the number of items to be covered under preferential trading. However, a consensus evolved to follow a product-by-product approach for preferential trading and this was eventually agreed by Pakistan which gave its consent for SAPTA in 1995.

The initial rounds of tariff concessions were nominal and touched very insignificant items which were scheduled in seven lists. There were about 350-400 items suggested for tariff concession. India presented a list of 106 items, Pakistan's list contained 35 items, Sri Lanka's 31 items, Maldives 17, Nepal 14 Bangladesh 12 and Bhutan 7. Subsequently more items were included in the list for preferential trading.

However, differences emerged about the extent of SAPTA being beneficial to every country in the region. Apprehension persisted that India may institutionalise the tariff reduction to suit its own interests and SAPTA may become an instrument of economic exploitation by India. The smaller neighbours dreaded the idea of competing with the gigantic market of India and feared being reduced to a producer of raw material for finished products with the label 'made in India'. Pakistan's lukewarm approach to prepare the list of items on which it would like to give preferential treatment put a question mark on SAPTA.

These apprehensions did not deter the Committee on Economic Cooperation (CEC), comprising SAARC's commerce secretaries and ministers to work out the modalities for finalising the second round of list for preferential trading. The list covered broader range of products with a focus on selected commodities like textile, jute, tea and handicrafts. The CEC worked on to do away with the prevailing tariff concession on individual products and offer concessions covering a spectrum of items under a single head. It also formalised regionally accepted norms for the custom authorities at the transit points to facilitate regional trading.

In order to stabilise the trading arrangement, India initially preferred to ease tariff concessions. This helped to gain in long run due to the high quality of goods and the large volume of trade. Thus India provided ten to fifty per cent concession in its list to its neighbouring countries to reap the benefits of its vast market. It was a case for quantity and access.

The concession in tariff offered by India covered items of special relevance for its neighbours. There were products like cloves, nutmeg and rubber for Sri Lanka; fish products, fertilizers and leather items for Bangladesh; pistachios and dry fruits for Pakistan; scrap and fish preparation for the Maldives. On the contrary, the regional partners offered only marginal tariff reduction ranging from 5 to 15 per cent on the items to be included for the preferential trading.

India enjoys exceedingly large balance of trade among the SAARC countries. However, this remains only 3.5 per cent total trading within the SAARC region. India feels that in order to give a fillip to South Asian economic cooperation there must be higher level of tariff reduction to make it compatible with the global tariff rates.

Even though SAPTA and SAFTA have became operational by doing away with the prevailing cumbersome trade practices, a lot of bickering persists about commodities to be put under preferential trading list. The charter of SAPTA remains indecisive about its tariff rates. This is one reason why entire first scheduled list of SAPTA touched only 0.3 per cent of the total SAARC's regional trade.

The rationale behind SAPTA and SAFTA is that the vast market of India would be opened for smaller neighbours to market their products at a nominal tariff, and for India, neighbouring countries would become its extended market.

The momentum generated at the various SAARC summits towards economic integration though may be astonishingly slow but the signing of SAPTA and SAFTA suggest the free flow of goods and services could be a reality in the region. The economic consensus perhaps may lay the foundation of political differences to be ironed out and pave the way for South Asia to become a dynamic region in the world.

Bilateralism and SAARC

SAARC, the forum to bring the seven nations of South Asia from conflict to cooperation has covered considerable ground since its inception in 1985. However, despite an impressive track record, more meaningful cooperation among the South Asian countries still remains a distant dream.

Since the beginning, SAARC has been plagued by tensions from within, which could be attributed to multiple factors. The prominent one being the colonial legacy which bore heavily on the newly independent states. Since they developed their national identities in the course of defining their sovereignty, social, political and economic problems started surfacing in these countries.

A general thread running in the entire region was the Indian involvement. All the countries were over awed due to India's unique position in South Asia. India occupies more than 70 per cent of the region. Its contribution to the total GDP is 73 per cent. India accounts for 59 per cent of the regions' imports and 67 per cent of its exports.

The concept of SAARC, therefore, became inextricably woven into the matrix of bilateral relations. However, there remained inherent weakness in SAARC's policy as its Article-10 (General Provision) prohibits discussion of bilateral and contentious issues. This clause was set to allay apprehension that the forum may not be used as an anti-Indian platform, and also of suspicion that SAARC as a bloc may not be used by India to promote its own leadership. Issues of bilateral conflicts were kept out of SAARC's purview due to fear of regionalising them.

The unsolved problem of international land and maritime boundaries, resource sharing, ethno-religious conflict, refugees' problem, security concerns were some common problem in South Asia. Frequent border skirmishes between India and Bangladesh, the ongoing debate between Bhutan and Nepal over the refugee issue, the irritants in relations between India and Nepal over the open border, general disputes and other sporadic events have constrained the growth of regional cooperation.

India-Bangladesh relations centres on water sharing, delimitation of land boundary, maritime assets and propriety of Talpatty Island. Trade and transit interests and power projects come in way of India-Nepal relations. India and Sri Lanka may have narrowed their differences over Tamil issue, but remain at odds over the fishermen problem, Tamil refugees and ownership of Kachatheevu Island.

The economic imbalance of South Asian countries hampers smooth functioning of SAARC. India's resource base and economic potentialities leads to apprehension that once the trade barriers are removed, Indian goods would swamp the markets of smaller countries of the region. However, it is the deep mistrust between India and Pakistan, particularly over Kashmir and its corollary as cross border terrorism, which has greatly undermined the growth of SAARC as a regional body.

Bilateral problems, which is chronic in the region, has often led to postponement of SAARC summits. The 11th SAARC Summit, scheduled to be held in November 1999, got postponed and eventually was held at Kathmandu in April 2002. Similarly, the 12th summit slated to be held in Islamabad in January 2003, finally was held in January 2004.

It is well known that bilateral tension among the South Asian countries is the formidable barrier to the growth of SAARC. Hitherto, it's realised that SAARC may not achieve its desired goal without harmonising the bilateral irritants. A consensus is emerging that bilateral problem among the SAARC countries should be discussed by widening the scope of SAARC. To make SAARC functional, the forum could be utilized to solve bilateral tensions which are causing impediments to SAARC's growth.

The Sri Lankan President Chandrika Kumaratunga gave vent to this thought at the 10th SAARC Summit where she underscored the need for discussing political issues, bilaterally or multilaterally, as they pose serious impediments towards building a climate of cooperation in the region. She insisted that SAARC must sit together even without either one – India or Pakistan – if such a case arises.

Mrs Kumaratunga emphasised that without getting contentious issues out of the way, or substantially diluting their impact, a wholehearted commitment to the lofty goals of SAARC would remain a mere wishful thinking.

SAARC made some attempt to reduce regional tensions by offering its forum to discuss ethnic strife in Sri Lanka and moderate the Indo-Pak differences. SAARC discussed the regional action plan concerning Himalayan river water resources and succeeded in making India and Pakistan avoid double taxation on bilateral trade and also help them to initiate cultural exchanges. However, these achievements are minuscule compared to the differences that persist among the nations on bilateral issues.

If SAARC has to move forward in the evolving intra-regional world order, it has to evaluate why it has failed to break the barriers of nation states and why it is unable to evolve an integrated regional personality as yet. The general perception is that bilateral tensions remains SAARC's Achilles heel and unless it is not ironed out, SAARC would remain a forum of periodic meeting of the head of the states. Despite the most sincere efforts, the record of SAARC in terms of its achievement is far from being outstanding.

There is a growing consensus that most intractable problems in South Asia could be settled by agreeing on certain broad principles within the regional framework. This will help not only in achieving regional cohesion, but also strengthening regional identity, enhancing regional security and propelling regional growth and development, which are the cornerstones of prosperity. If the future aim is regionalism then SAARC alone may help realise this dream.

SAARC – Retrospect and Prospects

As SAARC completes more than fifteen years of existence, to weigh the predicaments and prospects of the regional body would be prudent. The history of SAARC could be divided into four phases. The first phase 1985-90, was marked by great deal of enthusiasm to make SAARC operational; the second phase 1990-95, was marked by an economic agenda dominating the SAARC's proceedings; in the third phase 1995-2000, the pace of regional body slowed down as bilateral tension gripped the SAARC. The current and the fourth phase find SAARC getting rejuvenated again.

First Phase: 1985-89

Ever since the establishment of SAARC in 1985, serious attempts were made among the countries to formulate an integrated plan of regional action. The creation of a food security reserve, suppression of terrorism, people to people contact and common development programme were mooted during the first phase of SAARC summit. A great deal of enthusiasm was shown during this phase to push ahead the concept of regional cooperation.

The first summit held at Dhaka (7-8 December 1985) planned cooperation in agriculture, rural development, telecommunication, meteorology, health and population. Its ambit was extended to areas like sports, arts, culture, postal services, transport and science. In addition, SAARC members decided to link South Asian capitals through direct air services. They also agreed to a limited convertibility of currency to facilitate regional tourism. SAARC chairs were created in some universities of the member countries.

At the second summit held at Bangalore (16-17 November 1986), SAARC leaders endorsed to intensify economic cooperation. Here, it was agreed to implement an integrated plan for regional development and SAARC leaders called upon industrialised nations for rapid technological transfer to the developing states.

The third summit held at Kathmandu (2-4 November 1987), resulted in the establishment of the SAARC secretariat. An agreement was signed for suppression of terrorism and establishment of South Asian food security zone. SAARC leaders stressed the need to coordinate their national policies with a view to expand regional cooperation.

The SAARC summit in 1988 was postponed due to an abortive terrorist's coup in the Maldives and the presence of IPKF in Sri Lanka.

The fourth summit was held in Islamabad (29-31 December 1989), where the SAARC leaders called for efforts to study the causes and consequences of natural disaster and protection of environment. There was agreement on basic issues of food, clothing, shelter, education, primary health and population planning. The year 1989 was dedicated as SAARC Year of Combating Drug Abuse and Drug Trafficking.

Second Phase: 1990-94

During the second phase there emerged economic nuances of SAARC leading to formation of SAARC Chamber of Commerce and a consensus being evolved on South Asian Preferential Trade Agreement (SAPTA). The year 1990 and the decade of the nineties were dedicated as the 'SAARC years for the girl child'.

The fifth SAARC summit was held in Male on 21-23 November 1990 where four important institutions; Agriculture Centre at Dhaka, Human Resources Development Centre at Islamabad, Regional Tuberculosis Centre at Kathmandu and Regional Documentation Center at New Delhi were opened. An agreement was signed on narcotics and psychotropic substances. A special travel scheme was launched which exempted the formalities of obtaining visas within SAARC nations.

The sixth summit in Colombo, held on 21-22 December 1991, gave an economic twist to SAARC. Manufacturing services and industrial ventures were given a boost to start peripheral economic cooperation. SAARC stressed the need to expand the scope of joint ventures, buy back agreements, and joint marketing. The seeds of South Asian Preferential Trade Agreement (SAPTA) were laid at the Colombo summit.

The seventh SAARC summit which got postponed in 1992, eventually was held on 10-11 December 1993 in Dhaka. There, a consensus was reached to finalise the items to be covered under preferential trading. Pakistan initially showed apprehension towards SAPTA but later agreed to the preferential trading arrangement. The Dhaka summit laid stress on increasing the productive capacity of the region. Further, the Dhaka summit laid special emphasis on regional poverty alleviation programme and an agreement was reached to establish the South Asia Development Fund (SADF).

Third Phase: 1995-1999

In this phase, SAARC was seen taking off well in the beginning with the Delhi declaration in 1995 and making the preferential trade agreement SAPTA operational at Male in 1997. But SAARC's stock nose-dived in 1999 at Colombo where head of the states met for the first time after India-Pakistan demonstrated their nuclear powers in 1998. The increased tension between the two countries was evident when then Pakistan's Prime Minister Nawaz Sharif dubbed SAARC as a 'meaningless exercise.' Two SAARC summits in 1996 and 1998 were skipped due to continued bilateral wrangling.

The eighth summit which was postponed in 1994 was held on 2-4 December 1995 in New Delhi. In that summit there was a general consensus on removing trade barriers and improving trade and transit facilities in the region. SAARC leaders pleaded for cooperation in the area of science and technology and envisaged networking in the field of biotechnology and genetic engineering. They endorsed programmes for protection of environment, global peace, non-proliferation of nuclear regime and disarmament. Delhi summit showed concern towards increasing trade in narcotics, linkages between drug trafficking and organised crime, illicit arms trade and narco-terrorism.

The ninth SAARC summit was held on 12-14 December 1997 in Male where the South Asian Preferential Trade Agreement was finally made operational. The SAARC leaders there pledged to establish South Asia Free Trade Area (SAFTA) as a logical corollary to SAPTA.

The tenth SAARC summit in Colombo 29-31 December 1998 was held in the backdrop of nuclear tests conducted by India and Pakistan. This led the Sri Lankan President Chandrika Kumaratunga to advocate making use of SAARC as a forum for conflict resolution and discussing bilateral tensions to keep the momentum of regional body alive.

Fourth Phase: 2000-

This phase was marred by the Kargil incursion in 1999 and military coup in Pakistan by General Pervez Musharraf. This led to the postponement of SAARC summit in 2000. The failure of Agra summit between India and Pakistan on 14 July 2001 and terror attack on the Indian Parliament on 13 December 2001 further postponed the summit. The 11th SAARC summit finally was held on 4-6 April 2002 at Kathmandu. The summit was held in the backdrop of eyeball to eyeball positioning between Indian and Pakistani troops on the Line of Control (LoC) following 13 December Parliament attack. The summit also took place in the backdrop of the massacre of entire royal family of Nepal in a case of patricide on 1 June 2001. There weren't any major highlights in this summit except for General Musharraf's impromptu gesture on stage – shaking hand with Prime Minister Vajpayee.

The 12th SAARC summit which was scheduled for January 2003 finally was held on 4-6 January 2004 at Islamabad. The 12th SAARC summit was historic in many a sense. The soured bilateral relationship between India and Pakistan breathed a new lease of life when Prime Minister Vajpayee agreed to travel to Pakistan to attend the summit. History was made when Pakistan agreed to ratify South Asia Free Trade Agreement (SAFTA) at the 12th SAARC summit at Islamabad. But the path breaking moment came when India and Pakistan agreed to resume the dialogue process to resolve all their differences, including vexed issue of Kashmir.

The direction in which SAARC is moving, though gingerly, indicates that South Asia one day would assume an integrated personality of its own. However, its future lies on how SAARC unfolds in times ahead and mainly depend upon its approach to address their bilateral problems. Here it would be appropriate to suggest that, having Afghanistan and Myanmar within the SAARC's ambit may make SAARC broader and neutralise its tag of being India-Pakistan centric. These countries being on the frontiers of South Asia may facilitate SAARC in intra-regional cooperation, which in turn will open opportunities for further development of the region.

The business community in South Asia is agog to the reality of having high stakes in strengthening the bonds of regionalism. They are marching ahead to take the initiative from their governments. However, the political leadership is still unaware of the costs of non-cooperation. Their indifference to the narrowing of bilateral differences may serve short-term interests, but in the long run, their action remains detrimental to the regional growth.

It is highly significant that SAARC remain operational even when there is continued tension or there is a thaw in bilateral relationship in the region. It kindles the hope that SAARC could generate enough momentum to help develop a regional personality of South Asia.

Sub-regionalism in South Asia

Unhappy with the slow paced progress of SAARC, the idea of Sub- regional grouping in the eastern region of South Asia is being propounded. The lead is taken by the Indian Chamber of Commerce which is vociferously selling the concept sub-regionalism within South Asia. This comprises India's eastern states and northeast region along with Nepal, Bhutan, Bangladesh and Myanmar. The Asian Development Bank too has taken cognisance of the potential of this subregion and since 1997 has been advocating the case of South Asian Sub-regional . The foreign ministers of Bangladesh, Bhutan, India and Nepal have also given consent to the cause of South Asia quadrangle to give boost to economic cooperation within this region.

There are very impressive statistics for the natural reserves in this region. The entire region is a storehouse of abundant natural resources and untapped natural beauty. A large chunk of South Asia's natural wealth, be it coal, iron ore, bauxite, limestone, oil, natural gas, bamboo, agricultural products, lies in this region. It is being increasingly realised that, given the right initiative, the region could compete more astoundingly than in the framework of SAARC.

The eastern and northeastern states of India, if seen in isolation, constitute one of the poorest regions in the world. The northeast states have a history of insurgency and low level of growth and development. West Bengal suffers from over flow of labour force, Bihar and Jharkhand are known for social unrest, Orissa makes headlines for natural calamity or starvation deaths. There is little private investment and indigenous entrepreneurial spirit remains stifled in the region.

On the contrary, if the same region is viewed in totality, then it is found to be richly endowed with natural resources. West Bengal is India's largest producer of rice and fish, Bihar and Jharkhand is the richest state in terms of minerals and natural resources. Orissa is a treasure trove of historic monuments and exotic beaches. The 'seven sisters' of the northeastern region together with Sikkim and Bangladesh have untapped potential for tourism. The eastern rivers; Ganges, Teesta Brahmaputra, Meghna, comprise one of the wealthiest water resources and have potential of generating hydro-electricity which could become a 'powerhouse' in South Asia.

Given the right kind of infrastructure, investment, government initiative and information network, these states have high potential in terms of all round development. If the neighbouring countries; Nepal, Bangladesh, Myanmar and Bhutan were to economically linked with these states, the subregion can emerge as a formidable economic hub within South Asia.

The Indian Chamber of Commerce has put forward its suggestions before the Indian government to draw out the advantages of the region and reap its bounties. It has proposed to declare the northeast region a special economic zone and to integrate this subregion with the proposed Asian Highway, which is part of 'India's Look East' policy.

India is contemplating the revival of the historic Stillwell Road built by the British to create a road link between India and Myanmar during World War II. The road begins from Assam, passes through Arunachal Pradesh and upper Myanmar's Kachin state before ending in China's Yunnan province.

The road, however, has fallen into disuse and the seven northeast states have been demanding its reopening. The chief ministers of the region submitted a joint proposal to the Union government in 2002, to reopen the road to attract tourists and to increase trade with Southeast Asian countries.

The Indian Prime Minister Atal Behari Vajpayee, in his tour of Southeast Asian countries in 2002, had also laid stress on sharpening the nuances of India's Look East policy to bring the country closer to the Southeast Asian nations. Vajpayee in his deliberations had mentioned the grandiose scheme of an Asian highway that would change the face of the region. Former External Affairs Minister, Jaswant Singh, during his visit to Myanmar too had stressed the need to open the road links between the two countries to buttress economic cooperation.

Once the construction of the Asian highway is complete, the distance between India and the Southeast countries would shrink fantastically. Southeast Asian countries can become motor-able from India because there already exits a link road between Myanmar and Thailand which further stretches up to Yunnan province of China. In such case it would be possible to drive on the Asian highway from Afghanistan and westward to South China via India Myanmar and Thailand.

The necessity is being felt to draw out the advantages of geography and look at this subregion as a separate unit within South Asia. If this region operates as an economic zone, rapid trade and commerce would make it develop by leaps and bounds. This in turn would stamp out the scourge of underdevelopment from this part of the world

However, there are many bottlenecks in the development of such regional groupings. Unless a broad consensus emerges within respective government to harmonise their policies, this concept of sub-regional grouping may take time to evolve.

15
Resounding on South Asia

South Asia presents a picture of bewildering diversity. There is a schism of every kind present in the region, each nation has a different perception about the other. All the countries are engaged in the zero-sum game, where one's gain is the other's loss. Then there are certain myths being floated; like India being a weakling state, Pakistan a failing state, Bangladesh a hungry state. The biggest myth being India is blocking peace in the subcontinent. Inevitably these perceptions make regional reconciliation a difficult proposition.

Much of the tenure of present day antagonism has sprung due to the uni-focal approach to the nation building in South Asia. The current crop of leadership has almost brainwashed the present generation, so much so, that any talk of knitting the region together is considered as sacrilegious. However, underlying the diversities, there also nestles some remarkable degree of regional coherence. The irony is, more the diverse features are sharpened; more the regional coherence are lamented upon.

The future of South Asia cannot be de-linked from the global security environment. The war in Iraq has conclusively proved that US is the only superpower which would continue to maintain its supremacy in decades to come. The continued interest of the US in West Asia would maintain its military deployment on the Arabian Sea. The vast oil gas reserve in Arabian Peninsula and the Central Asian republics would entice US involvement in South Asian politics. So any security arrangement in the region cannot be accomplished without the tacit support of the US.

The other external player in the region is China, whose ambition is to be a global power. China's security concern is related to nuclear Russia on to its north, Japan in the east, United States in the Western Pacific and India to its south. In South Asia, the Chinese ring is all pervasive as Beijing remains the main supplier of arms to most of India's neighbours.

China has many unresolved problems with India, including the boundary disputes and the nuclear issue. India justified its nuclear weapons programme by conducting Pokhran II tests, saying its security threats directly emanated from China. The strategic disharmony that exists between India and China remains one of the biggest hurdles in achieving regional stability.

In order to make the region a peace dividend, India and China need to discuss the missile production and deployment issue and evolve a framework to resolve the boundary dispute. The two countries also have to talk about the level of deployment of conventional forces on their borders. Any comprehensive security plan in South Asia cannot be accomplished without the active participation of China.

Then, the conflict resolution between India and Pakistan is central to peace and stability in South Asia. There are three options before India to ensure peace in the region. It can either subjugate Pakistan or further fracture it, and if both cannot be done, then work in tandem with Pakistan and strive for peace and stability in the region.

Subjugating Pakistan could only be possible by going for a full-fledged nuclear war. However, given the uni-polar world, where US remains an ally of Pakistan and China playing a supportive role, Indian leadership needs to think over before war mongering and raising its volume to a deafening pitch.

Even if India achieves an outright victory over Pakistan, will it be interested in having a high deployment of security forces to keep such a region under its control? The sheer cost of maintenance of such a huge territory and resultant demographic metamorphosis, not to speak of social and other factors would be reasons enough for Indian leadership to detest from beating war drum. The geo-strategic reality of Pakistan and its nuclear capability should make

Indian leadership think hard enough before trumpeting any military adventurism.

The option to fracture Pakistan through a swift military action would also trigger a full fledged war. Even if India in this case achieves its objective, it would make Pakistan a further unstable country. A friendly and stable Pakistan would be far more preferable for India than an enemy state with nuclear capabilities close to its borders.

India's options are few; for war mongers it should be made clear that even though the military balance may be tilted in India's favour, it lacks clear-cut military superiority over Pakistan. The huge expenses of war, lack of external powers support, Pakistan's nuclear capabilities all call for refraining from any war mongering.

The only option for India is to work in tandem with Pakistan to bring regional stability. The responsibility also falls on Pakistan which has to accept India's position of a regional leader and act with it in close cooperation in pursuing such option. Pakistan also has to refrain from pursuing any policy that may harm Indian interests.

However, the third option can only be possible if there emerges an amicable solution to the Kashmir problem. The history of the last fifty years suggests that route to peace and stability in South Asia passes through Kashmir. India and Pakistan and people of Kashmir are the makers or wreckers of peace in South Asia.

If one goes by the global mood, it is clear that, if the regional players are unable to resolve the Kashmir issue, then the external actors would hand over a solution which may not be in the best interests of all the parties concerned. It therefore serves no one's interest to prolong the Kashmir problem.

The acquisition of nuclear weapon by India and Pakistan has created new challenges in South Asia. Some justify the 'bomb', saying it gives power, political leverage, reduced spending on conventional weapons and acts as deterrence. Others call it as sheer madness, pointing towards the enormous expenditure in pursuing the nuclear weapons programme. At the same time they warn about the adverse effects on the living being, in case the 'bomb' is used as a tactical weapon to win a war.

While India's nuclear programme is for acquiring regional superiority and to allay threat perceptions from China, it is the deep-rooted fear from India which seems to be the primary reason for Pakistan's nuclear choice. Both the states have a very amorphous nuclear policy and no clear-cut strategic doctrine for the use of their nuclear weapons. India had been talking about 'no first use' but after 13 December 2001 Parliament attack, it has backtracked from this position and has kept its nuclear options open. An early agreement on nuclear confidence building measures between India and Pakistan is must for regional stability.

There is also a need to address the total strategic disharmony that exists in the region. China has an aspiration to be a global power; India wants to be regional power while Pakistan's design is to deny India any regional superiority. The gap between India and China is enormous, and so is the bridge between India and Pakistan. It's a mad race in which all these three countries are involved and there is a dire need to stop it at once.

In post nuclear South Asia there is an urgent need for confidence-building measures between India and China and India and Pakistan to remove strategic disharmony and achieve peace and stability in the region.

Another feature in South Asia is the very close civil and military relationship. In Pakistan the military has extensive involvement and remains the single most powerful institution. Military agencies in Bangladesh too exercise important influence in national politics. In India, Nepal and Sri Lanka, the military plays an apolitical role but they remain indispensable due to continued internal and external insecurity concerns.

The sustenance of the military machine is heavily dependent on the import of military hardware from outside the region. This brings into picture the role of global armament industry which is constantly undergoing rapid technological changes. Almost all the nations in South Asia are heavily dependent on arms import, which they have to periodically upgrade in order to keep pace with the changes in technology. A vicious circle has thus developed in the region between insecurity and armament purchase.

It would be benign to accept that there are no vested interests among the so-called developed nations to keep the insecurity scenario boiling in the region. Any attempt towards demilitarisation is bound to attract opposition from those whose economy survives on armament exports. This glaring fact has to be taken into account while making any long-term peace arrangement in the region.

In South Asia, there is tension between India and smaller states. Each country has some conflict with India since they share a common boundary. India's size, population, resources and economy is source of envy to other smaller states. India's emphasis on bilateralism is viewed by its neighbours as a policy designed to keep them isolated. The geo-political realities inhabit creative thinking about improvising the future of the region. Unfortunately there exist no conflict resolution mechanism between the contending nations in the region.

SAARC, as a regional forum has been able to create some degree of consensus in taking a collective action on certain issues, but has been a total failure in addressing the issues of regional conflict. The irony is, SAARC is the only forum to mediate between India and its neighbours but remains constrained due to India and Pakistan tension. The concept of third party mediation is treated with disdain, Sri Lanka being an exception.

The region is witnessing gradual rise in communalism, regionalism and sectarianism. All the countries are under the grip of ethnic, sectarian and sub-national conflict. Unconventional conflict like insurgency and terrorism has been raising its ugly head. Such conflicts mainly arise due to deliberate discrimination by the states towards their specificities. The disgruntled elements find sympathisers from outside their national boundaries. This vitiates the security environment in the region. Much of the internal peace and stability would depend upon the approach the South Asian regimes adopt towards integrating their ethno-religious plurality.

There is shockingly low level of human development in the region as all the regimes have consciously neglected evolution of human security management. Human insecurity revolves around low income, poverty, illiteracy and unemployment. Children, women and the aged are the worst sufferers of this neglect.

Terrorism, sectarian conflict and natural disaster add on to the human woes.

Since none of the countries have made any arrangement of human security, the problem of migration and refugees looms large in the region. A carefully crafted human security plan may solve many of the problems that seemingly remain a source of bilateral conflict in the region.

Another redeeming feature is that, even though geographical lines have been drawn in the name of nation states, the entire region breathes the same air, drink the same water and till the same soil. They all live in the same socio-cultural firmament, sharing the vagaries of the nature and enjoying the benefits of common genetic memory. The dense fog in the winters, late arrival of monsoons, polluted rivers, felling of the trees, are all cause of common environmental concern. Surprisingly, it has not yet dawned upon the leadership to collectively strive for environmental security in the region.

In South Asia, some areas have problem of plenty while others suffer from scare resources. This peculiar development is present in all the nations where the area around the seat of power is much more developed than its periphery. There remains a huge potential for developing some areas in the region by augmenting its inherent economic strength. However, there is no comprehensive developmental plan ever being thought of for the periphery of the region.

There have been talks about formation of a sub-regional grouping in the northeast area of South Asia. This sub-regional grouping comprises India's eastern and northeast region, along with Bangladesh, Bhutan and Myanmar. This idea was mooted to mitigate the problem of underdevelopment. However, after the exploratory talks were held with the Asian Development Bank (ADB) in 1997, not much has happened about subregion grouping in South Asia.

The seven nations of South Asia have still to come to terms with peace. The subcontinent's preoccupation with past prejudices continues. Legacies of colonialism still haunt the region even though more than fifty years have elapsed since the de-colonisation of the subcontinent. The links between national and regional issues are yet to be established and there are practically no adherents for a comprehensive security plan for the region as a whole.

It would be diabolic to keep the peace process hostage in South Asia till India becomes invincible or Pakistan vanquishes India. History suggests that both countries have no other option than to reconcile to the existing realities and put a stop to the unhealthy competition of hating each other. The need is to roll down the sleeves, and work out a long-term regional peace plan with the support of US and China.

A logical step would be to establish a culture of peace and stability first and then start a meaningful dialogue at the bilateral and multilateral level to sort out the regional differences. The removal of the political differences is the first and foremost requirement for moving towards a meaningful regional cooperation. The second aspect should be to highlight the importance of economic development, human security and other facets of unity by recognising the common regional identity. Then there is a need to evolve the concept of regional security and agree to respect each others territorial sovereignty.

All this requires toning down of religious and national identity and acceptance of the over arching pan-South Asian identity. The simple logic is, as an individual each nation remains vulnerable but in combination they make a formidable force. If European Union can become a viable option then why a South Asian Union cannot become a United States of South Asia (USSA)? However, as long as the region remains engaged in a tug of war between nationalism and regionalism, the vision to make South Asia a singular regional identity would continue to be blurred.

The United Progressive Alliance (UPA) government which has came to power in May 2004 in India, has released a Common Minimum Programme (CMP) of governance, which also outlines the contours of foreign policy of the country. The new government under Manmohan Singh pledges to give top priority to build closer political, economic and cultural ties with all South Asian countries and remains committed to strengthen them more.

The CMP says that dialogue with Pakistan on all issues will be pursued systematically and on a sustained basis. On Sri Lanka, it supports peace talks that fulfill the legitimate aspirations of Tamils and other religious minorities within territorial integrity and solidarity of the island nation. With Bangladesh, it remains committed to resolve all outstanding issues and with Nepal it would like to initiate an intensive dialogue for developing water resources to create mutual advantages. The CMP says that it is committed to pursue border talks with China seriously and expand trade and investment with Beijing.

It seems that with the dawn of the new century, the frozen relationship among the South Asian countries has started melting. It remains to be seen how fast it may take closer to the vision of a South Asian Union. At this moment, pessimism and hope simultaneously thrive as soundings on South Asia.

Index

Abdul Ghani Lone, 51, 52, 53, 54
accession issue of Hyderabad, 41
accession issue of J&K, 41
Afghanistan, 150-162
    Ahmad Shah Masood, 151
    Dostum, 150
    involvement of Pakistan, 151
    Kashmir, 152
    King Zahir Shah, 151
    Mazar-i-Sharif, 150
    Mujahideen, 150
    Najibullah, 150
    Operation Enduring Freedom, 153, 160
    President Bush, 153, 160, 162
    reconstruction of, 152, 153, 154, 157
        9/11 attack, 35, 151, 152, 160
        Al-Qaeda, 151, 152, 160
        ethnic groups, 154
        Hamid Karzai, 153, 154
        Mullah Omar, 153, 160
        Osama bin Laden, 152, 153, 160
        US bombing, 153
        war against global terrorism, 153, 162
        warlords, 151, 154
    Russian interest in Afghanistan, 155-156
    Soviet withdrawal, 150-152
    Shias-Sunnis, 151
    Taliban, 150, 152
    tribal rivalry, 162
    Xinjiang province, 152
Agra summit of 2001, 30, 39, 44, 168, 209
All Pakistan Mohajir Student
    Organisation (APMSO), 18
Altaf Hussain, 19, 22, 23, 24
American interest (Kashmir issue), 33
armed struggle, 3, 4, 31, 56, 67, 69, 96, 162
arms import, 217
arms negotiations, 4
Article 370, 47
Asian Development Bank (ADB), 219
attack on Indian Parliament, 28, 30, 33, 45

autonomy, 2, 10, 45, 49, 56, 139, 178, 187
    administrative, 57
    geographical, 178
    political, 2

Baluchis, 2, 23, 165
Bangladesh, 95-109
    anti-India, 99, 101
    Awami League party, 96
    Bangladesh National Party (BNP), 98
    British secret documents, 95
    creation of Bangladesh, 95
        role of India, 98
    General Mohmmad Ershad, 99
    General Zia-ur-Rehman, 99
    Hasina Wajid, 98, 99
    Health Care, 107
    Indian military intervention, 95
    Jamaat-e-Islami, 100
    Khaleda Zia, 98, 99
    refugees, 2, 98
    supply natural gas to India, 100
    Zafrullah Choudhary (father of
        Bangladesh health care policy), 107
Benazir Bhutto, 43
Bhutan, 124-138
    census, 125, 126
    China's expansionism, 124
    code of Bhutanisation, 125
    code of conduct, 126
    constitution, 130
    constitutional monarchy, 126
    democracy, 126
    Drukpas, 124, 125, 131
    identity crisis, 124-126
    illegal immigrants, 125, 131
    influx of Nepali population, 124
    Lhotsampas tribe, 131, 132
    pro-democracy movement, 126-129
    Refugees Issue, 124, 125, 131, 132

Index

Royal Bhutan Army, 137, 138
Tibet, 124
bus services between Delhi and Lahore, 29

Chakma problems, 3, 102, 164, 166, 184, 180
Chandrika Kumaratunga, 196
Changing Profile (Indian Muslims), 14-17
   anti-Muslim politics, 16
   Babri mosque, 16
   Dalit-Muslim configuration, 16
   Godhra carnage, 16
   migration to Pakistan, 14
   Mumbai bomb blast, 16
   Muslim vote, 15
   voting pattern of Muslims, 15
China
   external player in South Asia, 215
   main supplier of arms, 5, 164, 215
Cold War, 31, 51, 70, 71, 155, 163, 172
Common Minimum Programme (CMP), 220, 221
communal riots, 14, 47
complete autonomy (Muslim), 10
complete autonomy (Tamils), 56
composite dialogue, 26, 28, 29, 31, 34, 38, 39, 44, 45
   bilateral talks, 34
CTBT, 33, 172, 173
Congress, 9, 10, 26, 27, 33, 40
creation of Pakistan, 11, 13, 23, 181
cross border terrorism, 3, 33, 205

D S Senanayake, 71
defence spending
   Bangladesh, 4, 163
   India, 4, 163
   Nepal, 4, 163
   Pakistan, 4, 163
   Sri Lanka, 4, 163
demand for Pakistan, 10-12
disharmony between India and China, 215

economic cooperation 5, 37, 39, 120, 135, 147, 197-203, 207, 208, 211, 213
Elephant Pass, 59
environmental problems, 6
ethnic movement, 178-179
ethnic plurality, 1, 151, 181

Farraka barrage, 5
forces of conflict, 1, 7
freely convertible currencies, 195

Gandhi, Mohandas Karamchand, 8
General Ayub Khan, 18, 43
General Zia ul Huq, 18, 32
Genesis of Kashmir Issue, 40
genesis of Pakistan, 27
global armament industry, 217
growing dissatisfaction (Muslims), 9
Gujarat riots, 2
Gujral Doctrine, 73, 118, 121, 166, 167

hate campaign, 28
highjacking (Indian Airlines plane IC814), 30
Hizbul Mujahideen, 48, 53
Human Rights, 186-189
Hurriyat Conference, 49, 50, 51, 54

India-Afghan Relation, 154-157
   cross border terrorism, 157
   fall of Najibullah, 156
   Kashmir, 152, 155, 157
   New Delhi-Kabul-Moscow, 156
   reconstruction of Afghanistan, 155
India-Bangladesh, 101-104
   anti-India activities, 103
   Bangla Bandhu, 101
   Chakma, 3, 102, 166
   creation of Bangladesh, 96-98
   gas, 104
   human rights, 104
   illegal immigrants, 3, 102, 105, 106
   northeast insurgency, 3
   Talpati or New Moore Island, 165
   water sharing, 3, 99, 102, 165, 166, 205
India-Bhutan Relations, 133-138
   anti-Bhutanese activities, 135
   anti-Indian militants, 135-136
   Chinese threat, 135
   enhanced economic assistance package, 135
   Gorkhaland Liberation Front (GLF), 134
   Greater Nepal, 134
   Indo-Bhutanese treaty of friendship, 133
   Operation All Clear, 135-138
      cease-fire call by ULFA, 137
   King Jigme Singye Wangchuk, 136, 137
India-Maldives Relations, 92-94
   bilateral trade, 93, 120
   economic cooperation, 92
   Maldives Institute of Technical Education (MITE), 92
India-Myanmar Relations, 147-149
   bilateral agreement, 148
   development of northeast region, 147

contain China, 147
India's Look East foreign policy, 147
maintenance of human rights, 148
India-Nepal Relations, 117-123
  AIDS, 119
  anti-India activities, 122, 123
  China factor, 120, 121-123
  environmental issue, 119
  Gujral doctrine, 118, 121
  harnessing of water resources, 118
  illegal border trade, 119
  King Tribhuvan, 121
  Maoist insurgency, 122, 123
  most favoured nation (MFN), 120
  plane highjacked, 122
  trade and transit treaty, 3, 119, 120, 166
India-Pakistan
  bilateral talks, 42-46, 168
  conflict resolution, 215
  drug-trafficking, 3, 37, 39, 167
  full fledged war, 216
  I K Gujral, 44
  Kargil, 44, 168
  Kashmir, 3, 4, 33-38, 40-46, 48, 51-54
  Manmohan Singh, 45
  Siachin glacier, 3, 38
  Sir Creek Island, 37, 39
  terrorism, 3, 4, 30-38, 42, 44, 45, 167
  tit for tat diplomacy, 166
India-Sri Lanka
  fishermen problem, 3, 165, 205
  Gujral doctrine, 73
  Indian Peace Keeping Force (IPKF), 73
  Indo-Sri Lankan accord, 57, 69, 72, 73
  Kachatheevu Island, 3, 165
  operation 'Mazhai' or rice bombing, 72
  Palk-strait, 3
  Ranasinghe Premadasa, 73
  Tamil refugees, 3, 77, 79, 165, 185
  Trincomalee and Colombo ports, 72
India's Role in South Asia, 166-169
Information Technology, 191-194
insurgency, 3, 4, 38, 44, 72, 115, 117, 120, 122, 123, 137, 147, 157, 180, 188, 211, 218
Islamic extremism, 32
Islamic Resurgence, 157-160

Jaffna, 59, 62
Jammu and Kashmir Liberation Front (JKLF), 2, 179

Kandahar, 30
Kargil skirmishes of 1999, 28

Kashmir committee, 49, 50
Kashmiri Pandits, 48

Lal Bahadur Shastri, 43
Line of Control, 29, 41, 51, 53, 103, 210
LTTE, 56, 58-70, 73-76

Maoist insurgency, 165
meaningful dialogue, 29, 30, 38, 220
Mohajir Imbroglio in Pakistan, 17-25
  Altaf Hussain, 18
  Kalashnikov culture, 18
  Muttahida Quami Mahaz, 19
  promised land, 17, 23
  rupture between Mohajirs and Sindhis, 18
Mohajir Quami Movement (MQM), 18, 23
Mohammad Ali Jinnah, 8, 9, 10, 11, 13
Muslim factor in Sri Lanka, 67
  Interim Self Governing Authority (ISGA), 58, 70
  Rauff Hakim, SLMC leader, 68
Muslim League, 8, 9, 10, 13, 19, 26, 27, 40
Myanmar, 139
  Aung San Suu Kyi, 139-142
    house arrest, 142, 143
    international pressure, 143
    new strategy, 144
    pro-democracy movement, 142
    released Suu Kyi, 143
  Military Rule, 139
    economic sanctions, 141
    ethnic minorities, 141
    General Ne Win, 140
    human rights, 139, 141
    military Junta, 140-143
    totalitarian state, 140
    U Nu, 140
  Students Struggle, 144-145

National Conference, 47, 49, 54
Nawaz Sharif, 29
Nepal,
  cease-fire, 111
  constituent assembly, 112-113
  emergency, 26 November 2001, 111, 116
  Girija Prasad Koirala, 111, 116
  Jana Andolan, 114
  King Gyanendra, 110
  King Tribhuvan, 113
  Maoist insurgency, 3, 110, 115, 116
    Baburam Bhattarai, 116
    kangaroo courts, 117
    Money for the movement, 116

Index

Pushpa Kamal Dahal (Comrade Prachanda), 116
   talks with the Maoist, 117
Monarchy, 112
Nepalese Congress Party, 110, 121
   overthrow the monarchy, 111
   prospects of democracy, 110
   Rana regime, 110, 113
   Sher Bahadur Deuba, 110, 111, 112, 116
   United Marxist Leninist (UML), 111
Non Proliferation Treaty (NPT), 172
Norwegian peace brokers, 63
nuclear deterrence, 5, 170
nuclear issue, 5, 170, 215
Nuclear Proliferation, 172
Nuclear safety in India, 174
nuclear tests
   India-Pakistan, 169, 170
   Ghauri, 169
   Missile Technology Control Regime (MTCR), 170
   non-proliferation treaty (NPT), 170
   Pokhran I, 176
   Pokhran II, 33, 176, 169, 215
nuclear tests in 1998, 28, 44, 176
nuclear weapons, 164
   acquisition by India and Pakistan, 216
   no first use, 217

Optimism-Pessimism Syndrome, 37

Pakistan
   non-NATO ally status, 4
   President Musharraf, 4, 19, 29, 36, 53
Pakistan nuclear designs, 164
partition of India, 8, 10, 11, 16, 37, 51, 52
Peace Battles in Karachi, 8, 19
peace plans (Chandrika), 62
people to people contact, 39, 94, 156, 168
plebiscite (Kashmir), 33, 36, 41, 43, 45
post Pokhran II diplomacy, 166
porous borders, 2
Prabhakaran, 61, 64, 69
pre-partition politics, 27
Problem of Ethnicity, 178, 180
   Baluch, 178
   Bangladeshi migrants, 179
   Bhutan: Nepali population, 179
   Bodoland, 178
   Drupkas, 179
   Kashmiri militancy, 180
   Mohajir, 178, 179
   Nepali elite, 180
   pro-Azadi movement of Kashmir, 180

Purvanchal, 178
Tamil ethnic group, 179, 180
Terai, 178
problem of migration, 2

Rajiv Gandhi, 43
Ranil Wickremesinghe, 60, 63, 68
RAW, 3
regional conflict, 70, 218
regional cooperation, 7, 149, 207, 220
regional power, 217
regional stability, 29, 215
Religion versus Reason, 181
   Babri mosque, 183
   bloodiest religious strife, 181
religious bigotry, 2
religious divide, 13, 184
Religious extremism, 165
religious fundamentalism, 2, 103
repressive regimes, 186
rights of the minorities in Bhutan, 130

S W R D Bandaranaike, 56, 71
SAARC, 198-213
   absence of a genuine climate of political trust, 199
   Indo-centric nature of SAARC, 199
   Phases of Saarc
      first phase 1985-90, 206-208
      common development programme, 207
      Drug Trafficking, 208
      food security, 207
      people to people contact, 207
      suppression of terrorism, 207
      fourth phase (2000-), 207, 209
      second phase (1990-94), 206, 208
      preferential trading, 208
      regional poverty alleviation programme, 208
      SADF, 208
      SAPTA, 208
      third phase (1995-1999), 206, 209
   preferential trade policies, 198
   South Asia Free Trade Area (SAFTA), 199
   South Asia Preferential Trade Agreement (SAPTA), 199
SAARC and bilateralism, 204-206
SAARC and Economic Cooperation, 201-204
separate homeland, 2, 58, 70, 161
separatism, 2, 72, 179, 180
Shimla conference of 1972, 43

Sindhis, 2, 18, 19, 20, 23, 165
Sirimavo Bandaranaike, 71
Soviet invasion of Afghanistan, 20, 32
Sri Lanka
    1983 anti-Tamil riot in Colombo, 56
    BC Pact, 56
    Chandrika Kumaratunga, 57, 58
    Chelvanayakam, 56
    IPKF, 57
    Liberation of Tamil Tigers Eelam (LTTE), 2, 4, 56, 58-70, 73-76
    S W R D Bandaranaike, 56
    Sea Tigers, 75, 76
    Sri Lankan Muslim Congress (SLMC), 57
    Tamil-Sinhala relationship, 56
    the Sri Lanka Freedom Party (SLFP), 57
    The Tigers, 65
    United National Party (UNP), 57
Sri Lankan ethnic crisis, 55, 72
Sri Lankan refugees, 2, 55, 77, 78, 79
    OFER, 78
    PAR/NAC, 78

Tamil ethnicity, 164
Tamil Fishermen's Problem, 74
Tamil insurgency, 165
The Maldives, 80
    agriculture, 84
    economic assistance, 85
    employment, 81
    global climatic changes, 81
    Indian imports, 85
    industry, 84
    Maumoon Abdul Gayoom, 89

    national emergency, 91
    political reforms, 89
    major source of income, 82, 84
The Maldives' Foreign Policy, 86
    environmental concern, 88
    historical ties, 87
    India, 86
    US' contributions, 88
two-nation theory, 23, 95

United Liberation Front of Assam (ULFA), 2, 134, 135, 136, 137, 179
United Progressive Alliance (UPA), 50, 120, 169, 220
United States of South Asia (USSA), 27, 220
US involvement in South Asian politics, 214

Vajpayee, 29

Wanni, 59
War against Global Terrorism, 35, 150, 160-162, 172
war mongering, 28, 215, 216
Women Struggle, 189
    reservation of seats, 191
    Sexual harassment, 190
    violence against women, 190
    women heads of states, 189
    women parliamentarians, 190
World War II, 10, 13, 212

Zulfikar Ali Bhutto, 18, 32